SIX ISLANDS ON TWO WHEELS

BY TOM KOCH

Bess Press
P.O. Box 22388
Honolulu, Hawaii 96822

For

Ingrid H. Wood

and for

Ruth K. Astmann

Cover and design: Z. Leimalama Harris

Illustrations: Bill Tomsa

Cover photo: Ann Cecil

Editing and typesetting: Revé Shapard

Library of Congress Catalog Card No.: 89-82129

Koch, Tom
    Six Islands on Two Wheels: A Cycling Guide to Hawaii
Honolulu, Hawaii: Bess Press, Inc.
224 pages

ISBN: 0-935848-79-7

Table of Contents

Maps

Acknowledgments

A number of people have aided and assisted in this project. I am, for example, indebted to cycling friends like John Daley, Ron Reilly, Jane Lewis, Betsi Timm, Karen Cisney and Roberta Baker, all of whom I've had the pleasure of riding with and whose own experiences have so informed this book. Guests riding with both Backroads and Island Bicycle Adventures all displayed an admirable patience when confronted, on their holidays by a cycling writer whose penchant for questions was balanced only by his insistence that they be answered. Over the years I've ridden frequently with the Hawaii Bicycle League, whose members--especially Eve DeCoursey, John Mathias, Patrick Clay, and HBL Tour Director Chuck Fisher, have been uniformly lavish in sharing with me (and others) their knowledge of cycling in general and riding these islands in particular.

Under the direction of Jane Eckelman, president of Manoa Mapworks, Inc, cartographer James P. Rounds took my vague request for a series of cycling-oriented maps which would "describe these islands at the bicycle's scale" and created a series of maps which do precisely what I asked.

Bill Tomsa provided the illustrations which inform the text.

The issue of what it means to be in an environment at the scale of a transportation mode was informed by two different sources. The support and guidance during 1988-89 of geographer Howard J. Gauthier, Jr., Ohio State University, made possible sustained research into the bicycle as a part of the transportation matrix and thus contributed significantly to the perspective this book adopts. Similarly, discussions with and encouragement from my friend Denis Wood, a cyclist and geographer, also encouraged and informed the whole.

Finally, I am indebted to the example of my aunt, Ruth K. Astmann, one of the best amateur athletes I have known. Her love of golf, tennis and skiing throughout her adult years has exemplified for me the joy one gets, in maturity, from activities too many think of as confined to the childhood years.

A Brief Preface

This is a book about cycling in the Hawaiian Islands. It's organization, route descriptions and maps are designed to give the interested cyclist or armchair traveler enough local knowledge to begin exploring on his or her own. Its maps and background information are designed not to replace the plethora of currently available histories, road maps, topographic charts and detailed travel guides but, rather, to focus on a single enterprise: cycling in Hawaii.

This is also a book about being in a place at the scale of the bicycle. It is about seeing the state's incredible geographic and cultural diversity at a speed and in a way which makes the physical and social environment accessible. Unlike motorists, bicyclists will not see Maui at 60 miles an hour in a quick, two-day flying visit. They will be in the heat on West Maui's rolling roads and feel the altitude in their lungs while climbing toward Haleakala. Because even good cyclists travel at speeds under 30 miles an hour, and most much slower than that, those who choose bicycle touring will have time to see and think and wonder about the place they happen to be.

This book is written with the firm conviction that cycling is a way to see and engage the environment and not necessarily an end in itself. Thus the routes and route descriptions are written for the dawdlers who like to ride and look, to stop, eat or simply rest at the beach instead of racing mindlessly to put on extra miles. When touring I average fifty miles or so a day, but the average route described here is shorter. Those seeking harder, longer days can string different routes together, of course. My intent has been to encourage the inexperienced rider while simultaneously providing background the competent cycling tourist can use.

This is a book about bicycling but it is also a collection of rides and the things which happened on them. It assumes that others share my interest in cycling not only to a place but through an environment's greater history. Thus I have tried to give background information—physical and historical—about the places one can cycle to and past rather than simply provide bare route information. This has been a learning exercise because I'm neither a Hawaiian old timer, a *kama'aina*, nor a fresh-off-the boat island *malihini* (newcomer). Since 1981, I've lived in Hawaii when I could and, when work took me elsewhere, returned when the job was done. Sections of these islands I know with the intimacy of long, local acquaintence but others I first met while researching this book. It is not a large state, but the richness and variety of the Hawaiian Islands are so vast that even native islanders are often surprised at the differences one finds island to island.

I have done my best to assure that all information presented here is correct. That means I've ridden extensively, read the work of others and relied on the advice, where needed, of other cycling friends. Ron Reilly of Island Bicycle Adventures, who leads tour groups to three local islands, has been especially helpful in keeping me up to date on road upgrades, construction plans and general conditions on the islands he knows best. As Huckleberry Finn disclaimed at the end of his tale, I've done the best I could and been as right as I know how to be.

But it is the nature of all guide and touring books that, like maps, each will be outdated even before the book is printed. Roads do change, stores are sold and nature takes its toll. Volcanoes on the Big Island, floods on Oahu, hurricanes on Kauai and the vagaries of local politics all assure that this book can serve best not as a touring cyclist's bible but rather as a resource, inspiration and general guide. Check with area bicycle stores, the Hawaii Bicycle Association, or local police if you have questions on specific routes or regions. I've included addresses at the end of each section to help the reader make his or her plans.

Enjoy your rides in Paradise. The local people in general will welcome tourists because it is good business and, I like to think, because most folk are warm and friendly. But, like people everywhere, Hawaiians appreciate the courteous traveler and dislike those who show no consideration for those who call a piece of geography home. "If only every tourist remember to show respect," one friend in the hotel business said to me, "everyone have good time. This our business but if they no show respect, no good for anyone." Good advice for *kama'aina* and *malahini* alike. *Mahalo* (thank you) for your interest in cycling Hawaii, and good winds on these quite magnificent roads.

A Brief Geology

These six islands are unique examples of a volcanic process mediated by wind and ocean erosion over time. They are the best known and most inhabited of 132 islands which make up the whole, long chain of geologic residue, traces of volcanic action over time. Since any trip in Hawaii will put the cyclist face to face with the physical fact of island forces and the geography of this region, a few words about how it all came to be—and what it might mean for the rider—are in order.

There are two versions of the Hawaiian Islands' birth, of the genesis of their geology. One is from the *Kumalipo*, the traditional Hawaiian creation story, and the other is based on modern geology. The Kumalipo's tale, a beautiful and complex text which linguists are constantly retranslating, is something like the western Bible's. In it Hawaii is brought forth from the dark by the agency of all-powerful, cosmic forces.

More prosaic is the geologist's view. Both versions agree that these islands were created, but modern scientists insist they were not called forth from the dark of a cosmic void but, rather, born on the unlighted depths of the ocean floor. Somewhere between 25 and 40 million years ago, fractures in the ocean's floor began to spew forth magma. These were the original, mid-Pacific, volcanic forces that caused the Hawaiian chain to build.

First these land masses grew under water, but as molten lava piled upon older hot rock, the islands emerged from the water to became visible land masses. To volcanologists, the general pattern is a story often told. The difference is that these volcanoes created land in the middle of the ocean and did not, like Mt. St. Helens in present day Washington or Vesuvius in Italy, vent their powers on already existing continental forms.

That means that it was indeed creation and not simply the transformation of low lands into mountain form. But these islands do sit, as must all surface land masses, on large subterranean anchors that float very slowly over the earth's hot core. These tectonic plates are constantly moving over time, and it is their travel which has caused the peculiar and remarkable shape of these islands in relation to each other.

Hawaii is rooted upon the Mid-Pacific tectonic plate, which has been shifting northwest since the first bit of magma spewed out from the continental floor. As the volcanoes roared (yes, there is a sound to it), the plate underneath was itself moving and so each new eruption placed its refuse in a different location on the earth's surface. It is rather like the cookie-making machine at Mrs. Fields' Cookies, in which a stationary dropper allots small islands of dough to a moving cookie sheet. But in the creation of these islands that dough dropper is in fact upside down—a volcano thrusting its lava up—and the moving sheet is a tectonic plate that has shifted, over time, from the southeast toward the northwest.

At first, in a rapid period of geologic creation, the islands appeared almost directly south of each other in the growing chain. But at a spot called the Emperor Sea Mounts north of Kauai, the sheet shifted and future islands began to arise east and south of their predecessors. Thus for the six islands that most people think of as the modern Hawaii chain, each new island has appeared in an almost lockstep fashion south and east of its predecessor. Kauai, the oldest of the six islands discussed in this book, is farthest north and west of the youngest land mass of all, the Big Island of Hawaii, which sits to the chain's extreme south and east.

But geologic Hawaii includes those previous geologic deposits as well as the currently inhabited islands and, in all, the Hawaiian chain of islands includes 132 points of land which were created in this process. The oldest have been worn down over time to atolls far north of Oahu, while volcanic eruption and creation continue to occur on the island of Hawaii itself. As the process continues, that activity will cease as well, but the volcanic growth will persist. Today, continued volcanic activity south and east of Hawaii is building a new island on the ocean's floor which eventually will appear in a fiery debut above the water sometime in the coming centuries.

Six Volcanic Islands

The result of this complex history is that the six islands discussed in this book are simply the most recent, best known and largest of inhabited Hawaiian land masses. They are also the newest. Most of those other, older points to the northwest of Kauai are small, eroded coral and lava remains, traces of the whole volcanic history whose most active period ended well before the important Ice Age began.

The volcano as a land form dominates each topographic map of these principal islands, and the results of that dominion create the geography that defines life in Hawaii, no matter how brief your stay. Oahu, for example, has two large, volcanic mountain ranges, the Waianae on its western end and the Ko'olau range to the east. Diamond Head, the island's most famous geologic landmark, is a volcanic crater, a mouth long silenced and the most obvious trace of the action that occurred here those millions of years ago.

Despite the appearances of independence, Maui and Molokai are, in fact, one land mass created by a single volcanic system that today is dormant if not necessarily extinct. You can see it in its glory on a visit to Haleakala, the progenitor of both islands. Hawaii, on the other hand, the southernmost piece of this geologic puzzle, is still growing, and its volcano system remains active indeed. Hawaii's Volcanoes National Park is testimony to the fact that, in geologic time, this island is a still growing and changing child. Eruptions that began in the early 1980s have changed the face of the island's southern tip and become one of this generation's most photographed natural events.

As these volcanoes grow, however, they also take back. Current eruptions have burned homes that stood in their path, pouring hot lava into the sea and extending the coastlines.

CYCLING THE REMAINS

What this means for the cyclist is an extraordinarily diverse landscape in which to ride. Low coasts and high hills dominate every island. The sharp thrusts of volcanic action have meant that most islands have coastal settlements and that roads will ring the island but can traverse the whole only in a few passes. This is because the volcanic pattern includes a "saddle" to ride through when traversing any one island. This is a lower-level path between the remains of volcanic action, and it is the route most cyclists seek when crossing any range.

On Oahu, for example, to go from north to south you can either fight the volcanic peaks, an impossible task for all who are not on foot, or cycle through the languid, lower fields up and down the more modern Kunia road. Molokai's ride from Kaunakakai to the western coast traverses the edge of a saddle on its gentle uphill side. There is no way around on the eastern ride to Halawa Valley, however. You have to ride up and over a strong, volcanic rise.

There are wonderful table-size relief maps of all major islands in St. John Hall at the University of Hawaii on Maile Way at East-West Road. These huge, three-dimensional maps are perhaps the best way to see the geography you will experience from the vantage point of your bicycle. Visitors are welcome to stop by and study these maps of the principal islands in the Hawaiian Chain but are cautioned that they are fragile and should not be touched, marked or otherwise disturbed. Location of that building is described in the Oahu Section's Ride Four.

Because these are tropical as well as volcanic islands, wind, wave and rain are crucial forces interacting with the land. The eastern side of each island has more rain and wind because prevailing weather is from the northeast and is accompanied by strong trade winds which hit each island's "windward side" first and hardest each day. That means there is more erosion on this side than on the calmer, leeward sections.

So when riding toward the rising sun, expect a rougher trip as you pedal into the wind and rain. Nature's force is fiercer on the eastern slope, but it also means a luxuriant, tropical vegetation born in the moisture of wind and rain.

Altitude is also an extremely critical factor in Hawaii, perhaps more important than the average visitor might expect. In the tropics and sub-tropics even a few hundred feet of elevation can make a difference in climate. In Hawaii that means every climb will include changes in plant life from palm trees and pineapple groves near the shore to pine trees and grasslands at medium elevation. Throughout the islands, location is defined by a combination of altitude and orientation to the prevailing winds.

So it makes sense, if you intend to climb, to keep a light jacket or sweater in the pack as well as, on the windward side, some rain gear. Even in the Big Island's Volcanoes National Park, still dominated by active lava flows, you will need a jacket at night and a sweater on chilly days.

Introduction: Getting Ready; Getting There

A SIMPLE TALE

Day One

John Daley was coming to Hawaii to escape Vancouver's wet, rainy, early winter season. He had purchased his ticket long months before and I'd promised he could bunk with me. We had been friends for years and, remembering the dreary bleakness of British Columbia in late November, I applauded his decision. But John was to arrive the day before a two-day Hawaii Bicycle League camping trip around Oahu, something I had been looking forward to for weeks. On the ride we would be logging perhaps sixty-five miles a day, and what was I to do with John?

He was a fair-weather cyclist, one of the legion who ride perhaps ten miles on a sunny, August afternoon. But balmy days had become a Vancouver memory and, since he did not ride in the cold and rain, it had surely been weeks—perhaps months—since John had ridden his bicycle at all. A two-day, 130-mile ride was out of the question for him, I thought. I could as easily expect my friend and guest to ride to the Sea of Tranquility on the moon.

I explained the problem to him by phone and said I'd understand if he didn't want to go along. The first day, I explained, we would ride counterclockwise from Honolulu to Malaekahana Point on the Island's northeast tip and, the next day, return across the Waianae Mountain range's low saddle to the populated, heavily trafficked, southern shores. "No problem," John said cheerfully. "I'm out of shape but can help drive the sag wagon and will enjoy the camping without the ride. You can pedal your heart out."

That was the plan but not how it ended. The day after he arrived, John rode my spare bicycle to the group's rendezvous point in Kapiolani Park and then spent the rest of that morning riding in the accompanying van, which carried the group's gear. But about 15 miles from our final destination, John grew impatient with his role. He turned the keys over to another man, unloaded my spare bicycle and rode it the rest of the way, cycling proudly into Malaekahana Beach Park that evening.

He was justifiably enthusiastic, exclaiming that his afternoon ride had been wonderful. The roads he had cycled were mostly flat and the wind had been constantly at his back. "It doesn't get much better than this," John exulted, as we stared at the setting sun. The campsite faced huge, rolling, North Shore waves, and the sky at dusk was bright and red.

We then looked at a map as I explained the next day's route. First, eight miles or so along Oahu's North Shore past several of the world's best surfing beaches, including the famous Pipeline. Then a stop at Haleiwa town for refreshments before a four- to five-mile climb up the hill to a Dole Pineapple station and, from there, a long, gliding downhill run past Schofield Barracks to Waipahu, Pearl City and finally back into Honolulu.

"If you don't mind," John said, "I'd like to ride again tomorrow morning. I'll stop when I get tired. Maybe in Hale'iwa."

Day Two
The next day we rode together for a while. When he was tired we stopped to rest and watch surfers slash and burn through lovely, large waves. Eventually we joined the other, faster riders waiting for us at Haleiwa, where the ride's climb began. John was offered his old spot in the sag wagon but to my surprise and, perhaps, his own, he declined. "I'll try the hill, thanks just the same."

With the rest of us he humped steadily from the North Shore to Dole's Pineapple Stand, which marked the beginning of a 12-mile, downhill ride on Kunia Road. He was not the fastest rider in the group but he was the proudest. "Now," he said firmly, "I've earned it," and proceeded to race and pound my aging Fuji Sundance downhill for the next ten miles in one of the most gloriously rural, exciting pieces of cycling on Oahu. Kunia Road from Schofield Army Barracks to Waipahu is a roller coaster ride where the momentum of the drops carries most riders to the top of the next hill and another swooping drop. It is that most precious of cycling commodities: almost effortless, always glorious, semi-rural riding and lightly trafficked road.

Finally, John decided he'd had enough when heavy automobile traffic again began to appear, and he chose to ride the van through the city and the last ten miles of the trip. The next day, however, he was back on the bicycle for a recreational ride and, from then on, averaged between fifteen and twenty-five miles in the city each day for the rest of his vacation.

Now, when John travels, he brings his own bicycle with him. He is still an average cyclist and still doesn't enjoy cycling in traffic. But he has learned to love to ride as a means of exploration and travel.

A BOOK FOR YOU, TOO

This book is for the John Daleys of the world. Most of us are, like John, a tad out of shape and nervous about giving up the automobile as a means of getting around. But you do not have to be a cycle champion—a Raul Alcala or Connie Paraskevin Young—to ride the roads and enjoy the world from the vantage point of two spinning, human-powered wheels. Just about anyone who can balance on a bike will enjoy seeing Hawaii from the saddle. Because the islands are small, they are the perfect size for the average cyclist, and the routes described here have been chosen to accommodate the beginning touring rider as well as experienced distance cyclists.

If you can ride only five, ten or fifteen miles at a stretch, that's fine. Maybe, like John, you'll ride twenty, thirty or fifty miles to-morrow. The routes detailed in this book break long distances into small components. The stronger rider may choose to cycle from Honolulu to Wahiawa and back in a day with no trouble at all. Others may decide to cycle five or ten miles through downtown Honolulu and call it arduous time well spent. The idea is to pick the distances you are comfortable with and the destinations which interest you.

Most people are like Daley and find themselves pleasantly sur-prised with what, in fact, they can do and how far they can go. But the secret of bicycle touring is simple—do what you can and not what others think you should do. Take your time. Rest, as John did, when you're tired. Stop and admire the boats along the shore, the trees which line Oahu's Old Pali Road or the points of solitude along Maui's Hana Highway. Leave the hard, hard training to racing riders and use holiday cycling for the pleasure it can provide.

This book is designed to help the rider—from novice to experi-enced cycle tourist—every step of the way. If you're still in the early planning stages, however, there are some simple decisions to be made: Which islands will you visit? Will you take an organized tour or ride on your own? Camp or stay in hotels? Rent a bicycle or bring one with you?

Which Island?

There are six major islands in the Hawaiian chain and each has its fierce and partisan devotees. *Maui no ka oi!* cry some, insisting that Maui is the finest island of all. Fanatical cyclist friends of mine, triathletes who train for endurance, insist that the Big Island, Hawaii, is heaven and fly there to ride long days on its many roads whenever they can. Over 80 percent of Hawaii's residents live, however, on Oahu, where last year almost 4,000 cyclists joined the Honolulu Advertiser Century. This is where the majority of the state's cyclists live, work, and train.

Each island is different and each is suited to different styles and abilities. Most have at least one good climb and all offer miles of off-road trail for those whose idea of heaven is dirt tracks traversed on knobby tires. All islands, with the exception of Molokai, also have areas of intensely urban traffic, but all islands, including Oahu, have stretches of beautiful, secluded, quiet road as well. Most people visiting the state try to see at least two or three islands in a visit, and this makes sense for cyclists as well.

Very strong riders will want the challenge of Maui's climb to Halekala's 10,000 foot peak, or perhaps will want to ride the Ironman race's 100-mile bicycle route on the Big Island. Intermediate riders will want nothing more than the long, lovely tour from Kahului to Hana on Maui or to amble from Lihue to Hanalei on Kauai. For beginning cyclists nervous about cycle touring, Molokai's minimal traffic and easy grades make it the best introduction I know.

It might help to think of the state as a series of themes—urban and rural, windward and leeward, upland and coastal—coming together as a thematic whole. This book begins with Oahu, moves to Molokai and Maui and then describes Kauai. The Big Island of Hawaii is left until last both because its size makes it the most complex of individual geographies and because, in a very real way, it is the key to all the rest. Physically, it is dominated by the active volcano which continues to erupt and spew magma along the southern coast. Culturally, the Big Island brings together in a single, isolated place the traditions of upcountry ranchers, agriculturalists growing coffee, macadamia nuts and other crops, coastal fishermen, tropical orchidists and general shopkeepers. It is last because, for me, this island ties together the state's many themes into a single symphony of culture, geography and social diversity.

Which island should you visit? The answer, clearly, is to ride each island. Failing the leisure to do that, choose the one which sounds as if it is most suitable to your interests, riding ability and available time. For those who are new to cycle touring, the answer might depend on where a particular group or organization is riding this month or this season.

TOUR COMPANIES

Two companies, Island Bicycle Adventures and Backroads Bicycle Touring, currently offer overnight bicycle tours on one or more Hawaiian Islands. The question of traveling alone or with a group boils down for many to the question of "how much luxury can I afford?" It costs more than $100 a day to be a guest with either group and, for many, that will be a prohibitive price. Organized tours take their guests to nice hotels and assure well-prepared meals along the way, but there is no doubt that a single cyclist can travel more cheaply along the same routes.

There are a lot of advantages to group travel. At its best, it is education, instruction and freedom from the planning solitary riding requires. Logistics are handled by experts who understand the problems of a touring rider and who have traveled your route before. For those who have only seven, ten or fourteen days of vacation, it means a set itinerary and the luxury of having things planned by others so vacation time can be used for relaxing. Professional bicycle tours include a sag wagon to carry the riders' gear and an experienced tour leader who supposedly knows the area, the roads, local history and the region. A good leader will encourage cyclists to do their best but also will applaud those who decide to ride in the sag wagon for an hour's rest. Caution is the best insurance for another day's ride. Further, routes are laid out with an eye not only to the region as a whole but in terms of safety, and that, for the new cycle tourist, may be a strong argument in the professional tour's favor.

Finally, joining a tour provides an instant community and a pleasant, companionable social situation in which people from various backgrounds meet and become immediately friendly. A major drawback, however, is that it is a group ride, which means an individual guest's interests and desires must sometimes come second. The route is planned, an itinerary is laid out and each day riders must follow that program. You may not change destinations at mid-day or choose to stay at Koke'e State Park on Kauai for a few days when the group is scheduled to return to Kapa'a. Going with a group means surrendering a bit of independence, a price some especially strong or experienced touring riders are not willing to pay.

Over the years I have bicycled past numerous groups and, while working on this book, I became curious about the experience. Because I usually ride alone or with a few friends, I'd never taken a packaged cycling tour, although alumni of them had told me how enjoyable riding as a paying guest can be. This book was a good excuse for me to see what it was like to travel under the direction of a professional touring company. So in October of 1989 I rode for a week on Kauai with **Island Bicycle Adventures**, an Oahu-based company, and the next month spent ten days on the Big Island with California-based **Backroads Bicycle Touring**.

I still prefer to travel alone, and to make travel planning easier for those who share this inclination I have included the names of hotels, hostels and campgrounds. But for those new to touring or who dislike the logistics of planning, these professional tour companies can be a boon. Choosing the appropriate company is crucial, however, and no two companies could be more different than **Island Bicycle Adventures** and **Backroads Bicycle Touring.**

Bicycle Tour Companies

Island Bicycle Adventures, which offers six-day cycle trips on Hawaii, Maui and Kauai, is run by longtime Hawaii residents Ron Reilly and Roberta Baker. Both are certified cycling instructors, and their tours have a three-fold mission. They are to be fun, Reilly says, which means enjoyable and accident free. But just as critically, IBA tours are structured to give guests as much background as possible on the area they will ride through. Both Reilly and Baker are passionate partisans of Island culture and geography who are constantly upgrading their knowledge of local culture, history, music and geography through university courses and outside reading. It is their pride that IBA guests have the opportunity to learn about the region while riding in Hawaii's diverse and changing landscape. In addition, IBA rides are structured to teach guests, most of whom are not experienced cycle tourists, about bicycle safety and correct cycle handling on the road.

Backroads, on the other hand, has one destination in Hawaii, the Big Island, and their tour is run like a good, well-managed Century ride, in which meals are provided and a hotel reserved for each day's end. They are facilitators, not instructors. If a bicycle needs repair, Backroads tour leaders can fix it, but it is not Backroads' aim or intention to teach bicycle safety or mechanics to their clients. Nor are its leaders knowledgeable about the local environment. Chris Sibley, tour leader on my ride, explained that it is company policy not to hire local individuals to lead their groups and, in fact, they rotate ride leaders to other destinations after a trip or two so nobody gets attached to a specific destination. The result is that their tour leaders are not familiar with Hawaiian customs, history, plants or sometimes even a specific day's routes. Guests are left to their own devices and, if they want to learn about the environment they are in, must study on their own.

On Your Own

In Honolulu, the **Hawaii Bicycle League** answers questions for those interested in island touring and, although they are Oahu-based, have a wealth of experience in helping Mainland riders who want to experience the islands. Their address is listed at the end of this chapter.

For those visiting Oahu, a ride with HBL is a good introduction to Hawaii. Every Saturday and Sunday HBL runs rides, usually beginning in Honolulu's **Kapiolani Park,** to some spot on the island. Each ride is led by a competent tour leader, and visitors (wearing helmets) are welcome. This is a fine way to have a semi-supervised bicycle experience. The "ride hot-line" telephone number is 988-7175.

On other islands—and on Oahu as well— it often pays to visit the local bicycle shop and ask where local folk ride or train. This is the fastest way to gain local knowledge and, for those interested in specific types of terrain (mountain bikers, for example), it is the local shop folks who are most likely to know. Bicycle store employees are, in my experience, almost uniformly friendly folk willing to share their knowledge and guide the newcomer to the safest as well as the most traveled routes.

Local residents on all islands use their bicycles for interurban transportation, and there is no reason a tourist can't do this, too. On Oahu, where I live, almost everything a visitor could want—hills, beaches, movies, restaurants and museums—is within eight miles of Waikiki's hotel strip and easily accessible to the sometime cyclist. If you choose to combine cycling with more general sightseeing, a bicycle allows the average tourist to visit all of Honolulu's most famous sights—from Makapu'u Point on the island's eastern side to the Arizona Memorial at Pearl Harbor. To facilitate this type of urban-oriented rider, rides to and through downtown Honolulu are included in this book.

On most other islands, the cities are so small that you can walk almost as easily as ride through town, but, wherever possible, a "city sites" section is included for the city lover reading this book.

Camping, Hostels and Hotels

If you're planning an individual trip, a burning question is "where should I stay?" There are hotels galore available in almost every price range. Which are best and what other options are available?

Camping, of course, is a viable option. There are scores of state and county campsites in these islands, although, for most, a permit is required. Each chapter of this book describing a specific island includes the names of appropriate parks and, at its end, a list of addresses, which includes where to write for state or county park information and permits. Campers are advised to plan ahead and wherever possible to reserve campgrounds before their trips begin, because the best—like the cabins at Koke'e on Kauai—are sometimes booked months in advance.

Like many regions on the Mainland, Hawaii boasts a Bed and Breakfast system in which you can stay at private homes for prices which range from between $35 and $70 a night for two. This is a nice way to travel, especially if you are interested in less traveled places. Many of those who open their homes in this way are not in central locations. I know people who are addicted to this type of board system and have made friends of hosts along the way. **Bed and Breakfast Hawaii's** address is, like the others, included at the end of this chapter.

Finally, **American Youth Hostels, Inc.**, maintains two locations on Oahu. One is in Waikiki and the other is a few miles away, across the street from the University of Hawaii at Manoa. The hosteling movement is for more than just kids—people of all ages can join, and the rooms, while plain, are uniformly well kept and very inexpensive in a region where most things are dear.

TAKE IT WITH YOU!

Whether you're traveling with a group or on your own, the next question is: should you bring your own bike, use a tour company's or try to rent a bicycle in the islands?

For those on packaged tours, it often makes sense to use the tour company's. A few people prefer their own even then, but if the company promises a decent bicycle, the choice, really, is yours. There is a charge for this service, however, and if the charge outweighs the cost of shipping your own bicycle to Hawaii, the answer should be to bring your own. Women who rented bicycles on both the Backroads and Island Bicycle Adventures tours said the machines themselves were acceptable but the saddles on those bicycles (Panasonics and Treks respectively) were very uncomfortable. They recommended, and so do I, that women planning to rent bicycles bring their own saddles and have mechanics put them on the rental bikes.

Personally, I prefer my own machine, even when offered a supposedly superior bike. My Fuji Touring V has been customized over the years to meet my every need and quirk, a benefit lacking in even the most expensive of machines. But many people who are less attached to their bikes find renting is more convenient.

Guests on both tours told me that a real advantage of renting their bicycles was a chance to learn about index-shifting, triple-cranks and the rest of modern cycling gear. Many rode old ten or twelve speeds at home, and they were surprised at how much easier hills became with the added gearing and the authoritative index shift system. On Kauai, I rode for a day with one woman who was so enthusiastic that she vowed, at trip's end, to buy when she returned home a new and fully equipped bike with the same gears and set-up as the tour group's rental bike.

Touring vs. Mountain bikes

On three of the six islands described here (Oahu, Maui, Hawaii) you can rent from local bicycle rental companies. For those who wish to ride for a day or two or to use a bicycle to tour, for example, Honolulu or Kailua-Kona, this spot rental system is ideal. The cost varies greatly, however, from shop to shop, from perhaps $70 a week up to more than double that amount. On some islands there is no choice but to bring a bicycle with you, because there are no bike stores or rental facilities on Molokai, Lanai or Kauai to support the occasional bike rider. Own, rent or borrow: the question is what type of bike do you want to use?

Mountain bike aficionados will find a lot of off-road miles to entice them on every island. There are woods, beaches, fire trails, parks and just plain country where fat tire bicycles excel. On some islands the "main road" is, in fact, a mountain biker's element, and those who choose fat tires for their basic bike will not be anything but pleased with the decision. Further, mountain bike clubs are springing up in Hawaii with organized rides and detailed, local knowledge of off-road trails. On Oahu, check with **The Bike Way** on Ward Avenue for more information.

Touring bicycles with 18 speeds and an extra-long wheelbase are my favorite mode of travel and will take the average rider over any terrain described in this text. I prefer the touring bicycle's slightly wider tire for its comfort on occasional off-road rides, but have seen even pricey Italian racing bikes being happily bounced over washboard roads by visiting cyclists whose passion for fine cycling machinery does not prevent them from punishing the bike on eccentric trails. The truth is, it doesn't matter a great deal what you ride as long as the bicycle is in good repair and has the equipment necessary for a safe ride.

It's also a good idea for the non-mechanically minded bringing their own machine to have the bicycle serviced before leaving home. It's no fun to leave on a bicycle trip and then to have mechanical problems. Tell the mechanic you're going touring and ask him or her to check the gears, cables, brakes and drive train.

File this expense under trip insurance and hope it's the last time you'll see a bike mechanic for a while.

BEFORE YOU GO

Training for the Trip

If you're ready to cycle Hawaii, you've probably ridden at least 25 miles or more near your home. Certainly you've read a guidebook or two and, perhaps, talked to individuals who have been where your itinerary is going to take you. That's great. But before you head out, there is one more thing to do: ride in familiar surroundings with your bicycle when it is loaded with panniers, sleeping bag and tent.

Bicycles handle very differently (especially with low riders on the front wheels) when carrying a full load than when they are unencumbered by the paraphernalia touring riders carry. It is not simply that a loaded bicycle is slower and climbing a bit trickier than when free of the added weight. Everything feels different. The machine is sluggish when you begin to pedal, faster on the downhills, harder to brake and more sensitive to weight changes when you're pumping uphill and out of the saddle.

The difference is easy to get used to, requiring only a day or two, but none of this is what a cyclist wants to discover in highway traffic in a new environment on an unfamiliar island. So pack the bags, ride a bit and then get a feel for how the bicycle will handle before ever leaving home.

If the bicycle feels very unstable, make sure the heaviest equipment is packed *at the bottom* of the panniers. The lower the weight the more stable the bicycle, and camp stoves, heavy cameras and heavy books should be loaded as low as possible.

Even if you're traveling with a tour or simply planning extended day rides, it also makes good sense to work a bit on hills and endurance techniques before leaving home. Hawaii has some wonderful climbs, and the better your physical endurance and riding technique, the more fun these exotic trips will be. Experienced cyclists know how to train, but if you're new to the game, ask members of the local cycling club (or even an employee at your local bicycle shop) to ride with you and criticize your hill work, cadence patterns, and gearing techniques. People love to teach, and most club members are flattered if someone asks for advice. Nothing makes a steep hill disappear, but the difference between a tiring and an exhausting ride is the proper gear and good technique. It doesn't take long to be schooled by an experienced cyclist, and time spent before leaving home will pay off in longer and less taxing vacation rides.

Before You Go: Outfitting

There are a few things every rider will need to ride safely in Hawaii. These include basic safety gear, water bottles, a tire change kit, a light for night riding and a helmet.

Everyone should have at least two water bottle brackets. If you rent a bicycle and it won't carry at least two bottles, then buy an extra bracket to fit. If you are not used to sustained exercise in the heat, you will need to replenish fluid levels frequently, and on many of the rides described here, water fountains and convenience stores are few and far between.

I usually carry fruit juice in one bottle and water in the other on even moderately short, local rides. The juice provides glucose energy and the water general hydration. Several times the combination has been used for first aid when I've found riders and runners on the road slipping into heat exhaustion. Cooling water poured on the victim's extremities and sips of fruit juice for glucose energy are, for those in such extremes, a critical roadside restorative. The idea, however, is to drink so that this medical emergency does not occur, to sip and replenish while riding (or running) before dehydration or heat exhaustion sets in. So drink in the saddle or when stopped at a traffic light and keep your water bottles filled.

Tubes, Tires and Patch Kits

A pump that fits on your bicycle's frame is also a very, very good idea. With it, be sure to carry an extra inner tube or two as well as a patch kit to repair tire punctures on those longer rides.

Hawaii's roads are often gravel strewn, and in off-road areas tree thorns are a hazard everyone has to live with. My record is three blowouts in a single, unlucky hour on Molokai, an island which at present hosts no bicycle stores.

Although these islands are relatively small, there is often a fair distance between gas stations and bicycle shops. The nearest gas station or cycle shop is often over an hour's pedal away, and that means a small blowout can become a rather serious emergency. On Lanai and Molokai, where there are no shops at all, a puncture without a patch kit can mean waiting hours for someone in a truck to give you a lift back to town. Then, of course, you'll have to waste another day traveling to Oahu or Maui and back for something as simple as a bicycle tube patch kit. The answer is easy. Be prepared.

Some folk stuff a spare inner tube into the back pocket of their cycle jersey, while others carry spare tubes, along with tire irons and a patch kit, in a small emergency bag which fits under the seat. Rental bicycles should be equipped with this type of gear; if they are not, buy the materials yourself and consider it simple insurance.

In my seat bag I always carry a Swiss Army Knife, three-way Allen key set, and a "Y-wrench" for emergency repairs and for tightening those nuts and bolts that seem always to loosen at the most inappropriate times. For years I've kept a copy of Tom Cuthbertson and Rick Morall's *The Bike Bag Book* with my traveling gear. About the size of the palm of my hand, this small, simple book is filled with great ideas for roadside repairs. Best of all, it explains, in terms even mechanical idiots like me can understand, how to handle, by yourself and with minimal tools, everything from a bent fork to a flat tire.

Lamps, Racks and Locks

A distance rider should carry some type of bicycle light for traveling at night. Reflectors are fine, but the law says bicyclists need illumination after dark, and, on unfamiliar roads, it helps to see as well as be seen. Even the best-laid plans will sometimes fail, and a day ride will sometimes—with flats, sightseeing or too much time at the perfect beach—become a dusk to evening ride. I have a six-volt battery light permanently mounted on my bicycle as insurance against such a time. There are also, however, good bicycle flashlights which clip on to the handlebars and weigh very little. For campers, they can double as a flashlight as well.

For Oahu-based riders, lights also are a legal and safety requirement in the island's two traffic tunnels. The Wilson Tunnel on the Likelike (pronounced "Lee-Keh Lee-Keh") Highway is long, narrow and not recommended, but the competent cyclist can safely (and legally) ride through the Pali Highway tunnel (see Oahu Ride Two) if he or she has a light.

I'd also urge you to have a rack attached to your bicycle frame. These are usually lightweight and inexpensive and enable you to carry the accoutrements of leisure almost effortlessly in cycling panniers. Carry racks can either be mounted over the back wheel or fitted as "low riders" holding bags on either side of the front wheel. The former is more popular. Like other serious touring riders, I have both, which lets me carry four bicycle panniers with weight distributed evenly front and rear.

On longer trips, a rack is a necessity to carry camping gear, sleeping bags and the rest of the things a distance touring rider needs. But even for day riders, a trip to the beach means snorkel, mask, fins and towel; a day trip means food, a camera and who knows what else. Some people cram all this in day packs on their back or insist that travel around the world requires nothing but a bulging fanny pack. Phooey. It just isn't so. A loaded backpack slung over the shoulders means you're carrying your weight too high. That can and will interfere with maneuverability in a tight situation. For day trippers wedded to backpacks, there is another, compromise solution. An elastic bungee cord or two will secure the pack, fins and even a six-pack of beer to the normal bicycle carry rack in a convenient and safe carrying position.

Finally, keep a good U-bolt lock on the bicycle. The added weight is worth it. A lock that can secure a bicycle firmly is the best insurance against thieves. Some people prefer cabled locks, but I lost a bike years ago to cretins with cable cutters and have used Kryptonite-style U-locks ever since.

Wear a Helmet!

That's right. If you don't have one now, shame on you. It makes no sense to spend hundreds of dollars on a bicycle, hundreds more on airfare and then not to insure your brains and life with a $50 ANSI-approved shell or helmet. Every statistic available indicates that bicycle helmets save lives. Accidents will happen, and they all do not involve automobiles. Sometimes, a rider loses control on the downhill, skids in the wet or simply zigs instead of zagging. If you have the misfortune to blow a tire, skid or pitch from your saddle, a helmet will give you the best chance possible of surviving without injury.

Wear a helmet, even if you're only renting a bicycle for a day.

Gloves and Cycle Clothes

While you're buying a helmet, consider a pair of cycling gloves.

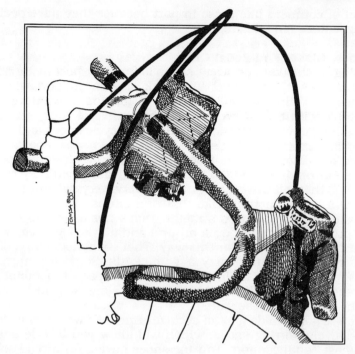

Style aside, gloves serve two necessary functions. The padding at the base of the thumb keeps the fingers from becoming numb, a surprisingly common problem for newer riders who grasp the handlebar tightly.

Gloves also provide protection in case of an accident. In even a minor spill, "road rash" can be a debilitating problem, and the most frequent type of injury is to the hand, which is used to break a fall.

Some riders wear only tee shirts, while others wear fancy cycling gear. A good cycle shirt made from Lycra costs under $20 in the mail-order catalogues. These are great. Easily washed in a hotel room, they dry out quickly after a Hawaiian rain shower, and two such shirts will last for a whole trip (alternating each day, of course). Tee shirts get wet and sticky, and don't dry fast, so an inexpensive cycle shirt or two makes sense.

Many people wear skintight, Lycra cycle pants, but I've never felt comfortable in them and for years wore plain non-cycling shorts. Cycle pants, like the fancy shirts, dry quickly after the rain and on long rides chafe far less than any other material. That's one reason why they're so popular. Whenever I was caught in a rain shower on the bicycle and had to finish the ride with damp, sticky shorts, I would promise myself a pair of the fancy, hi-tech skintights. Then I found a compromise for those who, like me, wanted comfort and normal appearance. There are now available specially designed cycle touring shorts which look like normal street wear, have chamois in the seat, use good synthetic materials and are extremely comfortable. Mail order catalogues and bicycle stores in most cities stock them as a matter of course. I like these in part because they have pockets, a clothing feature I'm addicted to.

Shoes, Cleats and Pedal Clips

Riding in sneakers or street shoes is fine for short distances, but on longer runs, their almost total lack of arch support will bother some people. If this is your first cycle trip, ride in whatever you're comfortable with but, if every night the arches of your feet feel like they're falling down, invest in a good pair of cycle shoes and consider it a "medical expense." That's how I rationalize my own pair.

More and more serious riders use specially cleated shoes that have step-in bindings to lock them to the pedal when they ride. The problem is that, off the bicycle, they are very, very difficult to walk in, requiring a gait something like that of a circus clown on stilts. For those who ride eight hours straight, that's not a serious disability, but for others who pause, walk around and maybe sightsee, it is very frustrating to be hobbled in this way. That's why local fans of these step-in systems usually carry a pair of "flip-flops" (cheap sandals called slippers in Hawaii) in pannier or back-pack to facilitate town travel when they get off the machine. If you use step-in toe clips, it would be smart to do the same.

If you're going to do a lot of cycle touring, it's worth considering a pair of bicycle touring shoes, which will allow you to ride and walk with almost equal comfort. Touring shoes have a firm, rigid sole, but are flexible. These have become my everyday shoe. Currently there are two styles--one for mountain bicycles and one for distance touring—and either will provide the added support a distance cyclist requires.

If you're not using step-in bindings, be sure to use pedal toe clips. These inexpensive beauties significantly increase the power of the leg's stroke by adding the "pull" up of one leg to the other's "push." Inexperienced riders typically fear they'll bind their feet to the pedals in a fall. They won't, but if this is a real concern, ride with the straps loosened or even removed until the fear goes away.

MOPEDS

These are two-wheeled, motorized and widely available on several islands. Many people rent them for a day or two, believing they are safe and convenient motorized vehicles which will carry them all over an island. A moped rider can use this book to scout out routes on islands like Maui, Oahu and the Big Island where rental agencies exist.

Be warned, however, that riding a moped is the worst of all worlds and requires real caution for safe use. They are too slow to be part of the fastest traffic flow but, because they are motorized, are not allowed in some places where bicycles can go. If you choose to ride one, be careful of the bicyclist who shares the road with you and know that your turning radius is, because of the moped's small wheel size, more restricted than a bike or motorcycle's.

Currently, rental agencies are not required to issue helmets with their machines, and this is a dangerous omission. If you choose to rent, insist on a helmet and if one is not provided, buy one.

I found a badly shaken up Australian couple trying to return to Honolulu from Hawaii Kai one day. They were in their 60s and had rented mopeds for a pleasant afternoon ride. Unfortunately, the woman had dumped her machine and gotten a concussion as well as some nasty bruises and cuts. She had tried to turn on a side street and wiped out, her husband said, on a patch of gravel. It's all too easy to do. They were returning from the hospital and when we met said that their Oahu stay had been ruined by the incident.

The message here is the same as for the bicycle. If you plan to ride on two wheels, wear a helmet, and if one is not offered through the rental agency, buy one for yourself.

This is a holiday—you've earned this pleasure. Now keep it safe by making sure that your brains are intact at vacation's end so you'll have something to carry all those memories home in.

CARRYING BICYCLES ON AIRPLANES

How do you transport a bicycle safely from one place to another? If you, like John Daley, live in Vancouver, is bringing your bicycle to Honolulu a major hassle? Happily, the answer is no.

Unless you're sailing to Hawaii, the bicycle must come with you by airplane and for all but the extremely wealthy that means flying commercial airlines. For those traveling by private jet, well, skip this section. Everyone else, however, be warned: most commercial airlines will charge an extra $20 for carrying your bicycle interisland and, from the mainland, the general charge is an additional $30. Further, there is at present no industry standard either for the cost of bicycle carriage or for packing requirements. Check airlines in your area and get the best deal you can.

To my knowledge only the Canadian carrier **Wardair** does not charge extra for bringing a bicycle to Hawaii. It doesn't even demand that your machine be boxed. I've flown with them several times, and each time my bicycle, simply rolled onto the airplane in Vancouver, arrived in good shape. Whenever possible I fly with them or interisland carriers **Aloha** and **Hawaiian** airlines, who allow bicycles being transported interisland to be rolled aboard without being boxed. Airline employees have confirmed informally my long-held conviction that boxing a bicycle is an invitation to disaster. Baggage handlers see a box and don't consider its contents. They see a bicycle and know this is a real thing belonging to a real person. I've never had trouble when allowed to roll it on an airplane but, even on Wardair, have had dents, dings and bent handlebars as a result of sending my Fuji in a cardboard container.

All Wardair requires (and this is virtually universal) is that the handlebars be pivoted 90 degrees from their normal position to parallel the top bar and that the pedals be taken off before loading. This allows the bicycle to fit into a narrower cargo space and assures that the pedals won't jam into some person's box of pineapples, spilling them all over the cargo hold.

Other airlines, **United** for example, define bicycles as "special" cargo, charge extra for their handling and then add insult to injury by making the passenger sign a release absolving the company of responsibility in case of damage. In addition they, like most Mainland-based carriers, insist the bicycle be boxed before it can be carried on board the plane. At least once a year I write and complain to these airlines that they want it both ways. If we have to pay extra for carrying bicycles, we shouldn't have to give up our right to compensation if a baggage handler drops that lovely Cinelli on its front fork.

For an additional ten dollars, United will sell the cyclist a bicycle box large enough so that—with pedals off and handlebars turned—any size bike will just roll in. Using these large boxes means the bicycle does not have to be broken down for travel and, if you are flying from the Mainland, it is probably a worthwhile purchase. If you buy it, it's yours, and that means it can go with you to your hotel, be stored there and used on the return trip. Still other companies insist the bicycle be boxed, but don't have cartons for sale. When making reservations, be sure to ask what the airline's policy is on bicycles and—especially for those traveling in a group—reserve a box if you need it. You can even buy a United box and use it on the alternate airline.

In Hawaii at present both interisland carriers **Hawaiian** and **Aloha** allow cyclists to wheel their bikes up to the counter and onto the airplane. They require but do not always enforce regulations requiring that pedals be removed and handlebars be turned. Between Molokai and Maui all this can be avoided by using the interisland ferry which travels between Lahaina and Kaunakakai every day. For more details, check the pertinent chapters of this book.

Boxing it Yourself

For those who must box the bicycle for their trip to Hawaii, there are several ways to prepare it for travel. Many people choose to get a used box from their local bicycle store—which usually gives them away—and do the job themselves. It's not difficult, really, but there are a few tricks, so if you've never tried it before, the best thing is to have your local bicycle shop do it once with you and you'll then know what to do in the future.

Normal-sized bicycle boxes require that the front wheel, saddle, handlebars and pedals all be removed. This means the front wheel has to be slipped onto a crank arm, the handlebars and saddle (attached to the seat post) tied to the top tube, the seat fastened to the same tube and, sometimes, the racks removed before it all will fit in a box that can be closed.

To secure everything together on the frame, I use old inner tubes, which have been patched and repatched into obsolescence, as my string. Usually I throw in a rag as well to separate handlebar and top tube so that the bicycle's paint job will be protected. Finally, I usually carry a magic marker and roll of packing tape in my panniers to make sure the box is appropriately marked and securely sealed. Paint large arrows in the "up" direction so a baggage handler doesn't inadvertently send it traveling upside down. It's your bicycle and its protection is your responsibility—seal the box and mark it yourself.

None of this is difficult, but it shouldn't be done the night before departure. That is not the time to discover that the box you picked up is the wrong size, that a binding bolt is frozen in place. So here is an item to plan ahead unless you're confident of both the bicycle's condition and your own mechanical abilities.

Tools to Bring

Fortunately, for most of this work modern bicycles require only three separate tools, which are also the basics of any spot repair kit. A "Y-key" wrench with the correct socket sizes will loosen any nut on the modern machine. An Allen key of the same design will handle the handlebar bolt, seat bolt and about anything else that may need tightening on the bicycle. Finally, a pedal wrench is a sound investment. This is a long-armed wrench costing under ten dollars, designed to fit your bicycle's pedals. The long arm gives good leverage and means not only will the pedals come off but that they can, at the other end, be reattached correctly.

Nothing is more embarrassing than to hit a new town, cycle in from the airport and kick off a pedal in the middle of a rush hour turn because it was reattached too loosely. Yes, it happened to me and I took a bad spill in the bargain. I had been in a hurry and had used a small vise grip to cinch the pedals. It wasn't sufficient to do the trick. The day after my fall I spent six dollars for a long-armed wrench that now resides permanently in my panniers.

Katie Laws, manager of Honolulu's **Island Triathalon and Bike**'s service department, says that the most common complaint among the many cycle tourists who stop at her shop is "clicking" pedals. In almost all cases, she says, the problem is not a bad crank or hub but pedals that have not been reattached tightly enough after being boxed. So if the pedals click when you ride, grab your wrench and give them another good tug. If that doesn't help, check with a local bicycle mechanic to see if there is, in fact, a real problem.

AT THE AIRPORT: HONOLULU

All of this is considerably less complex than reading it makes it seem. Traveling with a bicycle is really surprisingly easy. It takes a bit of getting used to, but after the first trip, it will seem routine.

If you've decided to go with a professional bicycle tour, a tour leader will probably meet you at the airport. If not, the choices, for most people, are to cycle from the airport into town or to use a taxi service.

Most people fly to Oahu first and spend a few days there before visiting other islands, although Oahu is becoming, for some, just a place to change planes on the way to Kauai, Maui or the Big Island. Because it is the first stop for most visitors, this book begins with Oahu and assumes it will be a cycling destination. It is still the state's most popular tourist destination and the place where over 85 percent of the state's population lives. Oahu also hosts a strong cycling community. Approximately 10 percent of the island's population—over 90,000 people—registered their bicycles last year with the Honolulu Police Department.

Campers will be pleased to know that there is a beach park a few miles from the Honolulu airport where they can stay. **Sand Island State Recreation Area** is a large camping area off Keehi Lagoon and only about three miles from the airport's baggage area. Those interested in using this facility should write for a permit before arriving (see the Oahu appendix). Be aware that gates at the site are locked each night, so those coming to Oahu on late night flights will have to make other arrangements.

Because the airport is in a very heavily trafficked area, my recommendation to all but the most eager is to let a taxi take you, your bicycle and your bags into town. At hotel or campsite your bicycle can be put together at leisure, the box stored for the next leg of the trip and your first ride will be more relaxed.

Honolulu has a wealth of station wagon-sized taxicabs serving the airport as well as the city. Ask for one from the airport taxi supervisor, who can be found at curbside outside the baggage area. After a six- or eight-hour flight, a Honolulu taxi is, for me at least, a necessity, and the $3 surcharge for carrying a bicycle (a fee set by the city) is reasonable. The average taxi fare without bicycle from Honolulu Airport to Waikiki is between $12 and $15, so the whole trip, with tip, will be under $20 to any of the many beach area hotels.

For those who insist on riding into town, refer to Ride Nine in the Oahu chapter of this book for the general route past the airport to downtown and then on to Kapiolani Park. There is a bicycle path on the north side of the highway, which goes part way into town. It is well signed and off-road, just to the mountain side of the west-bound lane. If you choose this path, be aware that it frequently crosses very busy intersections and exercise extreme care at each cross street because cars cannot see the cyclist at most traffic lights. This bicycle path (which is also used by joggers and the occasional moped rider) ends at Middle Street, and, from there, the cyclist will have to ride another few miles on Nimitz until Chinatown's River Road appears on the left. From Chinatown, Ride One (Oahu) will bring you into town.

On other islands, Molokai for example, station wagons are available as well, but there the traffic is minimal and—for those traveling interisland—the jet lag nonexistent. On Kauai, Molokai, Lanai and Maui, I usually ride in from the airport. On the Big Island what you should do depends on the airport you choose, its distance from your location, the time of day and how tired you are.

Koch's rule is bicycle in daylight if the flight took less than two hours. Longer than that on an airplane and I'm fit for nothing more strenuous than two beers and a nap. But, like most people, I also get anxious to be on the road, so the final decision ultimately depends on how I feel when leaving the airport and how disgusted I am at that moment with the automobile-dominated world.

Addresses and Information

BicycleTour Companies Serving Hawaii

Companies change their programs and offerings constantly, depending on demand. New companies may have entered the field, and older ones may have departed. The following addresses are offered without recommendation as places to begin the research for those who want to explore the idea of traveling with a group and a professional leader. For further listings, see the classified pages of cycle magazines.

Island Bicycle Adventures
569 Kapahulu St.
Honolulu, HI 96815
(800) 233-2226
(808) 734-0700

Backroads Bicycle Touring
1516 Fifth St.
Berkeley, CA 94710
(800) 533-2573

Country Cycling Tours
West 83d St. 140-G
New York, NY 10024
(212) 874-5151

Vermont Bicycle Touring
Box 711
Bristol, VT 05443
(802) 453-4811

Alternate Accomodation Sources

Bed and Breakfast Hawaii
P.O. Box 449
Kapaa, HI. 96746

For a modest membership fee, B&B will send a guide listing member homes--there on some on every island.

For information on hostels, write to

American Youth Hostels, Inc.
National Office
P.O. Box 37613
Washington, D.C. 20013-7613

AYH maintains two hostels on Honolulu. One is in Waikiki and the other near the University. Reservations should be made well in advance. Mainland branches of the AYH system can provide further information.

General Information

The Hawaii Visitors Bureau, a privately-funded agency, makes available a wealth of general information on the state. They have offices on every island as well as branches in several Mainland cities:

Hawaii Visitors Bureau
3440 Wilshire Blvd. #502
Los Angeles, CA 90010
(213) 385-5301

Hawaii Visitors Bureau
180 N. Michigan Ave. #1031
Chicago, IL 60611
(312) 236-0632

Hawaii Visitors Bureau
50 California St.
San Francisco, CA 94111
(415) 392-8173

Hawaii Visitors Bureau
441 Lexington Ave.
New York, NY 10017
(212) 986-9203

Guides and Histories

General information on Hawaii abounds. James Michener's **Hawaii** remains a superb and very readable background to the islands. Gavan Daws' **Shoal of Time** is perhaps the best and certainly the most widely recommended standard history currently available. It is available in most Hawaiian bookstores. Insight Guides **Hawaii** (Hong Kong: APA Productions) has for years been the general guidebook I most frequently recommended to friends. It combines a wealth of history and information on every island and has been a steady guide to the islands for a decade. Island Heritage, a Honolulu-based comany, now offers guidebooks for each island which are unseful introductions to each place. **The Essential Guide to . . .** (Kauai, Oahu, Maui, etc.) series offers good photographs, current information, beach listings and nice photographs in a size which will fit the typical bicycle pannier. Finally, Ray Riegert's **Hidden Hawaii: The Adventurer's Guide, Fifth Edition** (Berkeley, Ulysses Press) gives an encyclopedic list of hiking trails, beaches, campgrounds, restaurants and accommodations for all the islands. Most Oahu cyclists traveling interisland use this book to plan their travels, and it is one I can recommend without reservation to those who seek practical information.

Cycling: Clubs, Books and Guides

The **Hawaii Bicycle League** is a non-profit organization dedicated to bicycling in Hawaii. Its members, mostly volunteers, attempt to answer questions and provide assistance to visitors interested in bicycling in Hawaii. Its tour director, for example, regularly receives and responds to requests for information from cyclists from around the world. There is no charge for this service, or for participating in HBL's weekend rides on Oahu.

Hawaii Bicycle League
Box. 4403
Honolulu, HI 96812-4403
(808) 988-7175

There are no other guides to cycling this state currently in print. Outdated and out-of-print, but occasionally available in used book stores is the book I first read when I started cycling Hawaii years ago: Robert Immler's **Bicycling in Hawaii** (Berkeley, California:

Wilderness Press, 1978). Even rarer, less useful and much shorter was Linda McComb Rathbun's **Bicycler's Guide to Honolulu** (Honolulu: Petroglyph Press, 1976). Those who wish to combine cycling with hiking, or mountain bikers who want a description of Island hiking trails should read Robert Smith's **Hawaii's Best Hiking Trails** (Berkeley, California: Wilderness Press, 1982).

Indispensible to me is Tom Cuthbertson and Rick Morrall's **The Bike Bag Book** (Berkeley: Ten Speed Press). Nothing has taught me more about emergency repairs than this small, very slim, clearly written handbook, which costs under $5 and fits into the bottom of a handlebar bag.

Two good, general paperback books on bicycles, bike mainte- nance and bicycle touring are Richard Ballantine's **Richard's Bicycle Book** (New York: Ballantine Press) and Eugene Sloane's **The All New Complete Book of Bicycle** (New York: Simon and Schuster). Ballantine's book is a particular favorite of mine. Dennis Coello's **Touring on Two Wheels** (Nick Lyons Books), is a very basic primer on cycle touring that may be helpful to the novice who is nervous about traveling with a bicycle.

Cycling Oahu

INTRODUCTION

Visiting cyclists tend to avoid Oahu, seeking instead the glories of Maui, Molokai, Kauai and the Big Island. Honolulu, the city that dominates both Oahu and the Islands in general, is supposed to be too big and too urban for a vacationer's ride. The dense, almost constant traffic that rules much of the urban core from Pearl City to Hawaii Kai is just not what vacation riding is supposed to be about. As a result, many cyclists avoid the island where almost 90 percent of this state's residents live and avoid, in particular, the denser urban core, which non-cycling tourists visit with frequency and return to again and again.

Cycle Oahu. It's worth it. Forget what you may have heard. The south shore does have heavy traffic, especially during rush hour, but it is no worse and usually better than the traffic in many other large cities. Further, traffic eases off the main arterials, even during rush hour and within minutes of downtown and Waikiki are trees, paths and quiet woods which are a delight.

As a concession to rush hour, I try to stay off the major streets when traffic is heaviest—between 7:00 and 8:00 o'clock in the morning and 4:00 to 5:30 in the evening. But I've often barrelled through Waikiki, down King Street or along Kalanianaole Highway during those hours. In fact, as traffic backs up at those times, cyclists often find themselves passing motorists who must wait impatiently for traffic snafus to unbend. If the pace becomes intolerable, however, I stop and have a guava juice until the rush slacks off. But should you choose to ride during heavy traffic periods do not feel guilty or scared of people sitting in hot cars who watch enviously as a cyclist breezes by. State law gives cyclists the same rights as motorists, and you should not worry about your choice of the bicycle for transportation.

The City as Supersite

Honolulu is an urban center and suffers from many of the ills one expects to find anywhere more than 900,000 people of diverse races and backgrounds congregate. It also is an intensely urbanized, fascinating place with art, music, theater, dance, beaches and a breathtaking beauty that never seems to fade. Of all the cities I've known in 23 countries, 22 states and 10 Canadian provinces, Honolulu and its environs make up the most interesting urban environment I've ever seen. For me, there is no better way to see it all than from a bicycle's saddle. More than 90,000 bicycles are registered in Honolulu County each year, and more than ten percent of those bicycles are registered to commuters. In short, residents ride and so can you. Oahu and Honolulu are cycled every day, safely and enjoyably, by folk (like John Daley and me) with moderate riding skills.

The following routes include several relatively short city rides that avoid the worst of the trafficked streets, as well as longer runs along the island's coast and through its hilly interior. Destinations include the practical (where to pick up a camping pass), historical (Chinatown), cultural (University of Hawaii or the Academy of Arts), recreational (Waimanalo Beach), scenic (Manoa) and just plain glorious (Pali Lookout). The choice is up to you.

The intention is to convince you to use your bicycle both in Honolulu itself and as a way to see the island as a whole. I'm biased, of course. I love this place and want others to love it too.

Island Routes

The routes chosen here avoid existing bicycle paths and rely on streets like Kalanianaole Highway, King and Beretania, where there is sufficient room along the side of the road. Every study that I've read has argued that bicycle paths as they are now constructed are more dangerous than the road. They are too narrow, are badly graded, and include obstacles like joggers or skateboarders. Their general location is included here, but my advice is to stick with the streets. Also avoided where possible are side streets with lots of stop signs and bad cross traffic. My experience in Honolulu has been that major streets with sufficient curb width are the safest and best places to ride.

The worst streets are high-volume, narrow arterials, like Ala Moana Boulevard and Dillingham Highway, where the cyclist is at a disadvantage in the competition with trucks and cars for limited space. Where possible, these streets are avoided and, where they're needed, ways to ride safely are stressed. Nobody can decide but you what feels safe on a particular day and what does not. Each rider must decide what traffic conditions are acceptable and what destinations seem both safe and interesting.

If, however, you find yourself on a route which is just too much for your current cycling ability, move to the curbside and get off the bike. Go to a restaurant and take a break over some hot coffee or a cup of tea. Maybe a local cyclist will come by and ride a bit of the way with you or explain a different route. If you're still nervous, however, walk a few blocks until a less-traveled side street appears and ride on from there. That's what I've done many times while learning to ride in new

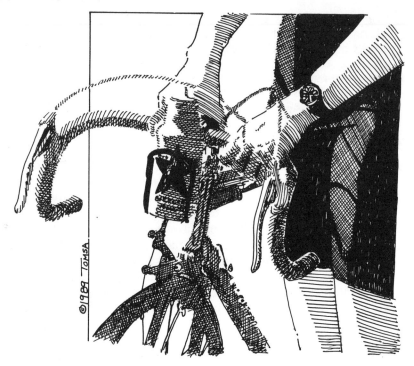

©1989 Tomsa

cities where the traffic patterns, routes and topography were simultaneously strange to me. You must decide for yourself what you are capable of, and nobody, other riders or drivers, will have anything but praise for those who assess their limits correctly.

Directions

Nobody in Hawaii talks about going north, south, east or west. Directions are taken from the islands' geography, and folks use prominent local landmarks to orient the visitor. So, when you ask kama'aina how to get from point "a" to point "b" on Oahu, they will probably say it is "diamond head" (roughly east) or ewa (generally west), mauka (toward the mountains) or makai (toward the shore). Because the northwest trades are so constant and so important to island life, people also talk about the "windward" side—an island's eastern side—and the leeward or western shores. So the Pali Highway is ewa and then mauka from Waikiki. From the University of Hawaii, however, Waikiki's Kapiolani Park is makai (toward the shore) and then diamond head side.

Starting Point

Let's assume you are staying in or near Waikiki, where the majority of hotels are, which gives a central point —**Kapiolani Park**—

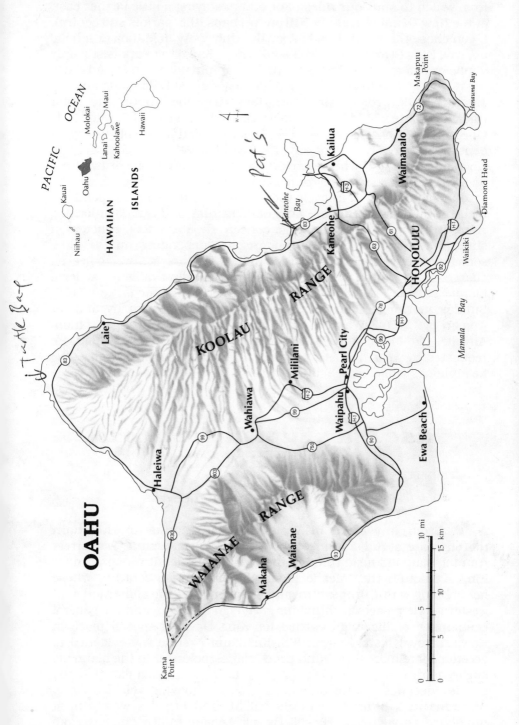

PACIFIC OCEAN

HAWAIIAN ISLANDS

Niihau

Kauai

Oahu

Molokai

Lanai

Kahoolawe

Maui

Hawaii

OAHU

KOOLAU RANGE

WAIANAE RANGE

Kaena Point

Laie

Haleiwa

Wahiawa

Mililani

Makaha

Waianae

Pearl City

Waipahu

Kaneohe

Kaneohe Bay

Kailua

Waimanalo

HONOLULU

Ewa Beach

Waikiki

Diamond Head

Makapuu Point

Hanauma Bay

Mamala Bay

to Turtle Bay

to Pat's

83

83

83

930

99

803

99

750

93

76

99

H1

H2

H1

H1

H2

H3

63

61

72

92

78

Kaena Point

10 mi

15 km

10

5

5

5

0

from which to start our rides. For others staying a little farther east, at the **New Otani** or **Kahala Hilton**, perhaps, the park is still central. If you chose the Youth Hostel near the University in Manoa or a hotel on, say, King Street in the Makiki district, Kapiolani Park is still only a mile or two away. If, however, you're camping at Sand Island Park, the ride into downtown will take a bit longer along Dillingham and Ala Moana Boulevards. Using the rides described here, the least trafficked route would be to Chinatown, and from there following Ride One in reverse order. The secret of Honolulu is that despite its urban density, it is really a very small town (at least when compared to Houston or Atlanta) where nobody lives more than a mile or two from one of this section's major routes.

Kapiolani Park is a lovely local park and the starting point for many of the **Hawaii Bicycle League** Saturday and Sunday morning rides. In the park near the large concert shell is a food concession stand where riders typically congregate, depending on the ride, sometime between 7:00 and 9:00 a.m. Visitors are welcome—no charge—and printed ride schedules are usually available at local bicycle stores. The "ride hot line" telephone number is 988-7175. Sunday mornings there is usually a second ride run by and for women by WOW (Wahines on Wheels), another HBL organization. Anyone, *wahine* or *kane* (male or female) is welcomed. Riders are requested to wear helmets, however, and are prohibited from using headphones while on scheduled rides.

Ride One: Kapiolani Park to Chinatown
Skill levels: Basic urban skills
Connects with Rides Two and Seven

From anywhere in Waikiki, cycle mauka to the main thoroughfare of Kalakaua Avenue, a wide, spacious one-way street running diamond head through the Waikiki district. It was named for King Kalakaua, the "Merrie Monarch" of the last century, whose hobnobbing with European royalty, insistence on the construction of western-style palaces befitting his sovereign majesty, and the general exuberance of his reign earned for King David a special place in Hawaii's royal history. In 1988, Kalakaua Avenue was widened to accommodate more traffic and pedestrians, making it in the planner's sugary phrase a "people place." At that time pedicabs, a fixture of the city for decades, were banned as "slower moving vehicles" from Kalakaua in a bitter City Council fight, and bicycles were almost prohibited as well. The Hawaii Bicycle League rallied support from cyclists to keep the right to ride this road and won with the support of

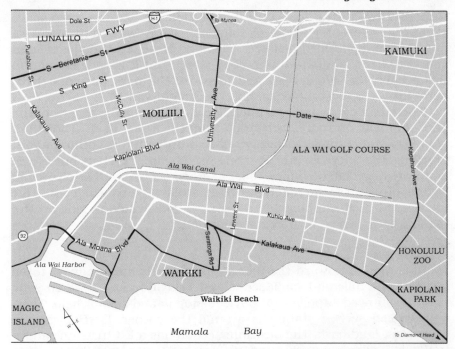

several cycling council members. Despite the volume of traffic funnelled through this area, however, cyclists will find themselves continually slowed by traffic lights timed to trap any traffic moving at even a moderate speed .

I usually ride down one-way Kalakaua on the left side of the street, one lane away from the turn-only lanes, until I see, on the right, the large, old and magnificent **Sheraton Moana Surfrider.** The Moana is one of the last of the old-style hotels on the island. When ships were the only way to approach Oahu and statehood a dream on the part of some, the Moana was luxury at the edge of the city, a beach resort near where "beach boys" with long boards rode the morning's gentle swells. In 1988 the hotel was closed for renovations, its furniture and fixtures sold to the public in a cash-and-carry island-style garage sale, and reopened the next year with a whole new decor which continues to echo the spirit of the 1920s and the memories of its earlier years. This is a place to stop and have a drink as the sun sets, to remember the days long ago when cases of hotel robbery or assaults on the beach were the province not of Hawaii Five-O but of a real-life detective named Chang Apana, the model for Edgar Biggers' fictional hero Charlie Chan.

Sheraton Moana

At the Moana, move to the left-hand traffic lane, preparing for a left turn at the next large intersection onto Kapahulu Avenue. The

Honolulu Zoo will be across the intersection, set back on green space signalling the outer fringe of Kapiolani Park. We'll return to this intersection again for rides over Diamond Head, to Makapu'u Point and elsewhere. Kapahulu is a busy street, but it is wide enough in this section for safe cycling and, because the park prevents right-hand turns for several blocks, nobody can cut you off.

There is a cycle path paralleling Kapahulu for the length of the park, but it is far more dangerous than the street itself. The gift of planners and transportation types who understand nothing about bicycling, the "bicycle path" is rarely used by local cyclists but is well patronized by skateboarders, roller skaters, people with strollers and legions of joggers who together create a moving obstacle course for us, the riders it supposedly serves. If you decide to ride on the "bicycle path," do so with extreme caution.

Date Street
Ride mauka (toward the mountains) on this street almost three quarters of a mile and you'll see **Island Triathlon and Bike** on your right. If you need supplies—or advice—stop in and ask for help. Their well-stocked service station is around the corner. IT&B is also a convenient landmark. The next intersection has a left turn lane and a traffic light where you will turn left (yes, ewa) onto Date Street. This is a secondary road paralleling the public Ala Wai golf course on your left and is not too badly trafficked. It's a pleasant if short ride of about a half mile before you reach the north-south corridor of University Avenue, which runs from the Ala Wai Canal into Manoa Valley.

University to Beretania Street
There's a traffic light at the simple, four-way intersection of Date and University, but even without street signs University is distinguished by the faded, narrow bicycle lane painted on its surface. Today we're riding only to the intersection with Beretania Street, the next major traffic light, which is two blocks mauka (toward the hills), but on Ride Four we'll go up University and explore the campus itself. For now, be ready to move to the left-hand turn lane at the next light, where a green arrow turn-signal directs traffic onto Beretania Street to your left. Turn into the near lane and settle in to riding one of the city's major arterials, which runs one-way across the city. King Street, its companion, carries traffic in the opposite direction toward Diamond Head, and this intersection is where the two streets meet. It is an intersection you'll come to know well.

As you ride ewa on Beretania, the street will narrow and widen several times until it settles, a mile along, into a comfortable city cycling route. Parked cars along this one-way street's left-hand side create a free zone which local cyclists use. Because there are frequent turn lanes, you have to be careful not to stay too far toward the curb and get sucked into a turning only lane along parts of this route. When we teach effective cycling on this road, students are warned not to ride too close to the parked cars but to stay a foot and a half distant from them at all times so that nobody will open a car door in their face.

You'll be holding steady on this street for about four miles, past Punahou Street, where you'll be a few blocks from one of the most famous and prestigious of private island schools (named, of course, **Punahou School**), Makiki Street, which becomes the **Tantalus** Mountain climb (a favorite training area for local riders and one described as Ride Five in this chapter), and Keeaumoku Avenue, which terminates at its makai end at the mammoth **Ala Moana Shopping Center**. Farther along, at the intersection with Ward Avenue, you'll pass the **Honolulu Academy of Arts**, a superb if small public art museum with a wonderful Asian collection. It's well worth an afternoon of exploration on its own, but for now just keep going past the State Capitol, with its huge statue of the Molokai martyr **Father Damien** in the front courtyard, all the way to Nuuanu Street, where a choice must be made:

The address you wrote to for county camping permits can be reached by turning onto Punchbowl from Beretania Street near the State Capitol. If you're not permit hunting, however, just stay on Beretania until Nuuanu, where a right turn leads to Pali Lookout and Oahu's windward side (see Ride Two). A left turn at this intersection carries you through the old city to **Chinatown**. We'll explore the harder route next ride, a 1,100-foot climb up a busy street and then through the quiet upper Nuuanu residential neighborhood to the Pali Lookout. But relax today and take the slower, easier route down Hotel Street to Chinatown.

Hotel Street

After a left turn onto Nuuanu Street, stay in the right-hand lane and stop at the intersection where Hotel Street breaks off to your right. All through this area can be seen vestiges of old Honolulu, but visit soon because they're fading fast. This was once sailor's town, an area of disreputable bars and tough bar girls, tattoo parlors and sleaze. When I first moved to Honolulu, Hotel Street's reputation was that of a racy, rough waterfront, and to stop in and buy a beer at some small bar was something of an adventure. No, it really wasn't dangerous, but there was excitement in the myth. Now it is being cleaned up, and nowhere is it all so clear as on this strip of Hotel to River Street. Thanks in great part to urban renewal, Hotel Street has been undergoing a face lift and is now trying for respectability; at least so far, the transformation is not complete. There are still tough bars, darkly lit little stores and a crush of humanity for whom Honolulu is not a mecca but a place in which life can be hard and something of a struggle day by day.

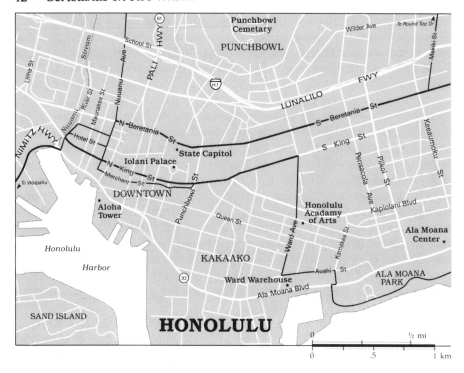

Get off the bicycle and walk down Hotel to your right for a block or two to get a feel of what was and what now is. At the intersection of Hotel and Kekaulike, for instance, there is still a block of ramshackle, old wooden buildings that are reminders of the way this whole area looked less than a decade ago. Nearby is the modern, concrete Chinese Cultural Center, which owes nothing in architecture or feeling to the world "Pake" (Chinese) workers knew and inhabited here fifty years ago. Side streets throughout this district each had their own feel and smell, but more and more that older sense is being obscured by a distinctive, urban feel. Renovated buildings abut older, dilapidated stores, giving a glimpse of what was until recently a forgotten city where transients, sailors and immigrants vied to satisfy diverse needs. An upscale future in which art galleries replace tattoo parlors and polite restaurants replace dark beer halls is equally evident, and existing together as these two do at present, it seems as if time itself is held somehow in the balance.

Chinatown

This is also the old Chinese area, the former center of community life for immigrants first brought in the 19th century to work the fields and build railroads. The Chinese community has been important in Hawaii's history, an integral component in the ethnic mix and a crucial addition to the local work force. Although Kung Fu Schools and traditional family association buildings have given way to Korean groceries or Vietnamese stores, you do not have to look very hard to find the markets or the people whose lives have been lived in this section.

Much of the area's past can be read in the history of Honolulu's oldest restaurant, the **Wo Fat,** which still stands at the intersection of Hotel and Maunakea. Started in 1882, the original building was destroyed in the great Chinatown fire of 1886, rebuilt shortly afterwards and destroyed again in another fire in 1900. Rebuilt again, the Cantonese-style restaurant survived, and in 1937 the current rather gaudy building was put up. It is a large structure, seating 850, and a place to stop for dim sum or a regular meal. If you do stop, take a moment to study the photographs of old Honolulu which hang on the restaurant's walls. In most American cities, "then" and "now" photographs like these would separate five or six generations. Here, middle-aged adults will remember when these images depicted their city perfectly. It is as if Honolulu has gone in a generation or two from the glory days of the mid-19th century fast into the 21st century.

A few blocks from the Nuuanu intersection, Hotel ends at River Street, a block past Kekaulike, where old men chat in Cantonese while watching the quiet waters of Nuuanu Stream flowing into the sea. Along River Street (really the stream) north of Hotel is the modern Chinese Community Center, with shops galore and a good Hakka-style restaurant where I've stopped for brunch. North of the statue of Chinese hero Sun Yat-sen, who lived here for a while, is a good, very inexpensive Chinese takeout stand (no place inside to sit down) called **The Royal Kitchen**. For those on a tight budget, it is ideal. Try some "char shu bao" (steamed pork buns) or shu mai (small, steamed dumplings) and eat them by Nuuanu stream with the old men whose perpetual domino game exists in harmony with the

blaring, boom boxes of younger folk who hang out here as well.

After lunch, ride slowly through the whole Chinatown area for a while or, if you prefer an even slower pace, try walking a few blocks after securely locking your bicycle to a post. Some people are Chinatown collectors and in whatever city they find themselves spend hours or days in that section of the city. If you're one of those, Frances Carter's *Exploring Honolulu's Chinatown* will be a help. There are Chinese fresh food markets, tattoo parlors, and junk or gift stores in profusion.

Just north of The Royal Kitchen and on the stream's other side is the **Izume Taisha Shrine**, on the corner of North Kukui Street. Over 80 years old, the Shinto shrine honoring Okuninushi No Mikoto often has services on the tenth of each month, according to Carter's guide. I've been there often on New Years Day to see crowds streaming in and out of the shrine as the white-robed priest helps local parishioners celebrate. It is only fair to mention, in an ecumenical way, that on North Vineyard street two blocks away is the city's most frequented Chinese Temple, dedicated to the goddess Kuan Yin. First established in the 1880s and, like everything else here, rebuilt several times, the altar holds a representation of the Goddess of Mercy sitting on a lotus blossom and flanked by, on the right, Wei Tor, guardian of the faith, and on the left, Kuan Tai, protector of truth.

Riding from here back toward Diamond Head and the beach, you pass lower **Maunakea Street** (near Ala Moana Boulevard), a re-stored block which has become a concentration of specialty and antique stores.   Along the way, at 150 Hotel Street, there is a wonderful, inexpensive Vietnamese restaurant with the best croissants in town. Vietnamese restaurants and stores are becoming ever more conspicuous in this area as Honolulu's newest wave of Asian immigrants moves into the city's oldest section and begins to revitalize it with their own restaurants and food stores.

For those with a taste for walking tours, two organizations offer the chance to see Chinatown with knowledgeable local guides. The **Chinese Chamber of Commerce** (533-3181) currently offers tours every Tuesday morning which end with an optional lunch at Wo Fat restaurant. The cost is $4 for the tour and $5 for those who want to eat with the group. **Hawaii Heritage Center** (521-2749) offers tours on Wednesday and Friday mornings.

Riding back diamond head from the Royal Kitchen you can take Pauahi, North King Street or Hotel Street. Technically, Hotel Street is now only for buses, but I've used it on occasion, forgetting the new prohibitions. All three streets turn right onto Nuuanu and then left almost immediately onto **Merchant Street**. This is one of those wonderful areas, like Maunakea Street, of 1920s architecture with detailed cornices and handsome brick. It also keeps the cyclist out of the worst of the major arterial congestion. Merchant runs past **Richards Street**, where the downtown **Post Office** stands, to Mililani and the **State Library** at the juncture of King and Punchbowl on your left.

The place you want to stop for state camping permits is on King Street almost directly across from the library. The address is included at the end of this section.

To Ward Avenue

A few blocks farther the traffic divides, with King Street continuing to the left and Kapiolani Boulevard—where the Newspaper Agency building stands across from Kawaiahao Plaza—forking to the right. Either will carry you to and past Ward Avenue, but I much prefer wider King Street and believe it the easiest to cycle. Staying on King, then, go until **TGI Friday's** restaurant appears on your right. This is the intersection of King and Ward. To the left across from the one-block **Thomas Square** is the **Honolulu Academy of Arts**, a landmark passed on the way out of town. Before turning right onto Ward Avenue for a half-mile, I usually stop in Thomas Square to see its magnificent banyan tree, which surrounds a fountain in the mini-park's center.

I have a particular affection for this tree and for banyan trees in general. The four-year-old daughter of a friend of mine calls them "Tarzan trees" because she can swing—"like Tarzan"—from the vine-like roots which hang down from the branches. As the trees grow, they root and spread in this way with the long, tough "vines" eventually planting and growing as additions to the tree's trunk. In places like Thomas Square, over time a tree can grow to incredible size and cover a vast area. Because I've lived near here for several years and visited frequently, I've watched as people of all ages stop, picnic or simply sit in silence near the park's fountain, dreaming away the day. Everybody swings from this banyan tree, some by tying the dangling roots into a makeshift swing.

Several years ago, in a late afternoon, the park was almost deserted when I saw an elderly man, bent like a question mark over his cane, shuffle up to the tree on its mauka side and stare critically at its immensity. It was as if he had known it when both were young and was deciding if the future was what either could have expected in the days when Hawaii was still a territory and Oahu an exotic destination. Surreptitiously he glanced left and right to see if anyone was watching him and, secure in his solitude, he nodded toward the tree, hooked his cane firmly over a wrist, and grabbed the branch which hung before him like a rope. Taking the weight with his arms, both legs wrapped around the branch, he swung once back and forth before landing in a crouch. I heard him chuckle quietly and say goodby to the tree and then, with some dignity, he continued on his way. I wanted to ask what it had felt like to swing again as he had when a child, to know if for a moment time had stood still or even reversed and if the flood of memories had been worthwhile or if the frailties of age which made his walk a haltering step had forced even further than memory can reach the joy such experiences once held.

But I did not approach and turned away, careful that he should not see me or know that his excess had been observed. I've thought about that moment many times in recent years. Somehow, it is a symbol to me of Honolulu today, with the old clinging tenaciously as

the newer roots and spreads. But also it reminds me of the type of urban epiphany one gains by cycling and stopping, meeting and watching.

From Thomas Square, I often stop on Ward Avenue at TGI Friday's to sit at an outside table and contemplate such things over a beer. This is one of my favorite oases in the city because it has had the courtesy and sense to provide a bicycle rack for cyclists. Makai on Ward a long city block is Kapiolani Boulevard again. For the very adept cyclist this street offers a fast route back to Waikiki. But like many riders I find the traffic as a rule excessive and prefer instead to continue down Ward to Auahi Street, just past **The Bike Way** (250 Ward Ave.), where I turn left and usually make an immediate right into **Ward Warehouse**. One local store in the warehouse, **Coffee Works**, which also serves sandwiches, is a hangout for half the people I know and another pleasant place to while away the afternoon. On the Ward Avenue side there is also a small shop selling excellent Japanese boxed lunches ("bentos"), which can be placed in a pannier and carried home or to the beach. If you are a strong-willed dieter (or don't drink coffee), continue along Auahi and turn right at **Kamakee**

Street, which runs between the large Ward Warehouse and, across the street, the equally large **Ward Centre.**

Ala Moana Park

I rarely ride Ala Moana Boulevard and when I do it is only on sections I know very well. It is generally safe for the average rider very late at night or very early in the morning when traffic is light. But during the day the traffic is usually horrendous and the curbs narrow to nonexistent in sections. I do, however, love **Ala Moana Park** with a passion, especially the section known as **Magic Island**. So to make park access safer and more enjoyable for new riders, I hereby offer a local-style detour.

The trick is to use the Kamakee Street shortcut and cross into the park at the traffic light at Ala Moana Boulevard. If you walk across (some cyclists do), be prepared to wait a few minutes. The traffic light favors the Ala Moana traffic and can take several minutes to change for park traffic. If you ride, turn right on Ala Moana, get in the left turn lane, and be prepared to turn left quickly into the park as soon as the light's green arrow turn sign appears because it is brief—active only for perhaps 30 seconds.

Then you are in the park, which is used by local folk for picnics, swimming, jogging, sailing, snorkeling and every other outdoor activity imaginable. There are tennis courts, exercise stations and a solid mile of pristine beach protected by the offshore reef against large waves in all but the worst weather. Local runners and triathletes practice in this region. Honolulu religious groups, companies and neighbors congregate for picnics on the weekend. The 19th century urban parks movement was begun to make sure city dwellers had a chance to enjoy open space, and in Ala Moana Park that space is used to the full.

Speed bumps in this inner park keep the traffic at bay, and a half-mile ride along uniformly superb, reef-protected beaches takes you to a parking lot just before the boat channel. This is the parking lot for **Magic Island Park**. Whenever possible I come here to fly a kite, watch the boats entering and leaving the Ala Wai Harbor, snorkel along these reefs or simply relax in the sun. Local kids surf in this area and fishermen cast their rods along the Island's boat channel. No place on Oahu speaks to me of the travel brochure life like this small pocket of tropical glory in the center of a fantastically urban environment. It is also, like much of Waikiki, man-made, a fabrication built onto once pristine shore now transformed into a human playground that seems, at this remove, almost totally natural.

If you don't turn in to the park peninsula, the road will bend to the left and end at Ala Moana Boulevard. Despite the traffic on this road, there is an easy way to dodge it. Wait for the light and just after it turns red for Ala Moana drivers, make your move. By timing the light, cyclists have a minute or two head start on all traffic and can travel the fifth of a mile required in carless luxury. Then, as traffic almost catches up, turn right into **Ala Wai Harbor** after crossing the canal bridge and past the boat repair area. The road bends past hundreds of private sailing boats (there is a three- to five-year waiting list for obtaining a berth) to terminate at **Duke Kahanamoku Beach,** where many local folk teach their children to swim.

If you wish to avoid that small beach and do not find the hundreds of boats docked here of compelling interest, turn left at the **Ilikai Hotel** and return to Ala Moana Boulevard, where the traffic is normally so choked as to be robbed of its fury. A quick right at the **Hawaiian Hilton** on Kalia Road has you heading Diamond Head past **Fort De Russy Beach Park** to Saratoga or Beach Walk Avenues where the road turns left. Up this road and a right on Kalakaua Avenue puts you a half mile from Kapiolani Park and close to all. A block north of this intersection is Kuhio Avenue, where many hotels are located and which may be more convenient than Kalakaua Avenue, depending on your exact destination.

This ride would put between 12 and 15 miles on the cyclometer, depending on detours and diversions in the ride downtown.

Ride Two: Chinatown to Pali Lookout
Skill level: Average urban skills, one long climb
Connects with Rides One and Six

This ride begins at the intersection of Nuuanu and Beretania Streets, where in the previous ride cyclists turned left at the light and headed for Hotel Street. This more arduous, hilly trip turns right at that same intersection and carries the rider up more than 1,000 feet in about five miles to the famous and breathtakingly beautiful Pali Lookout. Expert city-style riders can continue through the Pali tunnel and down to beaches on Oahu's windward side. Others, who do not choose to make the full run, can turn around at the Lookout and return to the Hotel Street area or go back into the city on King Street.

After the right-hand turn onto Nuuanu, the difference between this route and the Hotel Street section is immediately evident. Heading mauka, Nuuanu begins as a lightly commercial, heavily trafficked street which becomes rapidly residential. The higher you climb, the more prestigious and expensive the homes will be. The first part of this section has only a moderate incline, but, going through a traffic circle, cyclists find themselves on a steeper grade with moderately heavy traffic. This is a main artery that carries half the island's traffic from the windward side back and forth to the city. Stay on the right-hand shoulder and do not worry. Cyclists are a common sight, and drivers are fairly accustomed to our presence. Use lower gears as the grade steepens and remember that what goes up with difficulty comes down with speed and, sometimes, with grace. A little more than three miles up Nuuanu from Beretania Street you'll pass Dowsett Street. The *next* turn is **Nuuanu Pali Drive,** more familiarly known as **Old Pali Road**. Take this right-hand turn away from the traffic and into truly bucolic splendor. The hills are quiet, the homes superb and, if you just follow the road, you'll be riding alongside Nuuanu Stream where it has cut a deep ravine into the land.

After about three-quarters of a mile there is, on the road's right-hand side, a small clearing in the woods that looks like a painting of the elvish land of Rivendel in J.R.R. Tolkien's Middle Earth. This is on the lip of the ravine and is one of those small, serendipitous locations which make these islands so magical. It is a wonderful place to stop and rest for a minute, sip some juice and swallow a bit of gorp. If you're lucky, the clearing will be uninhabited and pristine except for fast food cups, beer cans and the standard refuse left by car drivers in scenic places. This is a favorite parking spot for couples, and sometimes you will find young people congregating in the area with ghetto blasters turned to ear-splitting levels. Auwe!

A little farther is a city water station with reservoir, another splendid sight where people stop. It looks so natural , this long field of water topped with green algae and a few lilies which grow along the reservoir's shore. It is large enough so that no tree can shade the whole and the effect is quite spectacular. It is worth riding the lower, trafficked section to find this exceptional and quiet piece of land. Nuuanu-Old Pali Road exits a mile from the Pali Lookout, and it takes a second or two to reorient as traffic zooms by at a noisy rate. Just ride on and endure. The lightly graveled shoulder continues for a little less than a mile and then it is there, the appropriate and well-marked Pali Lookout cutoff.

The View! The View!

There is a strong native cultural movement present today throughout the islands, an attempt to preserve the remnants of the traditional culture's best parts—language, dance, music and an ecologic awareness of man's dependence on the land—against the rush of fast food culture. A part of this movement is the perhaps inevitable nostalgia for older times, for the romantic era of warrior kings and subsistence lives. I encourage those who wish to preserve these remnants, but those who deify King Kamehameha and his line should remember the harsh brutality which also was a part of those good times.

Pali Lookout, for example, is the scene of one of the island's more famous slaughters in which defending, native soldiers were backed first to and then over the precipice by the victorious forces of the resourceful, brutal unifier of these islands, the great King Kamehameha I. That victory broke the back of the Oahu native

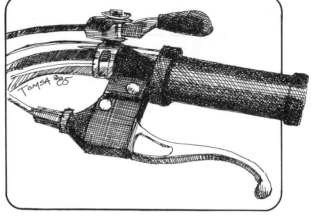

warriors' resistance and signaled the coming of one monarch's rule to Hawaii, from the Big Island to Kauai. From the Lookout's vantage point, the windward side can be seen below, with the growing town of Kaneohe in the distance and the ship's channel marked by a conical island called Chinaman's Hat offshore and to the left. To get there, however, you have to ride through the tunnel and down a winding road, a trip recommended only for expert cyclists able to ride for several miles at speeds of at least 30 miles an hour. We'll come back here at another point, but, for now, it is time to return to the city and the rest of the route.

Returning to King Street or Chinatown

Leaving the Lookout is easy. The road goes one way and empties into traffic heading makai toward the city. With four miles of downhill riding ahead, *it is prudent and important to keep your speed in check.* Accidents happen when folks ride faster than their abilities allow and wipe out on the downhill run. The secret is not speed, but controlled, safe speed on these long, downhill slides, so brake a bit as you roll along and it will be almost as much fun—if less terrifying— than a precipitous, forty-five-mile-an-hour plummet. On the left after just a mile will be a sign for the Nuuanu-Old Pali Road, and I recommend returning through that diversion, just the way you came. Coast back through that lovely section, and when it ends, turn left again, straight down *past* Beretania Street as far as Hotel Street (should you wish to visit Chinatown again) or turn *left* onto King Street. Riding King Street takes you quickly to the end of Ride One's route to Kapiolani Park.

Ride Three: Pali Lookout to Waimanalo

Skill level: Above average skills
Connects with Rides Two and Six

Better-than-average riders will want to use the Pali as a gateway to Oahu's windward side, and as a shortcut to campgrounds like Malaekahana on the island's northeast tip. It is not a difficult descent, but skill is needed both to ride through the Pali tunnel, which exits onto a steep, "U"-shaped bend in the road, and to safely maintain speed in an area with little shoulder and sometimes heavy traffic. The narrow, winding road on the windward side leaves little room for bicycles, so those who ride this section should be comfortable at sustained speeds of over 25 miles an hour in traffic.

Part of the route is visible from the Lookout, and new cyclists should take a moment to look down. The hardest section is right past the visible bend and, with that in mind, the only trick is to stay in the groove and keep your cool. A few people commute across this pass every day and other cyclists pedal it with frequency as a good, weekend training ride.

Here we go.

To ride through the tunnel safely and legally cyclists must have some bicycle lighting system. It is, as tunnels go, a short cut through the hillside, but to be rear-ended here would be an unpleasant experience indeed. So, if you decide to take this route, use a headlight and, unless you have a very good rear reflector, leg lamps to assure visibility.

Leaving the Lookout area, follow the traffic signs that indicate the tunnel and, if there is a long line of traffic, wait for a break. Do not ride here during rush hour unless you are extremely skilled. Mid-morning or early afternoon are far better times to push through.

Once in the tunnel, let speed increase but be aware that as you exit the tunnel onto Route 61 the road will drop and bend simultaneously—so keep control. Just go with the flow past **Kamehameha Highway** (Highway 83), where **Hawaii Loa College** will be (briefly) visible, and on the main **Kalanianaole Highway**. A left turn onto Highway 83 would carry you through often heavy traffic without a shoulder first to and eventually past Kaneohe. This route is used by some experienced local riders interested in heading quickly to the island's north shore and by a few very hearty commuters who daily travel between Kaneohe and downtown Honolulu.

For the moment, however, just continue past the junction with Highway 83 until **Castle Memorial Hospital** appears on the road's left-hand side. At this intersection bear right onto route Route 72, which is also Kalanianaole Highway. As you descend, **Bellows Air Force Base** will be on the left and **Olomana Peak** (altitude about 1,650 feet) will dominate the land to your right. Stay on Kalanianaole Highway to **Waimanalo Beach Park,** a few miles from Hawaii Kai.

This route and Ride Five complete an approximately fifty-mile loop of the island's dense, southeast corridor. From Kapiolani Park first to the Pali Lookout and then to Waimanalo is between 25 and 30 miles of extraordinarily varied bicycling terrain. I like this route both for its variety (downtown streets, the Pali climb, a tunnel, winding roads and then the beach) and for the park itself. Camping is allowed and all sorts of people from exotic places (Canada, Colorado, California, etc.) stop for a few nights. Usually I'll walk over to see any cyclists who have pitched their tents. The park is also heavily used by Oahu families who wish to picnic and swim during the day. Last weekend, for example, I visited the park and met a group of five women and two men who sat and sang Hawaiian songs for an hour, accompanying themselves on ukulele and guitar. They were not professional entertainers, they said. Just folk who sang in church and for the love of it—out of affection for the language and to take pleasure in the day.

Ride Four: Kapiolani Park to University of Hawaii & Paradise Park
Skill level: Basic urban skills
Connects with Ride One

If you want a fairly easy urban ride with only a modest climb through predominantly residential streets, then this ride is for you. It goes into and through Manoa Valley, where the University of Hawaii at Manoa stands, past Paradise Park, an often-visited tourist attraction, and ends at the Lyon Arboretum. This, for the botanically minded, is a University of Hawaii horticultural research and educational center and one of the island's unsung treasures. For those interested in a more arduous climb, this ride can be combined with a hump up Tantalus, which to mid-westerners living on the flats might seem arduous, but to British Columbians used to a glacial terrain will be a piece of cake.

East-West Center
From Kapiolani Park, our normal starting place, return to the intersection of University, Beretania and King Streets where the Chinatown ride branched off. This time continue in the faded bicycle lane up University and under the H-1 Freeway past its on-ramp. UH begins at the next intersection with a wide lawn and buildings whose

institutional architecture fairly screams "academe." Turn right at this light onto Dole Street and cycle through two more traffic lights to East-West Road, which terminates at Dole. Take a left and welcome to the East-West Center, which is a part of the University of Hawaii's campus. The first large building to the right, Burns Hall, often features exhibits of photographs, paintings or artifacts from some part of the Pacific Rim.

Its real treasure, however, is Alice, the Bento Lady, a University institution. Every morning from 11 to 12:30 each weekday this Japanese-Hawaiian woman sells Japanese boxed lunches (bentos) from the open doorway at Burns. For about $3 these bentos combine fish or meat, vegetables and rice in a container that fits handily into almost any bicycle pannier and can be carried anyplace (the beach, a park) the spirit moves you. Boxed lunches are now a Hawaiian institution, but hers, prepared fresh each morning, are unusually good. Her tempura vegetables (the batter recipe is a close secret which she will not share with anyone) are brilliant and the lemon chicken has just the right amount of tart spice to set off the sweetness of its meat.

Burns Hall is part of the East-West Center, a series of institutes whose purpose is to promote international understanding. A creation of the John F. Kennedy era, it is funded largely by the U.S. Congress with additional support provided by the governments of many Pacific Rim nations. One place to eat is just a bit down the road at another part of the Center. Jefferson Hall, a long, oblong building designed by the architect I.M. Pei, is the campus's most acclaimed piece of institutional architecture. It was designed around a huge, communal reading room which years ago held racks of newspapers from around the Pacific Rim. The whole point of the structure's interior was this meeting place which, sadly, has been closed to the public and transformed into private Center space.

Behind Jefferson and easily accessible is a small, Japanese-style garden you can walk through and eat in. It has a nice teahouse which, unfortunately, is closed to the public. Beside them both runs small, quiet Manoa Stream. This is a lovely area and, if a rain shower begins, the covered and beautiful **Thai Pavilion** is a perfect sanctuary in which to wait it out.

St. John Hall, mentioned earlier, is just past this area at the intersection with Maile Way. It is primarily classrooms, laboratories and offices, but cyclists are welcome to consult the large, table-size relief maps of Hawaii's major islands in the downstairs vestibule.

After that, if you wish to stroll through campus, a central walk-way directly across from the **Thai Pavilion** leads past **Hamilton Library** toward the Student Center complex. The university library is currently in deep trouble. It does not have adequate humidity control, and parts of its valuable Asian collection are endangered by creeping tropical molds. It is a form of official insanity that the State, which funds UH, has found money in its budget for new parking garages and a renovation of the Student Center but not sufficient monies to safeguard this library's unique collections.

Just behind the Student Center, whose good bookstore carries a complete selection of Island maps and a number of books on Hawaii, is **Manoa Gardens**, a University restaurant with outdoor, umbrellaed tables where most afternoons students (and faculty) sit and talk over beers. This is just off University Avenue and a nice place to stop and rest (even if you've hardly done anything at all). If you want to get on with riding, however, just continue up East-West Road and turn left at Maile Way after passing the spectacular **Korean Studies Center** on the right. Maile Way leads directly back to University Avenue at a traffic light, helpful in crossing heavy traffic. Go straight across University (a one-block long bicycle lane will guide you) and then turn right onto **Oahu Avenue.**

Bungalows

What a treat this area is. Quiet, residential, with beautiful homes that a generation ago cost perhaps $50,000 and now go for a mini-mum of $300,000. A **Quaker Meeting House** two blocks along on the left is one of my favorite residences in the city. Its covered porch, well kept lawn and solid, stone foundations give a feeling of permanence not unlike the sense one gets from attending a good Quaker meeting. Here form follows not simply function but sentiment, and often I pause for a moment before the Quaker site and think about their sensible philosophy which insists that individuals in a community through reasoned discussion can reach a consensus on any issue.

Several blocks away, near the intersection of Maile and University, is the **Manoa Valley Inn**, a lodge *cum* bed and breakfast which is perhaps the last of the early 20th century, Victorian-style houses on the island. It is on the National Register of Historic Places, and the furniture is straight 1920s, right down to the pool table with old-style pockets in the billard room. The effect of the billiard room, sitting room, and outside screened veranda is superb. One can imagine Charlie Chan interviewing a suspect in any of these rooms. Unlike other bed and breakfasts on Oahu, the Inn is a business with seven bedrooms, which in 1990 will begin at about $92.50 per night for a double. An Inn employee said they have had mountain bike riders staying there, and there is a place in back where bicycles can be safely stored.

Throughout this area you will see a profusion of bungalow-style homes that, at least for me, are objects of some interest. The bungalow is a one-story structure with a sloped roof, small windows and wide porch which, in its classic form, fills the front of the building. The design originated in India and was eventually carried to England by returning colonial civil servants. The classic form had small windows and a large, covered exterior porch to minimize the effect of tropical heat on the house's often dim interior. From England the style was eventually adapted to various climates in countries around the world. In California, for example, the classic bungalow's small windows were widened and its overhanging roofs shortened to take advantage of natural light in a more temperate region. In Vancouver, basements were added to create more room and allow for a central heating system. But here in Hawaii, and especially in Manoa, the old-style Indian bungalow with its overhanging roof-as-shade can still be seen. In keeping with the Island's ethnic mix, some have been modified to conform to a more Japanese aesthetic through the addition of shoji screens.

Oahu Avenue and E. Manoa Road

After a half-mile ride on Oahu Avenue there will be a busy intersection at **Alaula Way**. Traffic rolls through here at a good clip in both directions so *Be Careful* when turning left to the next lighted intersection where Oahu and E. Manoa Road meet. A right carries you down into a valley where the **Manoa Valley Theater**, an old Japanese language school and **Manoa Marketplace** shopping center reside. In the latter is the city's best coffee bar, where I often stop for an afternoon espresso, read the newspaper and stare at the valley's steep hills. Each afternoon, clouds pile up behind the tropical cliffs that enclose this valley and make it so beautiful. Then, at sunset, they often drift away as shadows drop from west to east like a curtain across the valley floor.

If you do not turn toward the Marketplace (or, having stopped, return refreshed for more of a ride), staying on Oahu Avenue leads to a slow climb to where the road again crosses Manoa Road. At this junction, on the left, is the famous **Waioli Tea Room** (3016 Oahu Road), where the Salvation Army maintains a classic and classy "grass shack" similar to the one in which Robert Louis Stevenson wrote during his tenure in the Islands. Over the years the Tea Room has alternated being first open to the public and then closed. At present, in late 1989, it is not serving the public on a daily basis but by the time you arrive perhaps it will be open again.

Paradise Park

In the end, Manoa Road leads to where we're going, so take that

TOMSA '89

one for now. Several miles farther is **Paradise Park,** which is filled
with exotic birds. In this high, verdant area, rainfall is heavy and
cloudbursts more frequent than on the coast or even at the
University. But a touch of damp is a small price to pay for such
unparalleled beauty. In the woods there are mountain apples, guava,
passion fruit and various berries along the trail that leads to **Manoa
Falls.** This is hiker heaven, a lovely and inevitably muddy area to
tramp along the upper reaches of Manoa Stream. From Paradise Park
you can also walk or ride to **Lyon Arboretum** and then up the steep
hikers' trails for Aihualama or Manoa Falls Trails. Hiking guides to
Oahu describe this area very well. I once rode a part of this on my
mountain bike but soon turned back. It was a muddy, slogging climb
and, somehow, it seemed inappropriate to me for a mountain bicycle
to churn up what was so fundamentally a hiker's path.

From here glance up and ewa for a moment. Let your eyes climb
up the hill and along the ridge where cars wind along about two
thirds of the way to the top. That is Tantalus, our next ride's
destination. It's not too difficult, and from this vantage point the
extent of climbing required to cycle the ride is clear.

To get back to the city from the Arboretum is easy; just retrace
the route, coasting down from where you left the bicycle to Waioli Tea
Room. From there continue on Oahu Avenue through the intersection
with East Manoa Road and, directly past the intersection, turn right
to stay on this road past the Quaker Meeting House. Most
automobiles go straight here, rather than turn right where Oahu be-

comes University Avenue, but I find the road too narrow and the traffic too fast when such a pleasant alternative exists. At Maile Way turn left again and immediately right onto University.

Ride Five: To Tantalus & Round Top Drive

Skill level: Average urban skills
Connects with Rides One and Four

Or you can climb Tantalus. On the Chinatown ride a future hill climb was promised at Makiki Street, which is easy to reach when returning from Paradise Park.

Just makai of University and Maile, turn right from University Avenue at the traffic light in front of the campus onto Metcalf and follow it down a slight hill to the next traffic light, which is Wilder Street. Turn right there and ride through a residential neighborhood past Punahou Street to Makiki Street and make another right-hand turn. Immediately after that turn a good, slogging, breathtaking climb begins and ends. This is a loop, a path which leads up the right-hand side as Round Top Drive and, after its summit, descends as Tantalus Drive. Tantalus is a volcanic ridge which separates the residential area of Pacific Heights from the community of Manoa. Local cyclists use this as a training route, and even experienced cyclists will appreciate both the angle of its ascent and the spectacular views of the city which break through at every twist and turn.

Those intent on their climbing are advised to bring a picnic lunch to reward the effort this climb requires. Much of the residential area passed through on this climb is a ghetto of the island's wealthy who simultaneously seek seclusion and spectacular views. Actor Richard Chamberlain's enormous house is nestled into the hillside here, I'm told, and some of the island's more prestigious (if less famous) families also reside at this exalted height. One of my favorite residents of this area is University of Hawaii history professor John Stefan, a dedicated cyclist who for years commuted each day to work on his bicycle. In the early 1980s I thought it an eccentric gesture, and now I remember with some shame my amusement at Stefan's transportation mode.

Gearing Up to Gear Down

This is a wonderful place to practice the use of your bicycle's granny gears if home does not require the full range of gears. The road twists and turns along the face of the hill, and each turn reveals a better and more glorious view of the city below. Perhaps two-thirds of the way up is the old Lover's Lane, a section overlooking Manoa

Valley where several generations of teenagers once parked and dreamed of how they would, well, conquer the world and its secrets. Maybe they still do.

The road eventually swings around and into Tantalus Drive, which climbs the ewa side of this quite incredible dividend of the island's once active volcanic age. I find Round Top an easier climb than Tantalus, but others prefer to climb the Tantalus Drive side. It's not a big decision. However you go, *Be Careful* on the descent. Gravity gives the gift of speed, and for those not used to hairpin turns where cars may drift outside their lane, it can be rather hairy. So whichever route you choose, check the brakes and descend with care. If you come down Tantalus Drive, stop and rest at the Makiki Forest Recreation Area. On both sides there are places to pull off the road, and, if this climb is arduous for you, just tell your cycling partner the stop is not because of shortness of breath but only to enjoy the view.

Mountain Bikes

Mountain bikers will love this area and the profusion of trails that it provides. Hikers' manuals and the local **Mauka** off-road mountain bike club will offer some suggestions on different Tantalus trails visitors safely can ride. Most bicycle stores in the city have a list of Mauka Club rides with the telephone numbers for ride leaders who can all be of assistance. As well, riders can stop by Jill Cheever's store, **The Bike Way**, 250 Ward Avenue, where several employees are active in mauka and are mountain bike "akamai" (savvy). In a pinch call The Bike Way at 538-RIDE for help.

Tantalus Return

From Tantalus, the return ride is really easy. Straight down Makiki to Wilder Avenue, left on Wilder through the Metcalf traffic light and left onto Dole, which leads again to University. On the way down University Avenue and back to Date Street, take a moment to stop at the **Church of the Crossroads** just past the freeway on-ramps. It has a red roof, red pillars and looks, amidst all this urban bustle, surprisingly serene. There is a huge, open inner courtyard in this surprisingly spacious and unpretentious church which houses a preschool and hosts in its meeting rooms a number of socially conscious local groups. It is, in short, an activist church, a facility which speaks to social as well as spiritual needs. For years I've found myself stopping here to spend a half hour when I needed to consider a problem in quiet surroundings.

Around the corner, off University on Coyne Street opposite the **Varsity Theater** is **Bubbies**, a local ice cream and coffee bar. Some believe it to have the best ice cream on the islands, but the boast is too much for me to make. It is good, however, and with a coffee is almost perfect after a long hill climb and fast descent from Tantalus and Round Top.

Then down University Avenue, left on Date and right on Kapahulu places you with a clear shot for Ala Wai Boulevard, which branches off on your right after the golf course and a traffic light. Riding along this one-way street, parallel to the canal, pays a scenic dividend: many canoe clubs practice on this water. The canal is really a drainage channel to keep the firm ground of Waikiki from reverting to the swamp it once was before being drained and reclaimed early in this century and then developed for the tourist trade. A number of side streets lead from this road into Kuhio Street and the rest of Waikiki, so, wherever you're staying, note the direction of the nearest side streets and use them to get back home.

If today's ride was only to Paradise Park and back that means a ride of perhaps 15 miles. If you rode Tantalus/Round Top as well, add another ten or twelve miles to the total.

Ride Six: Kapiolani Park to Hanauma Bay
Skill level: Good urban skills, some climbing
Connects with Ride Seven

This ride starts from the same Waikiki intersection, Kalakaua and Kapahulu, that the first ride described. It is also perhaps the single most trafficked bicycle route on Oahu, one used by commuters and leisure riders. Those who race like it for its long, fast Kalanianaole section. For the rest of us commuting, non-competitive cyclists the advantages are compelling. It is mostly level, generally well protected and takes the cyclist past beach park after beach park without the rigors of traversing major hills—except Diamond Head's solitary and benign half-mile climb. Hanauma Bay is at the top of Koko Head Crater, but if you're too tired, then consider this simply a ride to the suburb of Hawaii Kai or a few of the beaches that line the south shore from Queen's Beach to Lunalilo Home Road.

Those interested in cycling around the island will begin here as well, riding counterclockwise to the North Shore, west toward Haleiwa and then back along Kunia Road. The whole trip is about 124 miles, and local riders usually do it as either a long, long day or with an overnight stop. Some ride the reverse route, going out past Chinatown and beyond the airport to Pearl City, up Kunia Road and along the North Shore clockwise toward Kaneohe. A third option is to go from Kapiolani Park to Pali Lookout, from there to Waimanalo and then back onto this route to complete the approximately 50-mile circuit. Whatever option you choose, this is a crucial connector along the island's southeast corridor. It is also my lunchtime ride, which takes me from the city to the Hanauma Bay region and restaurants I like in Hawaii Kai.

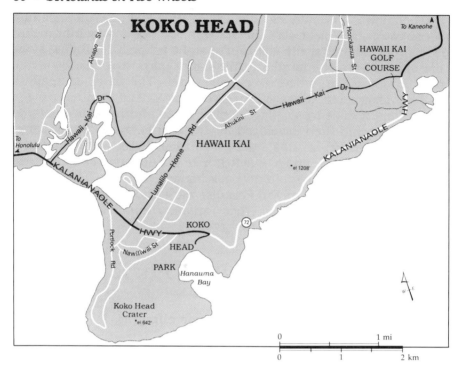

From Kapiolani Park

Go through the park on Kalakaua Avenue, keeping the beach to your right as you cycle into Kapiolani Park. The beaches are well protected, lovely and usually crowded with both tourists and local folk. Each stretch of sandy area has a different name and, often, clientele. A quarter mile past the intersection of Kalakaua and Kapahulu, for example, is **Queen's Beach,** where a covered, open concrete structure stands off to the right just above the beach. This is where a local fencing club practices foil, sabre and epee each Saturday and Sunday mid-afternoon. The surrounding beach area has become, in recent years, a predominantly male, homosexual hangout, but that does not dissuade anyone of any persuasion from sharing the area.

Traditional Hawaiian society was not homophobic, and, perhaps as a result, Hawaiian society always has been less stringent in its condemnation of affections between members of the same sex. As a result, in Hawaii transvestism and homosexuality are more generally accepted than on the Mainland. The Japanese influence, also strong through all parts of contemporary Hawaiian culture, might account for this relaxed attitude because, in traditional Japan, homophobia was also virtually unknown. Whatever the reason, the congregation of individuals with a specific sexual preference is not exclusionary—on the beach or in society— any more than Hawaiians have segregated its members by dint of race or creed. It is one of the island's great resources, this frank open-mindedness, a cultural asset which has made the islands a haven for individuals seeking a less prejudicial environment in which to live.

Just past Queens is a crumbled, broken down natatorium next to the city's **Aquarium**. The latter is spanking clean and a fascinating stop where the region's tropical marine life (algae, fish and mammal) is well described. The older natatorium, visible from **Sans Souci Beach**, is where the island's favorite son, Duke Kahanamoku, trained for his Olympic swimming medal more than sixty years ago. Ever afterwards, The Duke, as he was affectionately known, was Hawaii's goodwill ambassador to the *haole* (non-Hawaiian) world. After winning in the swimming pool he did much to popularize both these islands and surfing, its native sport, throughout America and the rest of the world.

Beach and Park

All this is visible to the right, while on the left and across the one-way street is still Kapiolani Park, one of the most wonderful urban resources imaginable. Across the Park, the **Waikiki Shell** hosts outdoor concerts, and nearby tennis courts are usually filled. Just past Sans Souci on the left is a large, open space where local kite-flying teams practice their two and three-person routines on any windy day. Elsewhere there are baseball diamonds, soccer fields and room left over for those who just want to walk, sit and soak in the sun and breeze.

Diamond Head

Kalakaua Avenue bends to the left past a circular fountain and comes, finally, to a well-marked intersection with Diamond Head Road. Take this right (a sign directs you to Kahala and Diamond Head) and a light climb of less than a mile begins with a very gentle, hardly perceptible rise.

On the right are two relatively new mini-parks, each with a spectacular view of the ocean and, on most days, of windsurfers and surfboard devotees skimming over the reefs. Continuing up the hill, which steepens and briefly narrows into a quarter-mile of work, the road crests just past the famous Diamond Head Lighthouse, which overlooks Kuilei Cliffs. There is a parking turnoff at this point, and below is a popular site for tournaments where you can usually see dozens of surfers or windsurfers slashing and burning through the waves. Should you wish to rest for a moment, pause here, just east of the lighthouse and reflect on the following sad story:

A Sailor's Tale

A few years ago a boat ran aground just off these

cliffs, a lovely sailboat with experienced skipper and crew who had crossed first from the Mainland and were in the process, that day, of completing an interisland trip. The skipper had recently purchased a new, electronic mate, a self-steering mechanism to steer the vessel where it had been programmed to go.

Alas, it worked too well. The skipper was so pleased with the gizmo's performance that she fell asleep before Diamond Head Lighthouse was visible in the night.

The gizmo, however, remained mindlessly alert and carried the hapless boat with its sleeping skipper directly toward the Lighthouse's point and onto the reef in front of it. The brute could be given a directional heading but, alas, held no information on when far enough would be too much.

It was, to say the least, an ignominious beaching, which ripped a huge hole in the vessel's side and, I'm told, killed forever the skipper's interest in new electronic gadgets.

Kahala

The route is simple and clear after the Kuilei Cliffs rest spot as Diamond Head Road is transformed into a lovely, half-mile downhill into the residential Kahala and Black Point districts, where beach homes cost several million dollars. Diamond Head becomes Kahala Avenue and narrows through this section which terminates at the **Kahala Hilton**. Just before the Hilton, by the way, is Waialae Beach Park, where novice windsurfers like to practice.

If you've come to either the Beach Park or the Hilton, however, you've gone just a bit too far for this ride. Kealaolu Avenue branches off to the left and parallels the golf course to an intersection where Waialae Avenue ends and, to the right, Kalanianaole Highway is ready to begin.

The intersection cannot be missed. A gas station is on the left, and the road has a turn lane bending to the right. Traffic is sometimes heavy here, but a cyclist in the right lane will have no trouble and, merging with the traffic's flow, will soon find a white-lined breakdown lane which marks the beginning of the Kalanianaole designated Bike Route.

Kalanianaole Highway

This road is a major highway to the windward side, and its first eight miles run out to Hanauma Bay, just past the residential suburb of Hawaii Kai. The route is clear—just head east and enjoy the procession of parks that appear to the right. Wailupe Peninsula is followed by Kawaikui Beach Park, Niu Beach and then, well, the names go on. On the left, residential communities march with an equal regularity up the mountain ridges from **Kahala** to **Aina Haina, Niu Valley, Kuliouou** and **Hawaii Kai.**

Caution
This is a signed bicycle route, not a reserved bicycle path. Cyclists have no special rights or privileges in what was designed to be and remains in law an automobile's breakdown lane. There are bus stops along the route and moped's buzz in and out of traffic, often presenting an even greater hazard than the traffic which whizzes by. Even worse, the supposedly inviolate breakdown lane, the "bicycle route," disappears occasionally and without warning, especially in the area near the **Aina Haina Shopping Center** and **Hawaii Kai Drive**. This is especially dangerous when heading from Hanauma Bay back to Kapiolani Park, but some caution is needed in both directions.

The state has slated this road for a major upgrade. They've tried for years, but now, in late 1989, it looks as if the work will really begin. With the insensitivity and insanity of typical, automobile-oriented traffic planners, the plan announced has been to put in more lanes to carry more traffic between Hawaii Kai and the city. The "bicycle route," which is, in most areas, currently wide enough for two riders, will be narrowed to four or five feet and bounded by a raised curb. Honolulu cycle activists are fighting a rear guard action to increase the section of the road they will be exiled to, and hopefully the scheduled "bike lane" will be expanded.

This new road, costing taxpayers millions, will not solve the suburban area's traffic snarls and is likely to create greater problems with the city's traffic flow in Kahala. Traffic planners on Oahu in particular and Hawaii in general believe that expanding critical arteries to make room for more cars somehow will solve the problem of too many cars in too small a space. But because the city's streets are finite and the major H-1 freeway already near gridlock, what they will accomplish with this program is minimal. It is as if a two-year-old scientist decided to increase the capacity of his milk bottle by pouring water into its mouth with ever larger and larger funnels.

Hawaii Kai
In Hawaii Kai, **Koko Marina Shopping Center** appears to the left just before Kalanianaole's climb to Hanauma begins at Lunalilo Home Road. To the right is the Portlock residential area, in which homes typically now cost upwards of $1 million and the views are spectacular. In fact, the views are nicer than many of the homes, whose value lies more in the land than the architecture of the miniature palace. The intersection is well marked with a pedestrian bridge. From here it is less than a mile's climb to Hanauma Bay and the Koko Head crater's top. In the shopping center is a modern

supermarket, a good place to buy snacks for a Hanauma Bay picnic, and at the ewa side of the center is a Korean-style, take-out restaurant whose large portions (vegetarian, chicken or meat) and reasonable prices make it a favorite pit stop of mine.

If you decide to visit Hanauma Bay but did not bring snorkel and fins, you can rent them for a moderate price at a dive shop near the Korean restaurant.

Hanauma Bay

The turnoff is very well marked for **Hanauma Bay Beach Park**, which has become one of the most popular of the island's marine attractions. This is a protected, sandy beach whose waters are a marine preserve in which schools of scores of different species swim among the coral growths. It is, literally, awesome when, for the first time, you float in four feet of water and see through a diving mask the marine world teeming with different types of life. Because it is a protected marine park, the fish, who are used to being fed and not fed upon, have no fear of human beings and swim past with what always has seemed to me to be the proper disdain of a sea-born creature for those of us who must live our lives on land.

I usually lock my bicycle at the park's upper level before taking the long walk down to the beach. The chain link fence in the parking lot on the upper level is a good place to secure your bike. Some people walk their bikes down to the sand's edge and lock up leaning against a tree, but I prefer to attach it to the top side fence.

To Sandy Beach and Beyond

Kalanianaole Highway continues from Hanauma Bay to the windward side, and it is sorely tempting to use this route to travel down the winding hill to Sandy Beach, Makapu'u Point and beyond. Many motorists and some bicycle riders use this route, and after the climb it seems fitting to ride the extra downhill mile into the wind and waves that await.

This is, however, a narrow, winding and precipitous section along the open side of a cliff. and should be attempted only by very experienced riders. The downhill turns along the road's edge, and strong crosswinds can feel like a huge, invisible hand pushing the rider into that 1956 Buick coming fast from behind .

My strong recommendation is that only experienced cyclists use this route and that everyone avoid it on the return. For those who do decide to ride down to Sandy Beach from this vantage point, be aware that there are several scenic viewing spots and traffic turnoffs along the route. Those caught in heavy traffic flow or who want to take it more slowly than surrounding cars would be advised to ride quickly from turnoff to turnoff, pulling in to let traffic by as they go. There is, however, a safer, alternate route to Sandy Beach on Hawaii Kai Drive (see Ride Seven) which is strongly recommended.

Returning to Kapiolani Park

The return to the city from Hanauma Bay is easy, retracing the route already described. This time, however, the wind is at the back and the hard climbs have been made.

On Kalanianaole caution is again required. There are sections where the "Bike Route" is a single foot wide and others where the route disappears to become a walkway over pedestrian-style bridges.

You can explore endlessly in this section, turning right at almost any major intersection to ride up and through a procession of valley neighborhoods, each with its own, unique character. For example, many people like to take a right off Kalanianaole past the shopping center onto Keahole Street and then a left at the next major intersection, which is Hawaii Kai Drive. Stay on this road, which circles the Marina complex and empties back onto the Highway. When I win a lottery I'll buy one of the townhouses along here, which have boat docks instead of traditional front yards.

The easiest way to get back to Kapiolani Park is to return precisely the way you came, with one exception. There is no turn down Kealaolu Avenue when returning from Hanauma Bay. Where Kalanianaole ends and the H-1 Freeway begins, take the Kilauea exit to the right, which leads under the freeway. There are several routes from here, but the easiest is to stay under the freeway until the far end of the Kahala Mall and then turn left onto Hunakai Street at the traffic light. There is a Jolly Roger Restaurant at this intersection's ewa-mauka corner. Hunakai is wide and easy, terminating at Kahala Avenue.

Hunakai Street ends in Kahala and a right-hand turn leads to Diamond Head, whose angle of ascent from this side is even gentler than it was on the outbound trip. Then a left-hand turn into Kapiolani Park leads directly back to the Kapiolani Park bandstand and the spot from which this ride began..

The round trip on my cyclometer for this route usually measures 25-30 miles, depending on the digressions and meanderings I don't seem to be able to avoid, even when marking routes for this book.

Ride Seven: Kapiolani Park to Waimanalo

Skill level: Average cycling skills
Connects with Rides Six and Three

This ride parallels the previous one as far as Koko Marina Shopping Center. It offers a different, safer route up around the crater and to the windward side, connecting with the Pali Lookout's descent mentioned in Ride Three.

At the Koko Head side of the shopping center, turn left onto Lunalilo Home Road. Travel along for about two miles past Kaiser High School to the intersection of Hawaii Kai Drive. A right turn here begins a moderate but not excruciating climb up what is locally called "Heartbreak Hill" but is neither so steep or so long as to be a heartbreaker. The summit is cleared after about a mile and immediately followed by a gentle ride down to Kealahou Street, where a right-hand turn continues the descent that terminates at Sandy Beach. A left-hand turn at this intersection leads to first Makapu'u Lookout and then Waimanalo Beach and, from there, up the windward coast.

At Sandy Beach, where local kite flyers sometimes congregate, are plate lunch trucks serving all manner of food, beverage and "shave ice." This is a frequent destination for the Hawaii Bicycle League's weekend rides, where I first learned this route.

Shave Ice, Plate Lunch

It sounds terrible and looks revolting but island "shave ice" is a wonderful idea after a hot morning ride. A rotary blade machine shaves slivers of ice off a block, and those shavings are drenched in one or a combination of artificial flavors and eaten something like an ice cream cone. The same problems attend: wait too long and it melts away; eat too quickly and a headache begins.

Plate lunch trucks are a feature of island life and a legacy of World War II. They first became popular during the war years as a way to assure that folk could find good, quick, hot meals while staying on the job for long hours. Women in Hawaii, as elsewhere, had joined the work force to push the war effort, and workers—men and women— needed good, inexpensive food to keep them on the job. It was from this need that "plate lunch trucks," serving local food on paper plates, was born. They still appear at every construction site, at major beaches and other sites where folk may get hungry or thirsty. None are noted for haute cuisine, all for hearty, filling meals consisting of, for example, rice, kim chee (spicy Korean cabbage) and beef stew.

These trucks are a good landmark for the return trip and, if you have come down from Hanauma Bay, it is here that, on the return, you should turn right to return to Hawaii Kai. The trucks are not, however, all-day stands and leave their location in the late afternoon. Even without their presence, it is an easy intersection to recognize, but folks often look only for what they expect and it is well to remember that even landmarks change.

Makapu'u Point

From the shave ice stop, continue north on Kalanianaole as it bends around and apparently away from the water, climbing around a curve and up a hill to Makapu'u Lookout. It is a glorious and dramatic spot with a sharp, fast downhill to Makapu'u Beach, where boogie boarders slash through short, steep waves, and hard, black lava rock stands in mute testimony to the volcanic history of this jutting piece of headland.

To the left is **Sea Life Park**, an arena-aquarium which Floridians and Californians will find familiar. Admission prices are reasonable, and it is open daily from 9:30 a.m. to 5 p.m. The Park is also a critical research facility and houses a restaurant where anyone can stop for a meal or a soda, although prices, unfortunately, are exorbitant.

Only strong swimmers wearing fins should attempt to surf at Makapu'u Beach. The waves are powerful and the jagged, volcanic rock on the beach's north side can be extremely dangerous. If you insist upon trying to body surf or swim here, start first at the side of the beach closest to the lighthouse, and as you develop both skill and courage, study how the local folk handle the waves at this beach. Others who, like me, prefer gentler waves and a longer ride will simply continue down Kalanianaole Highway a few miles to the Waimanalo Beach Park sign. This is where the **Pali Lookout** ride terminated and completes the southeast island route.

For those interested in riding farther along the windward side or riding counterclockwise around the island, the next ride continues from this beach to Malaekahana and the North Shore.

Ride Eight: Waimanalo to Malaekahana

Skill level: Basic urban skills
Connects with Rides Seven and Nine

This ride continues from **Waimanalo** along the windward side to **Malaekahana Beach Park** and the beginning of Oahu's North Shore. It is, with the previous ride, part of the local cyclist's counterclockwise, around-the-island ride, which takes approximately 130 miles and, depending on your strength, one or two days. Just past Waimanalo a short section of twists and turns through a residential district takes you off the main roads and through a pleasant but slightly confusing area. It is one of the more complex areas of the ride, so I have given careful and exact directions around and across secondary roads.

This is, incidentally, part of a route used by riders participating in the annual **Honolulu Advertiser Century** ride, held each year in September. Last year almost 4,000 cyclists rode from Kapiolani Park to Sandy Beach (25 miles round trip), to Enchanted Lake (50 miles round trip) or, for those wanting a distance ride, from Kapiolani Park to Swanzy Beach north of Kaneohe (100 miles round trip).

Twists and Turns

Just past Waimanalo Beach Park, turn left at a 7-11 store onto Oluolu Street. This will carry you away from the coast for a time and through a pleasantly residential district. After .6 of a mile make another left onto Hihimanu Street and, after another .6-mile ride, yet another left to Ahiki Street. In .7 mile Waikupanaha Street comes up and is a right-hand turn. This leads to Kumuhau Street in 1.6 miles, where another right-hand turn is needed. About a mile down Kumuhau Street, turn left at the intersection with Kalanianaole Highway. It's a busy intersection, so be careful.

Continue on Kalanianaole for 3.2 miles before making a right turn onto Keolu Drive. Congratulations, you've made it to the **Enchanted Lakes** area of the windward side. Don't be surprised if the area looks familiar. Episodes of *Magnum, P.I.,* and other popular television shows have been filmed here. There's a nice park in this area. Then turn right off Keolu Drive after 3.2 miles onto Wanaao Road and, from there, make another right after .6 miles onto Kailua Road at a traffic triangle. Can't miss it. There's a traffic light here as well. Be aware because, almost immediately, you'll turn left onto Kainalu Drive and ride it for 2.1 miles to Kainui Drive, where another right carries you to Kalaheo Drive, which becomes Kaneohe Bay Drive at Mokapu Boulevard. You'll stay on Kaneohe Bay Drive for a few miles. If you're riding with a friend, be sure to ride single file in this area where traffic bends past Aikahi Park and around the shore of Kaneohe Bay.

Continue up Kaneohe Bay Drive, cursing the traffic, until reaching the intersection with Kamehameha Highway. **Toyota City**, with its large car lot, makes this intersection distinct. Pause for a moment to pity the folk whose disposable income goes into automobiles, not bicycles, and then turn right onto Kamehameha Highway, also known almost universally as "Kam' Highway," which will carry you all the way to and across Oahu's North Shore.

Past Windward Mall, the highway passes Kualoa Beach Park near the Kaneohe Bay island called Chinaman's Hat, which is periodically visible throughout this route. The reason for its name is obvious—the island marking the northern entrance of this bay looks something like the traditional, slightly peaked cap which Americans in the 19th century associated with Chinese laborers.

Kaneohe Bay

Now that the route is clear—just follow Kamehameha Highway—it's time to pause and consider the astounding resource that Kaneohe Bay offers to residents and visitors alike. Although exposed to the constant northwest trade winds and waves, the bay itself is almost always calm. A long, high coral reef protects this area from the large swells which pour across the Pacific. A deep, north-south channel allows large ships to pass from Chinaman's Hat deep into the bay, while a smaller, more shallow east-west "sampan" channel has been

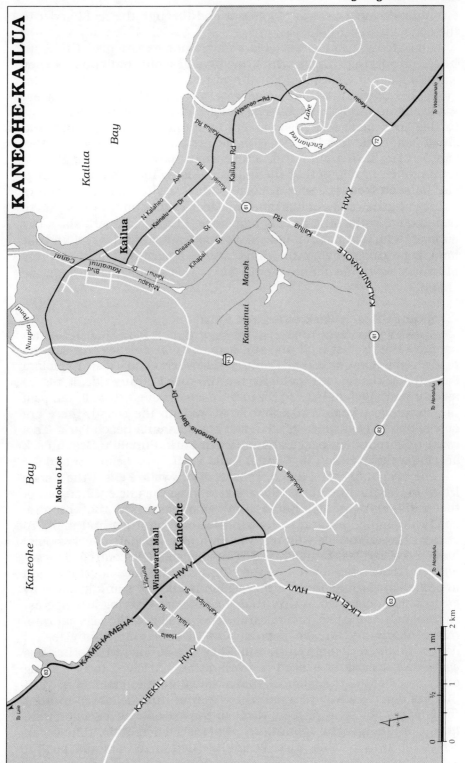

KANEOHE-KAILUA

cut for sailboats that wish to go out and through the reef barrier to the open sea toward Molokai.

Snorkeling in the channel is a marvelous experience. There are huge, lumbering turtles which become graceful balloons as they waddle from the exposed coral reef to first sink and then swim gracefully down into the deeper waters of this protected reef area. Waddling on land they look ungainly, but in the water these huge turtles are grace itself. Also present in abundance are shellfish and small fish. Local folk familiar with the area know precisely what fish can be caught in a spot and, often, when they will be biting. Most remarkable, to me, is that the outer reef is so high that each day it can be seen from the shore. Local sailors, fishermen and boaters often go to the reef, anchor and put deck chairs on it at low tide to rest and enjoy the sun. Sailing here once, I heard a superb slack key guitarist who had moored his small, wooden boat at the reef and sat happily picking away as the winds blew at almost 35 knots, carrying his music down the channel to the boat I was skippering through the channel.

Swanzy Beach Park to Sacred Falls

Cyclists may want to stop at **Swanzy Beach Park**, just past Chinaman's Hat, to rest a bit and stock up at a convenience store on the road's right-hand side. For Century riders who started in Kapiolani Park, this is the turning point for the 100-mile Century ride. If it is 50 miles from Kapiolani Park to Swanzy Beach (through Hawaii Kai, past the shave ice trucks, Makapu'u Point and up the coast), there are only about 14 easy miles left to reach Malaekahana Beach Park. It's a coast ride from here past Kahana Beach Park, Punalu'u Beach Park and Papa'akoko Beach to **Sacred Falls Trail**, just before Hau'ula.

The real name of Sacred Falls is **Kaliuwa'a Falls** ("the canoe leak," in Hawaiian). These Falls are said to be the ancient hangout of the traditional pig god Kamapua'a, who possessed the eccentric ability to change his form between that of a feral pig and man. To ancient Hawaiians the wild pig was an important part of ceremonial luau and other, less formal meals. Thus the god who controlled pigs— and could even become one—was a figure with some clout. Pigs run in profusion through most of these islands and are soundly hated by environmentalists, who worry that the pigs are starving less aggressive animals out of the habitat. Industrious fellows, the pigs eat rare, native plants and are so populous as to constitute, many feel, a danger to the food chain in Hawaii. They eat, simply, what other less aggressive species also need to live and are believed to be forcing other members of the island's animal kingdom into extinction. Most hunters don't really care about this. They're just delighted to hunt the feral pig (for sport or food) through the woods which stretch from here up the Ko'olau mountains. Nature's competition, however, seems far away on this nice, 20-minute detour to the Falls' pool. It appears calm and pastoral, but flash floods often send waves of water down from the hills. Mountain bikers especially will glory in the ride along an often dry Kaluanui Stream bed to the cool waters at the Falls' final pool. The whole area is rich with fruits and fragrances. There are Java plums, guava and kukui along this route. My sympathies are with the feral pig.

Laie to Malaekahana

Past Hau'ula and Laie Beach Park is the **Polynesian Cultural Center**. This is an incredibly successful tourist complex that I've never visited. It's most famous for its stage shows of Polynesian ethnic dances performed by Mormon students from around the Pacific Rim (Fiji, Samoa, Tahiti, Tonga, Maori New Zealand and Hawaii). During the day there are tours, and the Center's popularity can be gauged both by the immensity of its parking lot and the number of tour buses that regularly pass along this route. Beside the PCC is **Brigham Young University**, also known as the Church College of Hawaii, and a large **Mormon Temple** built in 1919 by Mormon missionaries who have lived in this area continuously since 1864. Visitors are welcome to walk the church's outer courtyards and landscaped grounds but not to enter the temple's sanctuary, which is usually closed to outsiders.

I prefer to stop for nature's show at **Laie Point**. Just past Brigham Young, take a right on Anemoku Street that leads to Naupaka and the small spit of land which is Laie Point. From here **Mokuauia** (Goat Island) is visible, and the waves crash into the local inlets with a force and size which, to an animist like me, are at once peaceful and terrifying. The quiet comes from the sheer natural power which so overwhelms that one can only acknowledge and surrender to its vastness. But, as a sailor, I'm always terrified by this show of the sea's strength against the land and take it personally as a warning that the ocean is never to be taken for granted.

Down the road another mile is **Malaekahana State Recreation Area,** a wonderful place for campers, who are warned to pitch their tents securely against the strong winds that sometimes blow in. Each night, steep, thick waves seem to grow from nowhere into an impressive size. Wave size, of course, is determined by the ocean floor's contour and the location of reefs, as well as by the wind. Unlike **Sunset Beach,** whose underwater geology creates long, huge waves, the shore topography here makes the waves appear to form close at hand and rise magically out of the sea.

Mileage Count

From Kapiolani Park along the route described this is a 64-mile ride. From Swanzy Beach, the 50-mile point on the Advertiser Century ride, it is only 14 miles to this point, and from Makapu'u Point perhaps 40 miles.

Ride Nine: To Haleiwa
Skill level: Good urban skills
Connects with Rides Eight and Ten

Malaekahana is where John Daley decided to begin his ride and tour the island's famous North Shore. On that trip he and I both lamented we couldn't spend a few days in this area. From the park you can have fascinating day rides to the Polynesian Cultural Center, Sacred Falls, Waimea Falls and the famous Sunset and Pipeline Beaches, where each winter some of the world's premier surfing competitions are held. Malaekahana is a wonderful base from which you can do any or even most of these things and be back at the campsite for dinner.

For those bound to destinations and schedules, however, cycling the North Shore is a piece of cake. The traffic is usually sparse in the park area, and Kamehameha Highway bends around the northern shore, which is precisely where you want to go. Past Malaekahana you ride first through Kahuku, a small but expanding community where house prices were, even a decade ago, relatively cheap. Now prices everywhere have skyrocketed and even in this area what was once a shack has become 20 years of mortgage payments. *Auwe*!

Aquafarms. Say What?
Past Kahuku and its golf course there is a quiet, pastoral ride on the highway over level roads. On the right will appear what the maps call Nudist Camp Road (a private road, by the way), and then a small shack where a local shrimp farm sells some of its produce. Unknown to most people, shrimp aquaculture is very big business in this area where, on hundreds of acres of low-lying land, local companies grow delicious shrimp, which are packed and sold on the Mainland and in Japan. This modest roadside stand has quite delicious, succulent shrimp and is a good, filling and inexpensive place to stop for a bite to eat.

There is also a farm somewhere near Kahuku ranch said to be raising frogs. I know this begins to sound like a Mark Twain tale, but my source is usually reliable. If there is a frog farm in this neck of the woods, I do only hope they're raising a prosaic and edible species and not the inedible but prolific Hawaiian cane toad. Imported to Australia in the 1930s to eat a specific, crop-threatening beetle, the Hawaiian cane toad decided the bug it was assigned to was unappetizing, but found the Australian climate agreeable and other local insects quite delicious. With no natural predators and an unlimited food supply, it multiplied freely and since has become a headache for Australians whose roads are periodically carpeted with thousands of the imported Hawaiian toads.

Soon you will pass the **Turtle Bay Hilton and Country Club** on the right. For kama'aina it is a weekend getaway resort and for visitors a "destination retreat." For both, the attractions are a good golf course perched, as is the complex itself, on the edge of the sea. Past the resort, the road runs mostly along the shore and past marshes for the next several miles. There are in this area small off-road gulches which mountain bikers may choose to explore. **Kawela Camp Road**, just past the Turtle Bay Hilton, carries the intrepid over several streams and up a winding road that, eventually, becomes a steep ride. I've not been on it in several years and have no intention of riding it again. If it is still tough I don't want to try it, and if road engineers have tamed it then it becomes the basis of another "if you'd done it five years ago"-style lament.

Sunset Beach

Do stop, however, at **Sunset Beach**, which is very well marked and easy to see. On the left is the Sunset Beach Elementary School and on the right is the ever-present sea. Stop and think what it is like to slash and burn through a 20-foot high wave and remember that, not too many years ago, Hawaiians surfed huge, ten- or fourteen-foot-long boards made of koa wood and not the short, high-tech things folk ride these days. A little farther, just over a bridge, is **Waimea Bay Beach Park,** another nice place to stop and rest. That's the problem with this route—each turn in the road is as beautiful as the last and the reasonable desire to rack on some miles (or kilometers) wars continually with the aesthetic demand that every mile be appreciated.

About ten miles by my cyclometer from Malaekahana this ride ends in **Haleiwa**. There is a small boat harbor which in summer is as peaceful as a Canadian duck pond but which in winter can sport huge rollers which keep boats locked in (or out) for days. There is an old-style general store just up the street. Be sure to get a shave ice here, sit on the store's wooden stoop, relax and smile at the incredible North Shore scenery before heading down island through the pineapple and cane fields.

For those who want more time in this area, a right-hand turn from Kam' Highway onto Waialua Beach road will carry you to nearby **Mokuleia Beach Park**. This is a nice beach, a nice park and a handy destination for a second North Shore day. Some Honolulu yclists ride to it directly from Kapiolani Park, reversing the route used here, with Mokuleia and not Malaekahana as their overnight campsite on a clockwise circumnavigation of the island.

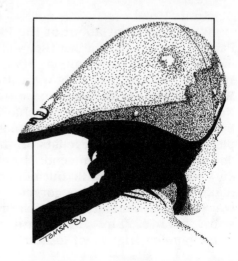

Ride Ten: To Honolulu from Haleiwa

Skill level: Moderate--a four-mile climb and some heavy traffic

Connects with Rides One, Two and Eight

From Haleiwa to Waipahu is one of the best rides on the island. From there into the city, however, another ten miles or so, the road is heavily trafficked, with confusing turns. It is not difficult but is recommended only for those used to cycling in traffic. Interestingly, the traffic and route are easier if you travel clockwise around the island because of the peculiar way the highway intersections are designed. Where it gets tricky we'll use some maps to show which way the traffic bends, and, with a little bit of planning, moderately experienced cyclists should be able to get through the interchanges with no trouble.

As you leave Haleiwa, about a mile down the road there is a traffic circle in which Kamehameha Highway (Route 99) heads south. There is also, in this area, a cane haul road that mountain bikers may love. I prefer the shoulder on Kamehameha Highway because a fairly steady, 4.5-mile climb begins at the traffic circle and continues straight to the **Dole Pineapple Pavilion**. Tour buses stop here so that tourists can leap out, take pictures of pineapples in the field and buy souvenirs before rushing off to the next stop. Cyclists, on the other hand, stop and buy pineapple because they are tired, thirsty and out of breath. They also stop because a hill has been crested, the downhill run awaits and, honestly, because cyclists like to stop wherever possible to brag, gossip, and chat.

Kunia Road

What they chat about at the Pineapple Pavilion, usually, is whether they will take the fast route down Kamehameha Highway into town or swing through Wahiawa past **Wheeler Air Force Base** and onto **Kunia Road**. You can ride Kamehameha Highway, but Kunia Road is probably the most idyllic piece of pavement for cyclists on the island and one I strongly recommend. The other way cuts out some city traffic but not enough to make up for missing this gorgeous trip. As you leave the Pineapple stop the road will soon divide. The left-hand turn is Kamehameha Highway (Route 80), and the

right-hand turn is Kamananui Road (Route 99), which takes a dip
and then bends left into Wilikina Drive. Follow Wilikina through
Wahiawa to a stoplight at Wheeler Elementary School, where a right-
hand turn puts you onto Kunia Road. Now relax and enjoy the rolling
downhill run as gravity carries you
back up the approaching hill,
assuring you an almost effortless,
roller coaster ride as a reward for
your labors. Traffic is minimal along
this section of the road, and that
adds to the pleasure of the
country's lovely scenery. Don't roll
out of control, do test the brakes
and watch out for cars or trucks
pulling into Kunia from the small
side roads.

If you find yourself singing as
the bicycle picks up speed and
seems to float up one hill before
plunging down another, sing
louder. That's what I always do.

Waipahu
After about 12 miles the
pastoral route ends as Kunia Road
flows into Waipahu's traffic rounds and urban traffic reappears. It's a
bit tricky here, and my friend John McCready laughs about the times
he has inadvertently ended up on the freeway. If it happens to you,
don't panic. Get to a safe spot, watch for a break in the traffic and
then ride to the nearest exit, which will be no more than a mile or two
away.

To avoid that, you want to go over the H-1 Freeway and onto
Farrington Highway from Kunia Road. Do not get into the right turn
lane too early because those first turns carry traffic onto the Highway
or a small cane road. Stay one lane away from these turns and ride to
the second Farrington Highway cutoff, which leads into a small traffic
circle that carries traffic to the east. The pace and volume of cars will
be brisk on Farrington and, indeed, all the way in to Chinatown. For
those who want a detour and a rest, Pearl City Tavern is the
landmark to look for on the right, a few miles diamond head on
Kamehameha Highway. It is a famous bar whose once-tough
reputation belies an eccentric decor and quite good food. The Tavern
is worth a stop. Families go there and so can you.

Pearl Harbor
The tavern is best known, at least to local cyclists, as a landmark
showing the route to a bicycle path which curves around Pearl

Harbor itself. Take a right at the tavern and, a bit more than a block south, on the left, is a badly marked entrance to the bicycle path, which carries as many joggers, strollers, walkers and kids as it does bicycle riders. Since it is a general use recreational path, caution is required if you do not want to collide with baby strollers or grim-lipped, serious joggers running three abreast. I rarely recommend bicycle paths because of the multiple use traffic and because I believe cyclists should use the road they have a right to. But the views of Pearl Harbor this route offers make it worth the time and, if traffic is heavy, the recreation path is a respite from the noise and press of cars.

You can also ignore the path detour, stay on Farrington, which becomes Kamehameha Highway, and ride it straight into town. Either way, stop for a moment at **Blaisdell Park**, which faces **Ford Island** in Pearl Harbor. It is a quiet, lovely spot, and since you've almost finished you've earned a moment's respite to savor the sight of the best natural harbor east of Hong Kong and west of Vancouver. Alas, it is closed to local sailors (security reasons, of course), and those whose love is boats and wind can only lament the glimpses they get of this great, protected natural resource reserved exclusively for navy vessels.

The Pearl Harbor bicycle path ends near **Arizona Memorial Place.** For those cycling clockwise from town and looking for the bicycle path, the Arizona Memorial is a convenient place to turn left. This carries you into Pearl Harbor and then begins the hunt for the badly signed bicycle path.

From the Memorial, everyone must ride Kamehameha Highway again. Stay to the right and get onto Nimitz Highway, the road below the viaduct. None of the roads are good, but Nimitz is the best of several bad choices and, I believe, the easiest route to bicycle. Traffic is typically heavy through the next three to five miles, carrying you past the **Honolulu International Airport** with the thousands of visitors (and thus car, bus and taxi drivers) who come in and go out each day.

There is a bicycle path on the north side of the street along much of this route, but its design leaves almost everything to be desired. The pavement is in bad shape and is littered with gravel and patches of broken glass. Its bends are so designed that one naturally rides into joggers, mopeds and cyclists coming from the opposite direction. Like other "bike paths" and "bike routes" it is a recreational facility shared by all and not the exclusive property of cyclists, which means speeds have to be kept low. I've taken it two or three times and won't again unless it is completely redesigned. If you do use it, be sure to stop at each cross street and listen for approaching cars. At most intersections, they'll be invisible until directly in front of the bicycle's wheel. The path ends at Middle Street and Nimitz, where you will have to cross at a traffic light and ride another mile or two into town.

On Nimitz, continue into town until River Street—the edge of Chinatown—appears. Near Honolulu Harbor's Pier 18, the road bends to the right and River Street is at the next light. I take this or one of the next available turns, head away from traffic through Chinatown to King and use this route to get back to Manoa, Hawaii Kai or Waikiki. From King Street to Ward or University Avenues returns you to routes described earlier in this chapter and completes the round-island trip.

Ride Eleven: The Waianae Coast

A detailed description of rides along the leeward Waianae Coast is not included in this edition. The most traditional area of intensely developed Oahu, this area ewa of Pearl City has in the past had a bad, if sometimes undeserved, reputation among Island cyclists for not welcoming outsiders. Many local, long-time Oahu residents have shied away from riding the area, and as a result much of the area from **Barbers Point** to **Kaena Point** has been terra incognita for most touring riders. Many argue the reputation is undeserved and, especially for cyclists, that this is an area worth exploring.

I do not believe in avoiding sections because of "reputation," especially when that name is built on social and racial differences. The truth is I'm not very familiar with the Waianae area because riding through Pearl City to Waianae is, from my apartment, a very long trek and I've put the effort into riding the other islands.

Another reason I hesitate to say much is that this part of Oahu is being developed and whatever is written today, in 1989, will be out of date by 1991. A huge development project is underway at Barbers Point, and the Waianae Coast area, long forgotten, is being eyed greedily by land-hungry developers. If the long-debated Honolulu light rail transit system ever is approved, that too will affect this area. Rather than writing what will soon be outdated, I prefer to give a general description of the area and let those who come to ride Oahu check out the current situation for themselves.

The search will be worthwhile because in this area are great beaches and fascinating areas from **Ewa Beach Park** at the southwest corner of the island to the barren and spectacular **Kaena Point** to the area's north. Ewa Beach is locally famous for its *limu*, an edible, even tasty seaweed. Used in local dishes, it is also known by its Japanese name, *ogo*. In the old days, Japanese or Korean women who carried bags to harvest the limu were as much a fixture of the beach as the waves that rolled quietly onto shore.

If you're interested, ask for some "limu poke," or fresh marinated fish and seaweed, at a fish store or supermarket anywhere on Oahu. When I'm out for an afternoon ride, I'll sometimes pack half a pound of this and, with a can of guava juice, ride to Sandy or Waimanalo Beach for a lazy afternoon's lunch.

North on Farrington Highway from Ewa Beach is the old **Hawaiian Electric Beach Park,** where the now defunct Oahu Railway and Land Company's narrow-gauge railroad once ran. From there it is a short ride to **Kepuhi Point,** where the famous Makaha International Surfing Championships have been held annually since 1952. The area has in recent years been eclipsed by the more famous North Shore sites, but for years this was the site for Hawaiian surfing. For a time, I sailed these waters and often pulled into lovely and protected **Pokai Bay,** where sailors are protected from the strong winter trade winds by the mass of Oahu that guards this leeward shore. Old legends tell of an eel-man with supernatural powers who inhabited the Bay, but what I remember best is snorkeling off the boat in the quiet and protected waters.

The largest town and central urban site of this area is **Makaha,** which means "fierce" in Hawaiian. The word comes, according to one study, from the days of prehistory when men from Kauai fought a pitched battle with local cannibals who were the region's original "savage" inhabitants and whose supposed ferocity gave the place its name. In the Makaha Valley today there is **Kaneaki Heiau,** restored in the 1970s, which was originally dedicated to the god Lono but which may have been refurbished by Kamehameha as a *hakini heiau*—a place of human sacrifice, to his god of war, Kualimoku. Just north of Makaha is **Makua Cave,** carved by the sea and, according to local legend, once occupied by a creature who could change at will between human form and that of a shark.

For those interested in this area and in movie history, an important stop is **Makua Beach**, where the film *Hawaii,* based on the James Michener novel, was shot. With traditional Hollywood logic, the film producers built a replica of Lahaina, Maui, on-site. It was, apparently, cheaper and more convenient to build the sets they needed in this then barren and largely unknown area.

Farrington Highway ends at **Keawa'ula Beach**, once known as **Yokohama Bay**, another nice surfing beach. I suspect that, as this region develops, the road to **Kaena Point** and around to the North Shore will be completed, but at present the dirt road is a mountain biker's delight of brush, rock and heat. It is also worth the trouble for those on touring bikes with a desire for off-road riding and a taste for the desolate and beautiful.

Kaena means "heat" in Hawaiian, and, with little rainfall and few wells, **Kaena Point** is hot, austere, rugged and gorgeous. One magazine appropriately called this area "Oahu's last wilderness." Ancient Hawaiians believed that a person's soul leapt from a rock in this extreme corner of Oahu into the next world, and even today there is a sense of departure and isolation to this area.

People have talked about its development for more than 100

years. In the 1880s, Benajamin Franklin Dillingham built a railroad which was to open up this region on the way to Kahuku and the North Shore. And, for a time, it worked as people came to visit if not settle. Eventually a road was put in to service the produce trucks which replaced Oahu's trains across the island but today that road is nothing more than a four-wheel track. Youcan still find the railroad's ties along the old roadbed, and it seems, sometimes, as if nothing but bicyclists and noisy four-wheel devotees will ever visit here again.

But this is Oahu, where land prices rise every year, and that means Kaena Point—sooner or later—will be developed into an area of condominiums and townhouse apartments. For now, touring cyclists with good gears and spare water bottles can still see it in a relatively pristine state, without condominiums, fast food hamburger heavens or "convenience" stores.

Addresses and Information

Camping Permit Locations

Oahu County Parks:
Dept. of Parks and Recreation
650 S. King St.
Honolulu, HI 96813
523-4525

Division of State Parks
1151 Punchbowl St.
Rm. 310
Honolulu, HI 96813
548-7455

Oahu Bicycle Shops

The Bike Way
250 Ward Ave.
Honolulu, HI 96814
538-7433

The Bike Shop
1149 S. King St.
Honolulu, HI 96814
531-7071

Eki Cyclery
1603 Dillingham Blvd.
Honoluu, HI 96817
847-2005

Island Spokery Bicycle Works
46-174 Kahuhipa
Kaneohe, HI 96734
247-5200

McCully Bicycle and
 Sporting Goods
2124 S. King St.
Honolulu, HI 96826
955-6329

University Cyclery
1728 Kapiolani Blvd.
Honolulu, HI 96814
944-9884

Hawaiian Island Creations
Pearlridge Center
Honolulu, HI 96701
488-6700

Island Triathlon and Bike
569 Kapahulu Ave.
Honolulu, HI 96815
732-7227 (sales)
734-8398 (service)

The Bike Planet
2639 S. King St.
Honolulu, HI 96826
949-8499
(also carries a complete line
of camping gear)

North Shore Bike Center
66-134 Kamehamea Hwy.
Haleiwa, HI 96712
637-3221

Wahiawa Bicycle Shop
823 Olive
Wahiawa, HI 96786
622-5120

_____ **Other Oahu Addresses**_____

Manoa Valley Inn
2001 Vancouver Dr.
Honolulu, HI 96822
800-634-5115 (toll free)
947-6019 (in Honolulu)

_____ **Other Guides to Oahu**_____

Exploring Honolulu's Chinatown, Frances Carter (Honolulu: Bess Press, 1988). A short description of places of interest in the old section of the city.

Insight Guides: Hawaii (Hong Kong: Apa Productions, Ltd., 1981). A general guide to the islands with a long and detailed section on Oahu in general and Honolulu in particular. My favorite island guidebook.

Bryan's Sectional Maps Oahu (Honolulu: EMIC Graphics: 1987). For those who will spend a fair amount of time on Oahu, this gives a complete collection of streets with a complete index. It is sold in bookstores and general markets.

The Essential Guide to Oahu (Honolulu: Island Heritage Press, 1988). One of a series of island guides which is well indexed and nicely illustrated.

Map of Oahu, James A. Bier (Honolulu: University of Hawaii Press).

Cycling Molokai

INTRODUCTION

On a washroom wall at the **Hotel Molokai**, two miles from the **Kaunakakai Wharf**, a grafitto pleads: "Don't let Molokai become Maui." I can see the writer's point. Although its parks are administered as part of Maui County, differences between the two islands are noticeable, almost vast.

Maui is bigger and hosts Lahaina harbor, which is so packed that even local sailors must anchor on permanent moorings several hundred yards off shore. A sea taxi service runs them back and forth to their boats. Kaunakakai's harbor is booming, too. Last week there were six boats at dock and one anchored off to enjoy the swells that barely rippled the waters behind the harbor's stone-built protecting wall.

Maui has condominiums and high rises. Molokai does not. On Maui you can find Pizza Hut, Burger King and McDonald's—many of whose employees are Molokai residents commuting to work each day on the 150-passenger *Maui Princess* ferry. Central Molokai has a bakery, Hotel Molokai, the Midnight Inn (pizza Thursday through Saturday nights), Hop Inn restaurant and Pau Hana Inn. There is one drive-in and little else, not even a 7-11.

In Lahaina and Wailuku, people have last names preceded by Mr. and Ms., while from Halawa Valley to Maunaloa Town, everyone on Molokai is on a first name basis: Joseph, Evelyn, Denis, Liualani or "da kine's cousin's bruddah." It's not an encounter group, but merely an island so compact—6,500 inhabitants—that last names are just not necessary.

Molokai's rich island cousin has large highways and stoplights to control the traffic, while you can ride from Kaunakakai up and down the island without ever seeing anything but rocks, trees, 'the occasional stop sign and warnings of falling coconuts and wild turkey crossings.

For me, Molokai is as good as it gets. Its attributes include a lack of traffic, friendly residents and its almost ideal size. A thirty mile ride will carry you from the port of Kaunakakai to either end of the island or round trip to the Kalaupapa Lookout with a side trip thrown in. Hills are high enough to require some effort but low enough to keep the vacation from turning into an endurance feat.

There are even motorists who will offer help in case of trouble but few enough cars that you can ride for perhaps half an hour without hearing the sound of a motor.

None of the rides are very difficult, although the climb to Halawa Valley, and the return from it, will be taxing to beginners. Because the traffic is minimal and the ascents so benign, all routes noted require no more than basic cycling skills.

People are discovering Molokai, traveling from Maui in small clusters on Sea Link of Hawaii's ferry, the **Maui Princess**, or flying over from Oahu for the weekend. Every other week or so overnight tours hit the island, and there is the usual traffic of local folk going from island to island.

In recent years a bicycle tour company, Progressive, has offered luxury tours for bicyclists on Molokai, although I'm told they may be giving up this business in 1990. The tours, at least for the present, stay at the old Sheraton Hotel, have sag wagons at the ready and generally travel first class all the way. Local residents tell me these tourists are good customers at area shops and that, each year, there are more of them. It's understandable, because for the tourist this is still the quietest and most accessible of Hawaii's volcanic homes. Its benign hills and general scale are ideal for those who see the world from the vantage point of two non-motorized bicycle wheels. Here are three tours for those who want to share the wealth.

Transportation

Molokai is not yet a primary destination, and there are no direct flights—thank heavens—from California or New York. To get here you have to either fly in (from Oahu or Maui) or take a boat.

Several regional airlines fly to this island—both from Maui and from Oahu— and there are often fare wars raging between carriers like **Aloha** and **Hawaiian** Airlines. A few telephone calls or a visit to the interisland terminal in Honolulu will give the current situation. Your bicycle may have to be boxed if you fly a smaller cargo plane or charter airline, so check before making a reservation.

From Molokai's airport it is a short, four-mile ride to Kaunakakai, where the two hotels are the **Pau Hana** and **Molokai Inn**. The former is near the ferry wharf and the latter, slightly ritzier place is a mile east on the **Kamehameha V Highway**. To get to the city from the Ho'olehua Airport, head east from the terminal onto **Maunaloa Highway** (it's the only highway around, actually) and keep heading toward the coast.

About 2.6 miles east of the airport is a turnoff for Kaia'e Highway, which heads toward Kalaupapa. A bit farther, the State Park is well marked. If your destination is Kaunakakai, however, just keep on Maunaloa Highway heading downhill into town. It becomes Kamehameha Highway, if the Hotel Molokai is your destination.

From the highway into town is a matter of three blocks. Turn left on Ala Malama, the only street you'll see which looks as if it goes anywhere. Just past the intersection about a half-mile there will be a sign for Pau Hana Inn, and a right-hand turn puts you in the hotel complex and at the reception desk.

By Sea

Even better is to arrive from Maui by the ferry. It leaves twice a day, once at about 7:30 a.m. and again at about 7:00 p.m. At present the **Maui Princess** is used primarily by Molokai residents working on Maui who have to be at work by 7 a.m., so the first trip is after local workers have been dropped off, and the second returns the Molokai folk to their homes.

Sea Link of Hawaii, which runs the ferry, is headquartered at 505 Front Street in Lahaina. Its owner, Dave Jung, has made a commitment to serving cyclists, so there is no extra charge for bicycles brought aboard his ship. The ship has a good cargo hold where bikes can be carried if the passenger cabin is full, but often ship employees just secure the bike in the cabin.

This is still, in 1989, a service struggling to find a niche for itself in Oahu's transportation world. I admit to a love of this service and a partisan belief in sea travel's superiority over air transportation. I am sorry indeed that an earlier experiment which had the *Maui Princess* running from Oahu to these islands has been terminated. On the *Maui Princess* you see the whales and you see the land at eye level. From the air you know that the world below is of potential interest but what you feel is the pressurized air in the cabin and what you see is the abstraction enforced by extreme altitude.

The Maui to Molokai trip puts you in the most spectacular of geographies. The sea trip gives spectacular views of Maui, Lanai and Molokai in the 90-minute run, and it will be, for many, the only chance to see these islands from the perspective of a boat upon the water. There is an added benefit to this sea trip in the winter months. From December through February, passage from Kaunakakai to Lahaina often means steaming past pods of breaching, leaping whales. These are humpbacks, which arrive each winter to bear and nurse their young before the spring's return migration toward the Alaskan shore.

It is an unforgettable sight, and, while you can pay local boat captains big bucks for a few hours cruise in these waters, the ferry trip covers the same region and provides a free whale-watching trip along with sensible transportation. One year I was running a charter sailboat in these waters and found a humpback whale surfacing alongside the 37-foot-long vessel. She dwarfed us, floating there, and then sank beneath the sea with nothing but a flip of a tail. The next morning, off the Molokai coast, a dawn sail showed us at least thirty leaping, breaching whales—mothers with their young—cavorting along the commuter's route between Kaunakakai and Lahaina. Rarely have I been so awed or sensed such a sense of alien purpose and grace as I did that day and now, each winter, I return and hope to be again amidst these wonderful animals.

If you've sailed to Molokai, take your bicycle through the gate, ride down the long wharf from the landing and turn right at Beach Place if you're going to Pau Hana Inn. If you're headed for the Hotel Molokai, however, continue on a block to Kamehameha V Highway and head right. That complex is well marked and under two miles away.

Finally, if you're staying at the Kaluakoi, take the early morning ferry and then follow directions in the next section to end up at the hotel resort in time for a late lunch.

Mountain Biking

There are no organized trails or clubs on this island, but there is, local folk say, a lot of off-road riding being done. I've met a few fat-tire fanatics on the road and all have recommended areas bordering on Kala'e Highway beyond Kualapu'u as the place to start. These locations include the state park and the wooded lands east of the highway where trails abound.   As well, halfway up Maunaloa Highway heading toward the airport and away from town is Maunahui, which terminates in a jeep road. Finally, there are hiking trails in Halawa Valley and no prohibitions that I know of for mountain bikers.

Be careful and please, ride with others. If you're injured, it will take time for someone to find you here. This is not like Tantalus in Honolulu where urban amenities are close at hand, so back-road, wilderness precautions should be your standard procedure.

Ride One: Kaunakakai to Kaluakoi
Skill level: Basic riding skills
Connects with Ride Three

This ride from the town breaks easily into three approximately six-mile segments. The first climbs to and past the airport, the second runs to Maunaloa town and the third is a fast, swooping descent to the island's northwest shore.

Outside of Kaunakakai there are no general stores until you reach Maunaloa, 15 mostly uphill miles away, so full water bottles are in order. If you forget, however, and are headed that way, the airport has a small snack bar.

Riding west from town, Kamehameha Highway becomes Maunaloa Highway, which you'll ride the whole distance out.

About a mile from the wharf on the left-hand, shore side is **Kapuaiwa**, a huge coconut grove planted by King Kamehameha during his reign. Originally there were 1,000 trees on this ten acres of land where the King had a summer home. Later, this area was also home to Prince Lot before he became king in 1963, reigning for only nine years in the Islands.

Today the trees still stand in splendidly straight, unnatural rows,

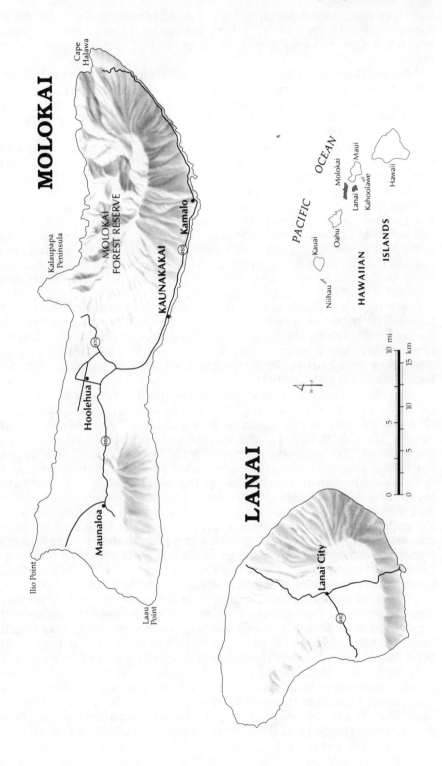

MOLOKAI

Cape
Halawa

Kalaupapa
Peninsula

MOLOKAI
FOREST RESERVE

Kamalo

KAUNAKAKAI

450

470

Hoolehua

460

Maunaloa

Ilio Point

Laau
Point

LANAI

Lanai City

440

PACIFIC

OCEAN

Niihau

Kauai

Oahu

Molokai

Maui

Lanai

Kahoolawe

Hawaii

HAWAIIAN

ISLANDS

10 mi

15 km

10

5

5

0

0

each tree loaded with dangling fruits. A sign warning of the danger of falling coconuts should be taken seriously. This is not a campground. A ripe coconut dropping 20 or 30 feet would cause a very unpleasant concussion.

Across the road from here is what local maps call **Church Row**. The island has an extraordinary number of Christian churches of various denominations, and some of the prettiest are right here. They are small, unpretentious and of mostly simple, late-19th century designs. The morning light just touches their rooftops, but by late afternoon they are bathed in warm sun. Riding here I always pause to enjoy these small testaments of a people's faith and to think about what missionaries brought to Hawaii, not just what they forced away.

It is fashionable to lament the changes which missionaries wrought in the Islands, for even casual visitors to condemn the puritan morality of those early immigrants. Certainly, Christian ministries of various denominations were part of the process of social and cultural change, and today many nostalgically lament what was lost. As clearly, early immigrants tried to impress upon the Hawaiians their own moral code, and the average 19th century westerner thought Hawiians needed help. They arrived here in tight, hot, European-style clothes and were generally despairing of what they found. The litany of their concerns is, from our perspective, merely quaint: horrified by the hula, which they tried to ban, frightened by near nudity which seems natural today on the tourists' beaches, Americans and Europeans were despairing of the native Hawaiian's lack of western-style industry.

But the Hawaiians were industrious—the fish ponds, heiaus and coconut groves which ring this shore are testimony to that. Westerners wanted and believed in a system of labor which would benefit not only the crown and its necessity for corveé labor but, as importantly, the common people as well. The religion they brought with them was an egalitarian one which promised salvation and a type of freedom unthinkable under the older system of hereditary royalty, traditional *kapu* (prohibitions) and subjugation to the ruling *ali'i*. The close harmonies of 19th century church music joined with the melodies of traditional Hawaiian to create the hybrid of intense, complex, contemporary music which is a Hawaiian resource of song *(mele)* and dance *(hula)*. Cycling by church row on a Sunday morning, I hear the voices in song and see the community which was forged through this merger of Western and Hawaiian traditions.

Yes, a past, a tradition, was lost in this change. But what was gained is not all bad and to condemn the missionaries as an evil imposition is to forget how quickly they were welcomed, how much they contributed to this region and to ignore the fact that they lived here, in a foreign land, so they could teach, often by example. That, I submit, is not dishonorable, and the results are evident in these small, unpretentious, well-used churches which focus the community's social and moral life in a way I can't help think is better than what came before, when the people were counters in royalty's game, their religion (and their labor) obeisance to an ali'i's whim.

Past the coconut grove and the row of churches, Maunaloa

Highway turns into a steady, gradual ascent of several miles' duration. Near its top, Dole plantation storage sheds stand in cleared fields to the left, while kiawe trees bristle to the right. A first cousin to mesquite, kiawe's wood is used for barbecue fires needing a strong, hot flame. The thorns, however, are like small, iron nails. Do not ride over tree branches if you can avoid them, even on a mountain bike. One fellow on a trip decided to off-road through a kiawe grove and, when he walked into town, found 34 punctures through tube and tire.

Left to Airport and Kaluakoi

Halfway up the hill the road branches to Kalae Highway on the right, leading to Kualapu'u and the **Kalaupapa Lookout**. The route is marked clearly, so you'll know where to go. This is a nice, hard climb of two miles, and a state campground (as well as spectacular scenery) rewards the industrious for their effort.

Stay on the main road, which bends to the left past the airport (whose snack bar can be the cyclist's salvation) and then becomes a two-lane highway rising toward **Pu'u Nana**, west Molokai's 1,380-foot-high peak. This is a steady 5.5-mile climb, and only spectacular views of the Pacific and long, lovely vistas of grazing land make it worth the work involved. I once rode this route during a forest fire that burned up to within several yards of the road, and I could not understand why I had two tubes blow within an hour. These were not simple punctures but long rips, explosions that decimated the rubber tube. At first I blamed shoddy workmanship, but then realized that

the heat from the fire had made the road surface so hot that the air in my tires, inflated that morning to their normal 90 pounds, expanded in the heat until they burst from the pressure. "High school physics," I said ruefully. "It was never my best subject."

The sailor and adventurer Tristan Jones remarks that he would be perfectly delighted if winds never reached above 25 miles an hour and if his sailings were never touched by storm. That is how I feel about this ride and about this island in general. It is the cyclist's equivalent of whitecapped seas that never become truly vicious. From the airport to Pu'u Nana, for example, is a climb of sufficient length to let the legs know they have to work but not so taxing as to be hard labor. As you work the gears, the bicycle sings but does not sigh. Riding here I sweat, but do not have to work too hard, and the road is naturally graded to create, upon the return, a truly glorious and long downhill run.

Just past Pu'u Nana, the road divides. The left branch leads to the small, one-street town of **Maunaloa**, and the right turn leads to the beach and its fancy hotel complex. The left-hand turn is worth the extra three miles of travel and leads to, among other things, a general store with cold juice and soda. An old plantation town now owned (like most of the island) by Molokai Ranch, Maunaloa is the subject of some debate these days. Local residents want to buy their residences from the company, which has not decided what it is going to do with the land it bought years ago from the folks at Dole.

Maunaloa's general store is filled with a wide variety of wares, everything from machetes to exercise equipment, confirming that this is a rural community where horses are picketed and graze in a family's back yard, where surfboards are planted at a small wood house's back door like an offering to the great God Surf. People live and work here in a variety of ways, and most of the daily needs of this diversity of interests are serviced by this store. The store also stocks a good assortment of juices, sodas and snack food. Since you've climbed over 1,300 feet you can feel proud and enjoy a cola with a candy bar. Across the street is the state's best kite store, **Maunaloa Kite Factory**, filled with an excellent selection of both locally made and imported kites. Its specialty, however, is Indonesian kites.

I usually carry a small parafoil kite in my kit. It weighs almost nothing, and where pride prevents me from "stopping to rest" I typically decide to pause and fly the thing when the winds permit. If you decide to do the same, be sure the kite has strong enough string. The winds at the end of this ride can be very brisk, and a 50-pound string may not be enough. Ask Joseph, the store's owner. His knowledge of kites seems almost encyclopedic.

Sharing the town's one-block business section with the kite store is the **Red Dirt Shirt Shop** (local designer T-shirts), **Jo-Jo's Cafe** and a jewelry store with locally made scrimshaw. Scrimshaw is carved bone and was once a common hobby in these islands when sailors incised whaling scenes (and personal memories) into whalebone. Now that it is illegal to buy whalebone in the U.S., modern scrimshaw is made from the bones of other, less endangered animals. Old scrimshaw costs at least the price of two Cinelli bicycles. Modern stuff, which can still be quite lovely, may cost less than a single bicycle wheel.

From Maunaloa town it's only a mile of mostly downhill back to the cutoff, where a turn at the Kaluakoi sign sends you on a straight, 4.6 mile descent that is heaven.

At the end of the run is the **Kaluakoi Hotel and Golf Club**, referred to by everyone (including its employees) as "The old Sheraton Hotel." It was, before being sold a few years back, officially known as the Sheraton Molokai Hotel, and on this island place names hang on. Whatever name you choose to use, the complex it describes dominates this landscape with golf course, condominiums and the rest of a resort location's debris.

Down the road a bit and past the hotel complex a half mile or so is **Po'olau Beach**, whose lovely sands and official campgrounds I recommend. It gets busy here, however, and you need a permit from County Parks division if you wish to stay legally. This area is known for its surf fishing and, sometimes, its surfing. On a clear day Oahu's Kaneohe is just visible through the haze a bare 35 miles across the channel. What is less well recognized is that this can be an excellent kite flying area. I've flown my parafoil from this beach, watched it unfold in my hand and shiver in the wind as it fills before climbing rapidly up and away. First it runs out like a fish on a line toward Oahu's Kaneohe Bay, just visible across the channel, and then the kite dances up, up into the air until it waves back at me from directly overhead.

I like this ride a lot, in part because of the pleasure gained from riding for several hours, but also because it is associated with memories of moments like that. Another of my joys is to roll into a nice hotel and, while sweaty and tired, sit down to a well-served lunch. You can do that at the Sheraton's restaurant on the beach. Some customers may blanch, but the hotel's waiters barely notice when a road-dusted rider, helmet in hand, orders a club sandwich ($6.25) or salad ($2.95 to $6.95). Great guava ices, too.

Because the hotel hosts escorted luxury bicycle tours, they are not put off by independent cyclists. The organized bicycle tours, by the way, spend several days at the Old Sheraton and one or two in Kaunakakai, but Maunaloa residents say they get trucked from the hotel up the hill and don't have to huff and puff it. That's cheating, my friends say. But then few of us stay overnight in such sumptuous digs.

The whole trip has been about 20 miles long, depending on exactly where the ride started in the Kaunakakai area. From the hotel the return is easy, but fill the water bottles before you go. Then head back to the road, turn left and start climbing to Maunaloa Highway. This is the hardest part of the trip, up an incline which is never quite steep enough to be a challenge (it's not Haleakala, after all) but is definitely tiring. Someone stopped to offer me a lift as I huffed along the last time I took this ride, but pride overrode comfort and sense. I insisted on finishing the uphill ride. But then I turned left onto Maunaloa and, after another two miles of very mild climbing, reached Pu'u Nana point. From there it is constant and glorious downhill all the way to the hotels, restaurants and beaches of town.

I loved every minute of the ride and knew, deep in my heart, that I am a puritan who could not have enjoyed the roller coaster return so completely had I not first humped up a few miles from the beach and my lunch.

Ride Two: Kaunakakai to Halawa Valley
Skill level: Moderate. some climbing
Connects with Ride One

Heading east from Kaunakakai on Kamehameha Highway there is, for 20 miles, a slightly rolling, winding two-lane country road with a fairly gentle but constant incline. That slight grade is made more noticeable by an ever-present, westerly trade wind which begins, usually, around ten in the morning and grows to a 20-mile-per-hour head wind through the afternoon. If you feel tired, it is because both wind and grade have conspired to make this a harder ride than it appears.

About 8.5 miles east of Kaunakakai there is a church on the right where everyone stops. **St. Joseph Church** was built in 1876 by Joseph DeVeuster of Tremelco, Belgium. He's better known today as Father Damien. He was the Leper Priest, the martyr of Kalaupapa, a man who found his religious calling ministering to the Hansen's Disease victims exiled to this island's north shore in the 19th century. Father Damien's work, life and history are described nicely in James Michener's *Hawaii* as well as in *Molokai*, a fictionalized tale of the Kalaupapa experience by Oahu author O.A. Bushnell. Gavan Daws' *Holy Man: Father Damien of Molokai* is a non-fictional description of Father Damien and his calling.

. Ordained in Honolulu in 1864, Father Damien was pastor to the whole island of Molokai, not just to the exiles' colony, and built several churches on the island's southern side, two of which remain.

St. Joseph Church is one of them, and it is an extraordinary sight. Small, elegant, with 19th century, European lines, it is a bit of Flemish simplicity planted right in tropical verdancy. From the old, iron door latch (no lock) to the thin windowpanes, its simple interior speaks of a plain, Christian faith.

Visitors are welcome and a guest book stands inside the door. Contributions to the church are used for its upkeep. One need be neither Catholic nor religious to be moved by the church, its beauty or the memories it invokes of an honest, selfless man.

Just down the road is another monument, this one to adventures in the early age of air travel. A wood-frame structure on the right marks the spot where **Ernest Smith and Emory Bronte** crashed into a kiawe thicket on the first transpacific flight from California. As airplane buffs will know, this flight in 1927 was, despite the rough landing, a stupendous achievement in its day and paved the way for the regular commercial flights that now ply the islands daily.

Six miles east of St. Joseph's Church and on the opposite side of the road is Father Damien's second, larger legacy, **Our Lady of Sorrows**. This is a more pretentious building than St. Joseph and has a huge, rough wood cross on its splendid lawn. This church is set back off the road a bit, a distance that enhances the church's lines. For me, however, it is less moving than the smaller, simpler, older church you visited ten minutes before.

Kamalo Harbor

Just about a mile past Our Lady is **Kamalo Harbor** and, across from it, a neighborhood store that carries ice cream, coffee, fruit juice and other cycling necessities. Stop and stock up. This will be the last chance for supplies all the way to Halawa Valley.

If you hang around long enough, local customers will fill you in on the battle over the harbor across the road. It is in many ways the story of Hawaii and its fights over access to coastal land. The only difference is that this one is written on a small, comprehensible scale.

The harbor was bought several years ago by off-island interests that are developing the boat basin as a commercial facility and have tried to refuse local residents the right to launch their fishing boats from its dock. In older times, the launch area was free, and folks used the harbor at will. Molokai activists now insist upon their right to the facilities and the necessity of a launching site in this area. The battle has become a court case with some hope of resolution if the state agrees to make Puko'o Harbor, six miles even farther down the road, into an east island, public launch facility.

You would think the coast had thousands of places from which to launch a boat, but because this southern coast is lined by a largely closed reef system, open spaces from which to sail or motor are limited. Thus harbors are defined, here, not only by their relation to land but more importantly by breaks in this reef barrier from which boats can safely come into harbor without ripping their hulls on the surrounding, coral shelf.

Traditionally the reefs also contributed to the artificial fish ponds that line the southern shore of this island. Molokai has the most fish pond sites of any of the islands, a tribute to the island's wealth and popularity in the old days among the ruling ali'i. Some of the ponds, whose structures are still in place, are believed to have been built as early as the 15th Century.

Within the reef barrier, which kept waves at bay, rocks were used to create artificial fences so that the shore side could be stocked with fish. The idea was to make a seawall tight enough to keep fish in but sufficiently porous that the sea water could move through and keep salinity and oxygen levels in the water high. Developed by and for the traditional society's ali'i, the ruling class, the fish ponds were built by conscription labor. The commoners of old carried rocks out along the shallow water to build these wonderful, serviceable ponds which they then stocked by hand with fish.

The builders, of course, never got to (legally) enjoy the fruits of their labor, which were the exclusive preserve of island royalty. Now you will sometimes see a fishing boat bobbing gently in one or another pond, harvesting in democracy what in tradition was reserved for the royalty.

Puko'o

Past Puko'o the road slowly becomes more hilly and difficult, climbing from Murphy's beach up the hills on a badly winding road to **Pu'u o Hoku Ranch**. In 1987, the road was paved, and you can thank that advance for the somewhat increased automobile traffic which now rides here as well.

Think of what it would be like to cycle up a warped washboard. That is what this road used to be like. Mountain bikers loved it and so did I because very few cars and no tour buses came through. Those that tried drove very, very slowly, which is what a cyclist likes to see.

This is not an easy part of the route, however, whatever means of travel you choose. If it were not so lovely, with progressively better and clearer and more rocky views of the shoreline amid trees and bamboo whispering in the wind, nobody would make the trip. In the distance you can see Maui with progressive clarity while climbing to the last point before the Halawa Valley descent.

Two miles from the road's end there is a spectacular lookout from which glimpses of the final, switchback descent can be seen. The last two miles is a weaving, curving mountain ride that requires some caution and skill. But what a place to end a trip! Deep in the forest and yet on the coast, there is a hike from here into **Halawa Valley**'s waterfall. It is reportedly among the most beautiful ambles south of Kauai's Na Pali Coast.

No, I've never done it. After cycling up and down the hills, even a moderately arduous hike (remember you still have to ride back) has seemed too much to consider when I could just luxuriate in a place so beautiful.

The odometer reads about 30 miles to the Valley's floor from town, but the return—after the first two-mile climb—is downhill. With the winds behind for a change, the return ride is exhilarating. Afternoon trade winds push at your back, and the morning's climb becomes an afternoon downhill back to Kaunakakai.

Ride Three: Kaunakakai to Kalaupapa
Skill level: Moderate
Connects with Ride One

The third ride is up the center of the valley from Kaunakakai, first toward the airport and then branching left at the Kualapu'u sign. It leads to the Kalaupapa Lookout, which brings you to a spectacular vista almost 1,600 feet above the island's northern shore. For those wishing to camp or ride mountain bikes at **Palaau State Park**, this is the way to go.

The round-trip distance is perhaps 16 miles, and it is at best a half-day trip. But the view itself and the chance to visit the Hansen's disease community earn this route a section of its own.

From the Lookout you can see the isolated north coast peninsula called **Makanalua**, "The Given Grave." For sixteen years, until he himself died of the disease, this was Father Damien's domain. When he first came, this was a refuse dump for an ill and despairing humanity, withered by disease and torn from their community. Father Damien's presence assured at least a modicum of medical care, but his real contribution was in caring. Neither this Belgian priest in his funny clothes, the physicians who visited so sporadically nor the royal families who ruled this island could do anything to diminish the horror of the "wasting disease," which progressively killed the nerves and resulted in progressive disfigurement. What Damien did do was live within the medical prison's confines, treat the ill as human beings and, by example, insist they recognize their own humanity.

Perhaps nobody has captured better the fear and hatred the idea of exile contained for Hawaiian residents of the 19th century than Jack London. He was feted throughout the islands when he visited and then violently condemned for the stories he wrote about his trip. It was a scandal of the day, and old newspaper records are filled with the disbelief that one who had been shown so much aloha could have reacted with so little taste.

What angered many native readers was London's sympathy for native Hawaiians' feelings of betrayal when exiled to Molokai and, I suspect, his ability to articulate the feelings of those who chafed under the dominion of *haole* (foreigner) business and political interests. This is clearest, perhaps, in his story "Koolau the Leper." London, who stayed at Kalaupapa for several days, makes clear that, for the native Hawaiian, the concept of segregation was a political as well as a medical act. The story's opening lines, spoken by a native narrator, state the argument clearly: "Because we are sick they take away our liberty. We have obeyed the law. We have done no wrong. And yet they would put us in prison. Molokai is prison." His story is the tale of a Kauai man who, suffering from Hansen's disease, refused exile because it meant separation from his wife and son. It details his and his family's flight into the Kauai mountains and the successful guerilla war Koolau waged against the officials who attempted to capture him and send him away.

The story is important in part because the resentment against foreign (non-island) interests remains today on the part of native Hawaiians. Of more topical interest is a revival in the 1980s of the idea of segregating AIDS sufferers in much the same way that Hansen's Disease victims were segregated here a century ago. It was suggested, at one point, that removing those with AIDS disorders would stop the spread of this century's debilitating illness, just as 19th century Hawaiians believed isolation was an answer for their medical plague. Fortunately, as the hysteria over the modern illness decreases, the idea of banishment has slowly died down as well.

So, at least for me, Kalaupapa stands as a lesson hopefully

learned: fear of disease added banishment and ostracism to what was, in the last century, another painful, debilitating and ultimately fatal disease. Neither fear nor ignorance could stop the spread of the infection, but as Bushnell's book makes clear, fear and ignorance did compound the sufferers' pain.

This is now a restricted area. You cannot enter the settlement or wander around unescorted without permission. even though Hansen's disease can now be controlled, Kalaupapa is a community whose members were born when their home was an exile and have chosen to remain in its confines today. This is not a museum or simple tourist attraction but a community, home, shrine and village all in one. Some people fly in on tours with Air Molokai (flights leave from the Molokai airport at 9:15 a.m.) or take the famous **Molokai Mule Ride** from Kalae stables (to which you can bicycle). The $25 per person fare includes a pass to the inhabited area of Kalaupapa, a picnic lunch and tour of the grounds.

Local hotels will be glad to assist with arrangements for those who wish to fly, take the mule ride in or be met at the settlement after a hike from **Kalaupapa Lookout**. This is a three-mile trek descending 2,000 feet and, while spectacular, not for those who dislike heights or who are just beginning to get into good physical condition. Remember, those who walk down from the Lookout must later return the same way.

Another non-cycling trip is the **Molokai Wagon Ride,** which takes its customers to **Heiau Ili Ili o Pae**, a traditional place of Hawaiian worship off the coast road. This is a doer's ride, the brochure says, where "traditional Hawaiian net throwing" is taught along with coconut husking and other classic arts. I've never taken it, but I promise myself on each visit to Molokai that the next time I will take this trip. Arrangements can be made through local hotels.

Molokai is also a lovely place just to sit, think, relax and read. For those seeking less sedentary, non-cycling activities, sailboats are for charter out of **Kaunakakai Harbor,** and there is good scuba diving off the coast if you can find a local diver willing to act as guide. Be warned, however, that there are currently no dive shops on the island, so you will need to bring tanks and equipment with you and replenish them on Maui.

Snorkeling along sections of the south coast is said to be a real delight, especially if a small boat is available to carry you west of the harbor. Nobody, of course, should try snorkeling or diving alone. Ask at the hotel desk, and somebody's cousin's brother or sister may be able to help with a boat and the local knowledge necessary to safely explore the island's aquatic side.

Addresses and Information

_____ Addresses for Molokai_____

For State Park camping permits:
  Division of Parks and Recreation
  Kaunakakai, HI 96748
  553-5141

For County camping permits:

(Molokai is a part of Maui County)
  Department of County Parks and Recreation
  1580 Kaahumanu Ave.
  Wailuku, HI 96793

For information on state campgrounds on Oahu:
  State Department of Land and Natural Resources
  465 S. King Street
  Honolulu, HI 96813

_____ Ferry Service information_____

Maui Princess Ferry
Sea Link of Hawaii
505 Front Street Suite 203
Lahaina, HI 96761
 661-8397 (on Maui)
 653-5736 (on Molokai)

_____Accommodations _____

  Pau Hana Inn, Kaunakakai, Molokai Hawaii
  Hotel Molokai, Kaunakakai, Molokai, Hawaii
  Kaluako'i Hotel and Golf Club, Molokai Hawaii

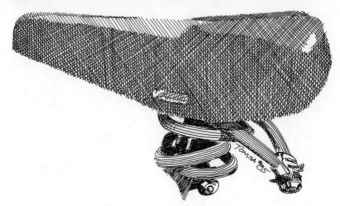

_____ Recommended Reading_____

A.O. Bushnell's *Molokai* (Honolulu: University of Hawaii Press) is a fictionalized story of Father Damien's refuge. Bushnell is a fine local writer whose novels are filled with local flavor and color. Usually, copies can be found in used book stores on Oahu and, of course, purchased new as well.

Gavan Daws has written extensively about Hawaii, and his *Shoal of Time* is considered by many to be the best general history of the state. His *Holy Man: Father Damien of Molokai* is, like his other works, an honest historical treatment of a complex and difficult subject.

Jack London's *Tales of Hawaii* (Honolulu: Press Pacifica, 1984). London, who visited the colony in the 19th century, was strongly affected by the exiles' plight, and this collection includes several stories about Kalaupapa.

Cycling Maui

INTRODUCTION

According to the map of Maui's routes and roads, planning a jaunt across the island's terrain should be a piece of cake. There is a coastal road that swings pleasantly counterclockwise from Wailuku to Lahaina; the Hana Highway is a clear ribbon along the northeast coast. By contrast, the climb from sea level to Haleakala's crater is sure to be for most a difficult, tortuous bear of a ride. But at least the road is good, a straight shot of clearly marked highway. Finally, there is the road around the southern half of East Maui, which, really, doesn't look too bad. Sure, there's a short climb and a bad stretch of road, but it all ends, the map says, with a six mile, zig-zagging descent to Makena Point or with good highway up to the Ulupalakula ranch area and onto Kula Road.

None of these routes are what they seem, however. It is not that the cartographer lied, but that maps cannot always tell the whole truth. The route around West Maui (Kahului to Lahaina) is a graveled roller coaster of steep ascents, declines and hairpin curves too small to be detailed on any but the largest-scale topographic map. No cartographers will describe the route's chief hazard of a pack of dogs waiting at mile 12.5 to terrorize the unwary rider, because the days in which map makers detailed such dangers—"there be dragons here"—are long, long gone. From Ma'alaea Harbor to Wailuku, head winds are often fierce, making what the maps promise as an easy eight miles an endurance feat into 30- or 40-mile-per-hour winds.

Once, I'm sure, there was a clear road to Makena Point from

Ma'alaea Harbor, and maybe that road still exists. But it has been redesigned so many times to accommodate the growing hotel and condominium trade that, despite an hour's search and past knowledge, all I can say is that it seems to have disappeared. So, too, the road down from Ulupalakua to the Makena area, which is private and now off limits. Do not blame the cartographer when reality does not jibe with the two-dimensional world. But don't plan a trip assuming anything but good faith from the shorthand in which the map maker must work.

This chapter is an object lesson in what maps can never really say.

Maui is the most popular cycle destination in the Hawaiian Islands and one of the best-known cycling sites worldwide. The straight, tough climb from Wailuku to the summit of Haleakala ("Race to the Sun" is the annual event that celebrates it each September) and the stunning, speedy descent from the top have been described in articles for years. The Hana Highway, which traces the bulge of East Maui for 54 miles of often turning, rising, hilly splendor, is another piece of "cycleania." But the best—and the worst—of these routes is something locals know all too well and cartographers not at all.

Maui's most famous routes are so well described that I hesitate to puncture the myths and suggest what resident riders long have known. There are better roads to ride than Haleakala Highway and even more beautiful (and less traveled) roads than the one leading to Hana. Those trips are worth all the praise that has been heaped on them for years, but they do not begin to describe the rigor and beauty that is cycling on Maui. This chapter, then, will be a somewhat eccentric view of cycling what is, perhaps, the best-known bicycling island in the world. Alternate routes for Haleakala are suggested, and rides rarely touted elsewhere are advocated here.

Arriving: Kahului Airport

There is an airport near Hana that caters to small, local planes, but for those who don't travel by private plane, there are really only two ways to get to this island. One is by the **Maui Princess** ferry, which arrives in Lahaina each morning and returns to Molokai late each afternoon. It's a wonderful trip, described in the Molokai chapter, and heartily recommended to all. Most people, however, fly commercial airlines to Maui, either from another island or, increasingly, directly from the Mainland.

Most cycle tours begin near Wailuku/Kahului, two small, coastal communities that have grown over the years into one urban location which sits on the isthmus separating Maui's western and eastern parts. The airport is no more than four miles from town and an equal distance from a good county campground. Both town and campsite offer immediate access for riders heading to Lahaina, Hana or the summit of Haleakala.

In 1989 new runways were being completed at the Kahului Airport which will allow larger jets to land. This addition promises to add the European trade to what has been a predominantly North American and Japanese tourist destination. With that construction come new, larger terminals, more efficient baggage handling, air conditioned passenger lounges and the rest of modernity's comforts. Soon you will not have to walk in the sun on the runway's tarmac to board or disembark from the jets which bring thousands of visitors to Maui. Hydraulic boarding ways will be the order of the day.

I liked the funky, old-time feel of Maui's airport a few years back when the baggage area resembled a Mainland bus station and the whole was contained in a long, tin shack. But the up side is that, with others, I now can grumble about how good the old days were and what a shame the tourist economy has forced it all to change. When you hear these complaints, nod sympathetically and know that most who make them are working in a profession or trade that has profited from the ever greater volume of tourists deplaning daily. The good old days were not, in fact, so swell, and those who wail this island lament usually do so in a ritualistic way.

Airport Transportation
Taxi cabs are available at the airport's entrance, but the town and campgrounds are both so close that it makes no sense to do anything but ride your bike from the terminal.

For those arriving from the Mainland, it makes sense to pack cycle pants and shirt in a pannier carried onto the airplane. While baggage handlers unpack the 400-seat jet, nip into a washroom and change into cycle duds so that you'll be ready to ride in the hot, moist, tropical day when your bicycle is at last unloaded.

Cyclists arriving interisland are presumably already dressed appropriately, and if you've flown **Aloha** or **Hawaiian Airlines**, you will find your bicycle almost ready to ride as it is unloaded from the airplane. Neither carrier requires that the machine be boxed, and many of Hawaii's baggage handlers don't object if the pedals are left on at loading time.

Those on tight travel schedules will note that the first flight from Oahu arrives in Kahului before 7 a.m., and you can fly out of Honolulu and be on the road to Hana, Lahaina or Haleakala before 8 a.m.

Most cyclists arrive too late in the day for a long, tough ride, and for them there are, really, only two directions to cycle. Either pedal about four miles on the Hana Highway Road to **H.A. Baldwin Park** or turn toward town and the hotels of Kahului, which are three miles in the opposite direction. Both routes are well marked.

For campers who have ordered their permits by mail and are eager to be at the beach or strategically located for the next day's ride, H.A. Baldwin Park is wonderful. Leave the airport and follow the traffic out of the airport and stay with the flow as it bends left onto **Kaolani Place**. This leads to a well-marked intersection with the **Hana Highway** (Route 36). Turn left onto the Highway and, in thirty minutes or less, Baldwin Park will appear on the makai (ocean) side of the coastal road. Supplies can be purchased a mile farther down the road in the town of Paia. Both park and town will be described in this chapter's Ride Six.

Kahului/Wailuku

For those heading into town, turn *right* at the Hana Highway sign and ride past the well-preserved **Kanaha Pond,** which is a designated Wildlife Sanctuary. Once it was a royal fish pond, but in this ecologically egalitarian age has been transformed into a refuge for the migratory Hawaiian stilt. This is the famous *Himantopus mexicanus*, better known locally as the *ae'o.* I've been by there many times and have never seen one, so take on faith the assertion by experts that they really do vacation in this area and deserve their lush, marsh-like vacation home.

Other species nest here as well, and bird watchers may ooh! and ah! appreciatively at the opportunity to keep them under close observation. If you think life is about spotting rare types of birds, consider picking up Andrew J. Berger's *Bird Life in Hawaii,* a good, basic book on the island's aviary history and population.

Technically this is still the Hana Highway, but almost immediately the name changes, as you approach town, to **Ka'ahumanu Highway.** Just before it does, however, you will see **Andy's Cycle and Sport Shop** in a small shopping complex on the right. If your bike has a problem or you forgot some equipment, this is a good place to pick up supplies while asking for local directions.

Ka'ahumanu Highway, named after the favorite wife and queen of Kamehameha the Great, runs straight through Kahului and Wailuku toward **Iao Valley**. It is the main drag, what transportation experts call an "arterial," and the traffic on its surface is often fierce. Hundreds of tourists in rented automobiles travel along it each day, zipping up Haleakala or out to Hana in an afternoon, and they love to drive this road at high speed. Huge cane trucks and other commercial vehicles also clutter the asphalt, joining the thousands of full-time Maui residents who need to enter or leave these two towns.

All this makes for busy rush hours, which leave cyclists doggedly pedalling on the extreme edge of the road while trucks, buses and cars whiz by without a thought. I like Maui and love cycling in most places, but hate riding rush hour anywhere within five miles of these towns. Last time I was almost killed by a woman in a big rental car who swerved toward me across a full traffic lane, missing my bike by a hair. The five kids who littered her Toyota had turned its back seat into a juvenile battleground, and she, apparently, was remonstrating with them and not watching the road at all. As I bounced off the shoulder and onto the grass, I saw the driver, half turned and screaming as she raced to some hotel swimming pool in town.

The message is: ride carefully in the Wailuku/Kahului area. There are too many cars for the available road, and many drivers are going to be distracted. The secret of safe cycling is, as ever, to ride carefully and consistently, observing all signals and not presuming motorists will show any sense or courtesy at all.

In Town

Kahului and Wailuku are the supply depots of Maui. Goods flow in through the harbor at the edge of town, where cruise ships dock and Japanese fishing vessels refuel. **Kalana O Maui**, the county's office buildings, where camping permits can be picked up, is on the road to Iao Valley. Ka'ahumanu Highway also hosts three shopping plazas, two of them side by side. If Lahaina is the arts and crafts center of this island, then Kahului and Wailuku are its prosaic heart.

Entering town from the airport, for example, you'll find Kahului and Ka'ahumanu Shopping Centers on the mauka side of the road. The former is home to local supermarkets and stores, the latter houses typical, mall-style companies including a small Sears outlet and a Waldenbooks.

In Kahului Mall is **The Island Biker**, a cycle shop nestled next to a mediocre, Japanese-style restaurant which has the advantage of being relatively inexpensive. I like this small bicycle shop in great part because its helpful owner, Bob Nooney, is more than willing to haul out his well-used topographic map to brief touring cyclists. On my last trip we spent half an hour going over changes in various routes. I recommend the shop and its courtesy to all.

In the back of Kahului Mall is **Christine's Restaurant**, a local eatery that serves an early morning breakfast and closes at 2 p.m. Their mahimahi burgers are pretty good and the chocolate milk shakes simply great. A milk shake is one of the best and most delicious rewards I can think of after miles of tiring and dehydrating road. If you've never indulged, try it this trip.

Across the street from this mall, the area's three major hotels stand side by side. All three face the highway with their backs to the beach and sea. In the old days, airline stewards and stewardesses usually stayed at the Maui Hukilau, and some who fly this route still recommend it. The Hukilau, now called the **Seaside Motel**, is where I like to stay. It is part of a small, Hawaii-owned family chain, not fancy, but friendly and competitively priced, a reasonable alternative for those who believe that tents and bedrolls are to be used only in dire necessity. Cyclists can almost always get a first floor room, which means they do not have to lug their bikes up and down the stairs.

Ride One: Kahului, Wailuku and Iao Valley

Skill level: Basic cycling skills
Connects with Ride Two

I recommend the practice rarely, but this is a place where it pays to wake up just before dawn. Watch the light from your hotel or campground as it swings from a whisper of sun into a grand chorus of sunlight highlighting Iao Valley. The center of the park is a 2,250-foot-high pinnacle surrounded by the walls of **Pu'u Kukui**, whose summit reaches up almost 5,800 feet. At dawn the view is briefly clear of clouds, which will soon swing in to obscure the sight. The whole show takes perhaps half an hour and is worth the lost sleep.

The Iao Valley area is a perfect tune-up ride. If you've not ridden in the tropics before or have not loaded up the touring bike in months, this is an interesting and not too taxing ride on which to check out stamina, equipment and will. From Kahului Shopping Center to the Valley's Park is only a five-mile jaunt ascending perhaps 1500 feet. From there you can explore the Valley and, along the way, the reaches of Wailuku while purchasing camping permits for the rest of your island stay. Iao Valley and the town's environs means a not too taxing 12- to 15-mile day.

From **H.A. Baldwin Park** it is a six-mile ride on the Hana and Ka'ahumanu Highways to the Kahului Shopping Center, across from the town's hotels. Those who have chosen the soft life of beds and air conditioners swing out from their posh retreat and right onto Ka'ahumanu Highway toward Iao Valley. It cannot be missed from this side of the island. Like Haleakala itself, the summit of **Pu'u Kukui** is a brooding, omniscient presence so dominant that you are instantly oriented in relation to it from almost any spot, and it is hard ever to be truly lost.

The first mile of Ka'ahumanu in town is almost flat and very easy. It leads up a well-paved and well-trafficked road into the beginning of an ascent. Traffic is urban in this area and, if heavy, civilized by stop-lights and a well-marked road. Another mile up the hill, just past a McDonald's on the right (I'm no great fan of the Golden Arches but they surely are landmarks you cannot miss) will be the area's only "skyscraper," the nine-story **Kalana O Maui,** where the county administration does its business. A left at this intersection puts you on a short road to Lahaina (see Ride Three) and the island's leeward side. It is at this building that you should stop to pick up camping permits and pause a moment to consider and praise the recently retired mayor of Maui county, a dedicated chap with the wonderful name of Hannibal Tavares.

Maui County's Mayor

Tavares is often praised and almost as frequently damned by local folk for the changes that occurred on the island during his tenure in office. He is better known internationally, however, for a political campaign to stop the United States military and its friends from using Kaho'olawe Island, which sits a few miles off this coast, as a target range. Kaho'olawe is (like Molokai) a part of Maui County and, historically, an important site to native Hawaiians. It is filled with *heiaus*, traditional Hawaiian religious or ritual sites, and ancient middens. More recently it has become littered with the ordnance of American, Canadian, Japanese, Australian and New Zealand navy gunners.

That, many Hawaiians believe, is an unacceptable aggression against the *aina*, the land. Kaho'olawe has been appropriated and placed off limits by the federal folk, who turned it into the passive target America and its naval allies use for shelling practice. Tavares— and many other Hawaiian citizens—want this silliness stopped. As

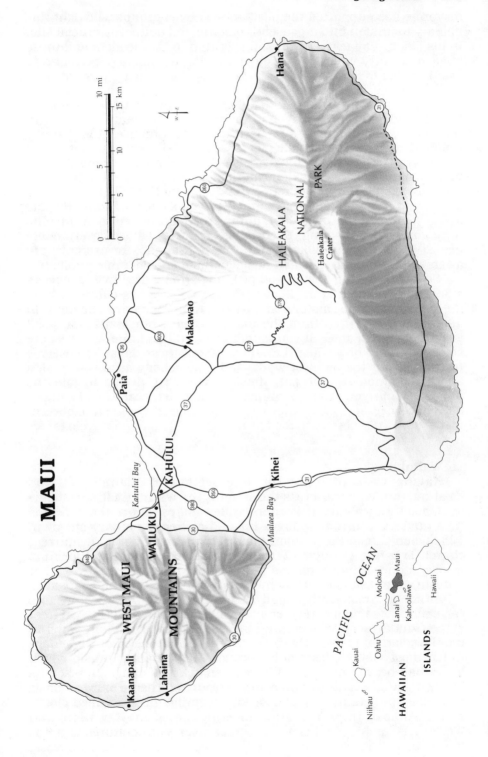

mayor he has supported the position of activist groups who fight this military incursion into a peaceful, historic and culturally crucial site. In his official capacity, Tavares has written to U.S. leaders and those of each country which participates in RIMPAC military exercises to ask them not to bomb what is a peaceful and inoffensive piece of Maui real estate.

Mayors are not supposed to tell heads of state what to do. It is, in theory, bad form for a mayor to instruct the Secretary of the Navy that a local island is not to be used for target practice. It is virtually unheard of for a county official to write to the prime ministers of other countries to ask, politely, that they stop the bombing of his municipality. Tavares has done all this and to good effect. Because of his actions, and those of other activists, several U.S. allies—including Japan and New Zealand—have in recent years declined to participate in the yearly shell game, which dumps more ordnance each time the navy guns start shooting. Even those countries whose governments persist in taking pot shots at Kaho'olawe (Canada, for example) are aware of his campaign, which has generated considerable publicity.

So if you're going to stop and pick up permits, drop by the mayor's office, and let them know if you support the island's efforts to limit the use of a fragile, historic site as the target for navy shooters. In 1989, Tavares retired from the mayoral chair, but Maui is a small island in a small state. If you're interested in this issue, chances are somebody will know where he's hanging out these days. He deserves recognition for this activist work, and if somebody asks you to sign another petition to stop the shelling, you may decide to join the protest. While you're at the county building, let local officials know, one concerned activist to another, that the county and state governments could do more to make Maui a habitable place for cyclists.

Wailuku

Kalana O Maui is at the intersection of High Street and Ka'ahumanu Avenue. Across the street is the **Wailuku Library**, home to a good Hawaiiana collection. A few steps down the block is **Ka'ahumanu Church,** where a grass-thatched sanctuary stood in 1832 when Queen Ka'ahumanu herself worshiped here. The current church is a fine example of 19th century ecclesiastic architecture, whose stone solidity makes an interesting contrast to Father Damien's more simple but, to me, more moving labors on Molokai.

Although the church usually is closed during the week, visitors can sometimes find a caretaker who will let them in. But the real treat is the Sunday service, when the invocation and hymns are sung in the Hawaiian language. Hawaiian is a beautiful, melodious language which most visitors hear only through the popular music which blares half-heard from car radios or in snatches of a nightclub act. Its thirteen sounds rush together into a recurring theme of a few basic phonemes punctuated by almost imperceptible breaks called glottal stops. Almost from the first meeting between Hawaiian and Westerner, music has been a bridge between both cultures and it is in the music that the richness of the mix is most evident. The close,

19th century harmony of prosaic church music is enriched by the smoothness of the glissando of vowels which end all Hawaiian words.

There is good, sometimes great Hawaiian music to be heard in these islands. Most of it is the result of a happy marriage between the missionary's 19th century religious music—simple melodies with a 4/4 beat—and the complex, rhythmic traditions of Hawaiian hula and chants. To hear a service where Hawaiian is sung is to hear a snatch of history and to feel the power that missionaries and residents knew when these two potent traditions first met in the days of square-rigged whaling vessels as fast clipper ships raced back and forth across the Pacific in the 19th century's China Trade.

Up the street and a bit closer to Iao Valley is the **Bailey House Museum**, built by Edward Bailey in 1941 when he was headmaster of the Wailuku Female Seminary. Also known as Old Bailey House, the building is made of twenty-inch-thick stone covered with plaster and, for some reason I've never understood, goat hair. There is a beautiful view of the isthmus itself from the the museum's yard.

A Bit of Botany

From Old Bailey it is about three miles up valley to Iao pinnacle. This is a lovely, climbing, winding road with reasonable traffic and the hint of cool which comes in the tropics with even moderate altitude. Along the way, pause to look at the trees, which appear to be pine but are, in fact, *Casurina.* What at a glance appear to be pine needles are, in fact, a plant stem. They are not native to these islands but can be found in abundance on several islands, Oahu included. In the distance other trees will appear to have silvered leaves. That is the characteristic sheen of the Kukui tree, whose nuts have been a mainstay of island pharmacology for generations. A mile before Iao Valley's parking lot is a sign signalling Iao Valley Lodge and a restaurant called **Mark Edison's Place.** Don't stop now, however. It's a brief rest stop for the return, and Iao Valley itself is only a mile farther up the road.

Iao Valley and Needle

Immediately entering the Valley itself there is, on the right, a rock cliff in which people claim the image of John F. Kennedy can be seen. At *Pali 'Ele'ele* (Dark Gorge) tourists stop and gaze intently, many apparently assuring their friends/spouses/parents/siblings that yes, of course they recognize the face that has become a symbol of civil integrity in American political history. Many dutifully photograph the site.

Others are always seeing things that I miss. They find the image of Christ in a cloth, lovers in clouds, and presidents in natural, soft stone. In cloth I see fiber, in clouds I see vapor, and in rock I see, well, rock.

Iao Needle

The other big attraction is Iao Needle, a 2,250-foot lava rock pinnacle that sits smack in the valley and is itself surrounded by **Pu'u**

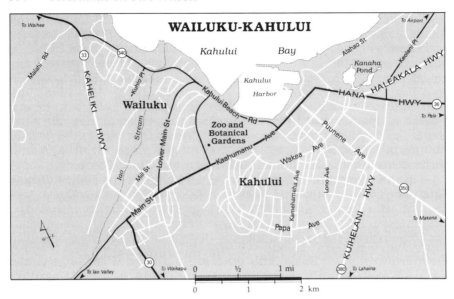

Kukui. To me it looks like a hand's third finger raised in belligerent protest (to whom or what doesn't matter) and, each time I think of that, I smile and nod to myself. It is, perhaps, the cyclist's symbol, a finger throw at the encroaching world, and should be made into a T-shirt design if not a medallion for adventuring bicycle riders.

Climbers with more ambition than sense have mounted repeated assaults on the pinnacle, but it is a dangerous, difficult climb and one not recommended to anybody who possesses a particle of sense.

The surrounding valley, filled with hikes and wandering space, is well worth the time it takes to explore. There are pools of cool, fresh water that run from the rainy heights down through this area and toward the isthmus before joining the surrounding ocean.

Kepaniway Gardens

The return from Iao needle is all downhill and thus imbued with that lovely feeling of having gravity as an aide on the descent. To prolong the pleasure, stop at **Iao Valley Lodge** next to **Kepaniway Heritage Gardens**. The lodge's rooms are priced competitively with those in town, but have no TV because, in a valley like this, it would be sacrilege to spend one's time watching "Wheel of Fortune."

Mark Edison's Place is a restaurant in the complex that looks like the dining hall of an upscale, Mainland summer camp. Beautiful wood and a huge picture window onto the gardens make it a wonderful rest stop. The restaurant's picture window looks out upon Kepaniway Heritage Gardens, a county park celebrating the island's ethnic diversity with formal gardens and pavilions representing history's waves of Chinese, Japanese, European and American migration to Maui. It's pleasant enough, but like so many other formal homages it seems artificial in an area whose human history is so evident. To *see* the multi-cultural history of Hawaii (or any island) simply look at the folk who surround you (folk with names like Juanita Chen Mendez Kopinski) or *listen* to a church service whose various parts are presented in English, Chinese (or Japanese) and Hawaiian.

The name Kepaniway, by the way, commemorates a rather bloody battle fought on this site in 1790 between Kamehameha I and the then-rival chieftains of Maui. With the help of military advisors John Young and Isaac Davis, The-Unifier-Of-These-Islands decimated his local opponents in what by all reports was, quite literally, a slaughter. The name Kepaniway means "the damming of the waters" and was given to the area because, local historians say, so many bodies piled up in Iao Stream that its flow was blocked by the carnage.

Ride Two: Ma'alaea Harbor & Honoapi'ilani Highway
Skill level: Basic urban skills
Connects with Rides One and Four

Leaving the battle site and the valley, zip downhill and back toward town. At Ka'ahumanu Church, if you hang a right, the road leads directly to **Honoapi'ilani Highway** (Route 30), which cuts across the island isthmus to Ma'alaea Harbor and the leeward shore.

When trade winds are gusting, this 6.5-mile semi-rural road has a strong tail wind urging the rider on. Winds funnel through the isthmus, channeled by Iao Valley and Haleakala, to blow at times with real force. Truth be known, this is not a great road for cycling. The shoulder is minimal and the winds sometimes tricky as you sail past working plantations with the West Maui mountains always brooding to the road's right and Haleakala beckoning across the isthmus to the left.

Still, I prefer this road to the more heavily trafficked Mokulele Highway (Route 350), which commercial vehicles tend to use. In 1989, Route 380 was resurfaced and is now graced by an excellent and wide shoulder on both sides of the road. This road runs from the Kahului Airport and joins the Honoapi'ilani Highway near the isthmus. It is now probably the best route for cycling across the isthmus, although the Honoapi'ilani Highway, with its continual views of working fields, windmills and vibrant agricultural life in the shadow of the mountains, remains the most scenic.

The road climbs a few hundred feet to Waikapu, a few buildings and a country store that stand beside the road, and then down past **Maui Tropical Plantation** to the opposite shore. The plantation is a sixty-acre agricultural park open daily and with no admission charge. It sports a tram ride and roads that wind through fields of coffee, guava and mango. There is also a market where visitors can buy foodstuffs grown in the park area.

Kahului-based riders who want a slightly longer tune-up ride than Iao Valley offers but who don't want to circumnavigate West

Maui in a single day will find the Plantation a compromise destination. By riding first to Iao Valley and then to the Plantation before their return, enough miles will be added to this route to satisfy an intermediate cyclist. The ride back to Wailuku/Kahului will often be handicapped by strong head winds, so beginners may wish to make this a separate excursion.

Ma'alaea Harbor

Honoapi'ilani's terminus, **Ma'alaea Harbor**, is built on a lovely bay near where humpback whales often play during their busy winter months of residence. The harbor is home berth to a variety of tourist-oriented vessels that specialize in whale watching, fishing, and sight-seeing. From the harbor's public beach you have a grand seat for the contemplation of a whole range of ocean life. Swimmers, boats and whales all slide past in a fabulous panorama for the rider who chooses to rest in indolence against a mature palm tree.

For those needing refreshments and food, there is a restaurant nearby and a country store (closed Monday) where soft drinks and junk food are available.

From here it is about 15 miles to Lahaina and less to Makena Point. See Ride Four, Lahaina to Makena Point.

Heiaus, Zoos and Gardens

If you choose to save Ma'alaea for another day, there are other, closer destinations to explore in the Wailuku area. Returning from Iao Valley, for example, a left on Main Street leads downhill to the beach road and a left from there leads to Kuhio Place, just past a bridge over Iao Stream.

Here is the entrance to the archaeologically significant **Haleki'i-Pihana Heiaus**. The Haleki'i was used during Maui King Kahekili's reign in the late 18th century, and Pihana, about a hundred yards from it, was a sacrificial temple. If you want to know more, diagrams on-site explain the layout of the temple's walls and buildings.

If you do not turn in search of these traces of that long-gone age, lower Main Street carries you to the harbor and its coastal park, which, I hasten to add, is nothing special. The road here is well trafficked but sufficiently wide so that the cars should present no problem. Just before the harbor, the botanically minded may want to take a right onto Kanaola Avenue and the **Maui Zoological and Botanical Gardens**.

Neither is a magnificent example of natural, wild ways well preserved. The zoo is small and insufficiently funded. The botanical garden beside it appears mundane and unexciting to any who are not cognoscenti of horticultural arts. To those in the know, however, it is in fact something special. The garden is punctuated by low mounds of plants growing on what seem like miniature hillocks. These are what professionals come to admire because they demonstrate the method of Rene Silva, the botanist who created them.

I visited with University of Hawaii botanist and algae expert Jane Lewis, who told me Silva is a local and largely self-taught botanist who can grow plants whose propagation has frustrated other experts

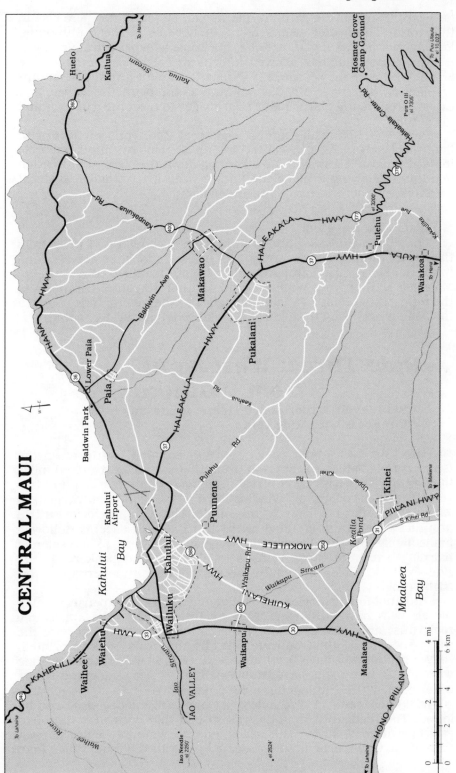

CENTRAL MAUI

To Lahaina

Waihee River

KAHEKILI HWY

340

Waihee

Waiehu

HWY

33

Iao Stream

IAO VALLEY

Iao Needle
el 2250

el 2524

To Lahaina

HONO A PIILANI

30

Maalaea

Maalaea
Bay

Kahului
Bay

Baldwin Park

HANA HWY

Paia
Lower Paia

36

To Lahaina

Kahului
Airport

Kahului

Wailuku

380

KUIHELANI HWY

Waikapu Rd

Waikapu

400

Waikapu Stream

MOKULELE HWY

350

Puunene

Pulehu Rd

Keahua Rd

HALEAKALA HWY

37

Baldwin Ave

Kaupakulua Rd

400

Makawao

Pukalani

HALEAKALA HWY

37

Kealia
Pond

Kihei Rd

Upper Kihei Rd

S Kihei Rd

Kihei

31

PIILANI HWY

To Makena

KULA HWY

37

el 3200

Pulehu

Waiakoa

Keokea Ave

To Hana

378

Haleakala Crater Rd

Puu o Ili
el 7305

Hosmer Grove
Camp Ground

To Puu Ulaula
▲ el 10,023

To Hana

360

Huelo

Kailua

Kailua Stream

N

W E
S

4 mi

6 km

0   2   4

0   2   4   6

for years. Many of the garden's plants can be found nowhere else in the world. The secret seems to be in his use of these mundane-looking mounds as a planting site, but some whisper privately that it is local magic that has allowed him to succeed where others have failed. Whatever the reason, his happy facility for growing what others cannot has made Mr. Silva as rare as the plants he serves, and experts from many places make pilgrimages to meet the gardener and his garden.

From the Botanical Garden and local Zoo, you can return to hotels or Baldwin Park by continuing up Kanaloa Avenue a half mile to Ka'ahumanu Highway or by returning down the street to the Beach Road and following it along the harbor until it terminates, again at Ka'ahumanu, across from Kahului Mall.

Distances traveled

The ride to Iao Valley and around town is about 12-14 miles from the hotels and a not very arduous 24 miles if it includes travel to and from Baldwin Park campgrounds. If you included the route to Ma'alaea Harbor from Wailuku, add another 13 round-trip miles to the total. It is honest to add five miles to the mental mile count if the head winds back from Ma'alaea were even moderately severe.

Ride Three: West Maui from Wailuku

Skill level: Experienced riders; numerous hills
Connects with Ride One

Ride Two is a faster, easier route to Lahaina, a trip down the Isthmus to Ma'alaea Harbor and, from there, an easy thirteen miles to Lahaina. This trip, by contrast, is longer, badly marked and traverses a roller coaster of winding road whose condition ranged, in early 1989, from mediocre to miserable. This counterclockwise trip around West Maui is filled with steep, short ascents followed immediately by equally short declines which end at a succession of hairpin turns. For those unused to climbing and back roads the ride—only 40 miles in reality—seems endless and perhaps a bit frightening.

It is not for the novice or for someone riding an expensive racing bicycle with narrow, narrow tires. Sections of the road are simply rock, dust and gravel, although the county has begun to pave the worst sections of this road and, by the time this book is printed, those sections will have been improved. Still, however, this is a ride where mountain bikes have traditionally been a blessing and where water bottles (three at least) remain a necessity.

In 38 counterclockwise miles, not one convenience store can be found. The road until recently was so bad that cars were forced to travel for miles at the cyclist's speed, and the views presented at each turn of the trail (parts did not deserve to be called a road) range from beautiful to spectacular. Even with improvements, it will remain a narrow back way, and improved road surfacing will make the ride easier for cyclists without creating a super highway where traffic dominates the scenery.

Another nice feature is that, once on the road, it is impossible to become lost. From Wailuku to Lahaina the road has virtually no detours, and directional landmarks are clearly evident. For the first ten miles or so, Haleakala dominates, but slowly, mile by mile around the West Maui shore, Molokai becomes the principal view until, finally, near Lahaina it is Lanai that youwill continually see. The slow speed demanded of 12-degree ascents and the need to ride cautiously on the downhill sides of each hill give plenty of time for the rider to ponder the minutia of this world.

I love this ride and recommend it to riders of moderate ability who have moderate endurance and good climbing skills. When I rode this route for the book, in the spring of 1989, I was returning after several inactive months on the Mainland. I was out of shape, unused to the heat, carried no water and was generally ill-prepared. Thus mine becomes a cautionary tale of all the things a cyclist should not do. My only gesture to common sense was that I wore my helmet, stopped frequently to rest and knew I was behaving like a fool.

From Baldwin Park

Coming out of the park, turn right onto Hana Highway and follow it into town. Just past the three hotels and across from the malls is an intersection where the Beach Road bends to the right. Take the turn and ride around the harbor. The road here is very good and leads straight past **Nehe Point** to what appears, at first, to be an easy and sensible climb.

These are the suburbs of Wailuku, where the country club and golf course can be seen. **Wahieu Beach Park** is just to the right and, in **Waihe'e**, there is a single general store. There is currently talk, rumors really, of a new development in this area. If it happens it probably won't be for several years and that means there is still time to see this incredibly

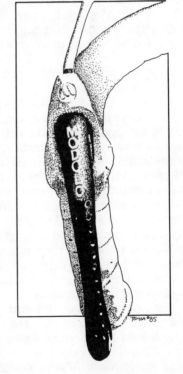

peaceful stretch of slowly ascending road before it becomes spoiled.

Near the store, where I had planned to stock up on fruit, juice, and carbohydrates, two local fellows lounging by a pickup truck asked where I was going on a bicycle. When I said Lahaina they asked if I knew the road, and when I nodded they suggested that I was crazy. "It's a long way, bruddah," one guy said. "You do dis fo' fun?"

the other guy asked and, embarrassed, I had to say yes. Put so baldly, the idea of cycling terrible roads did sound a bit odd, even to me.

We had such a nice chat that, when leaving, I forgot to buy any food. It wasn't until five miles beyond that I discovered that of my three water bottles only one was even half full. I'd already finished the second, and the third had been reserved for juices. So add to the list of potential bicycling hazards folk so pleasant they make riders forget to stock up on supplies.

The road continued to climb and I continued to sweat from **Waihe'e** to near **Olai.** The latter is about 12 miles from Kahului, and the road through this section twists and turns to progressively spectacular views of Kahului Harbor and Haleakala. At mile 12 (measuring from the Kahului Mall) I found a beautifully landscaped stream and rock garden on the left-hand side of the road. It is private property, but the owner was out watering his plantings beside that water-filled, lovely stream. He kindly filled my water bottles from his hose and cautioned me (as I do you) not to drink from hillside streams because many of them are polluted.

Feral pigs run wild in these hills and, he said, have polluted many of the waters. His water, on the other hand, came from an old native well and was absolutely pure. Since few things are worse than to cycle tough terrain while suffering from diarrhea and cramps, I heeded his advice and was even more grateful for the water he was glad to spare.

Where Are We

It was in this neighborhood that what became a commonplace of the trip began. Motorists heading in both directions would pull up next to me and ask where the road they were on was headed. Since there is only one road around all West Maui, it seemed obvious the cars were headed either to or from Wailuku/Kahului or Lahaina. But locked in their cars and held to speeds of less than 20 miles an hour by the twisting, narrow mountain terrain, all these drivers felt lost.

That was a boon to me. When my water bottles were empty I relied, like Blanche DuBois, on the "kindness of strangers" and existed on what I could extract from motorists who stopped to ask me for directions. What they really wanted was assurance. Used to wide lanes with lots of directional signs, many drivers apparently found a narrow, winding road whose terrain absolutely limited car speed to a low-geared crawl an extremely unsettling experience.

I was happy to oblige and each time explained, politely, that the road was a circle and that they were certainly headed in the right direction and need only forge ahead. On a circle, after all, it is impossible to be really lost. Then I'd ask, nonchalantly, "I seem to be out of water, here. Would you have anything drinkable to spare?"

The normal response was, "Geez, nothing but this half-dead can of cola," or "Sorry, just some of this weird pineapple/coconut juice which isn't very good." Fine, I would reply. No problem. All contributions were gratefully accepted. Two slurps of coke, a half-dead can of 7-Up and the dregs of pineapple/coconut juice mixed with a bit of pineapple and guava nectar were what kept me going. One mother with several kids handed me half a peanut butter sandwich. When her three-year-old protested this intrusion into his personal larder she said, "I'll give you the whole sandwich if you'll take my kid, too." The other half of the sandwich looked inviting, and I was prepared to bargain for a bag of potato chips as well. But it didn't matter. I lacked a child seat and helmet, and she had neither juice nor water to spare.

Dogs

It is rare to find dogs roaming loose in these islands where leash laws are in effect. The exception is on this road just past the landscaped yard--the only one for miles. As I was leaving the drinking hole, a driver going toward Kahului stopped to warm me that a pack of dogs was nearby, chasing everything in sight.

They were at mile 12.4 and uncharacteristically organized in the attack. A white one picked up the point while their leader, a black monster, ran beside me with his teeth so close to the front tire that spittle dripped on the wheel. Four or five of their fellows brought up the rear as I pedaled on, terrified out of my wits, screaming " Sit! Stay! Heel! Get away! Go chase a car, not me."

I'm never sure if I prefer the dogs that chase me to be large, well-fed beasts like these fellows were or scrawny and pitifully hungry curs. With the former you can assume they're not hungry enough to want to do real damage, but then I always wonder, what exactly have these carnivores been eating? Salad and granola make no animal look that sleek. If they're half-starved, of course, I can understand their desire to take a bite out of passing cyclists, even if it is difficult to sympathize with the idea of becoming some canine's meal.

In any case, the thing to do is continue to pedal slowly, shouting forcefully at the dogs. "Show no fear," the books instruct. I try not to, but my voice tends to break like an adolescent's at moments like this, and that, I suspect, may be a cue the dumb beasts understand too well.

These sleek dogs lost interest in me after about 100 yards. It turns out they are a well-known feature on that road. When I asked one of the employees at the Seaside Motel about the pack she said, cheerfully, "Those are my cousin Mendez' dog. They do not bite nobody yet." Local bicyclists from Lahaina to Kahului all had a similarly laconic view, holding that, until a cyclist is in fact devoured, the Mendez dogs should be considered a minor annoyance and not a serious threat.

Mile 13-25

Past that hazard, the road degenerates into a seemingly endless series of short but steep ascents and descents joined by hairpin, 160-degree turns. There is no way to build up speed on the downhill because it's going to be only a quarter mile until the road turns almost back onto itself and begins again to climb two to three hundred feet into the next convolution. Each section of this part of the route is only a few hundred feet in length and it is slogging, hot, dusty work.

What makes it even more interesting, especially for those on non-mountain bikes, is that large sections of the road are nothing but gravel and dirt on rock. If it was ever paved, the pavement has disappeared. Twice I had to get off and walk the bicycle over bad patches where my tires simply skipped and spun without traction.

One joy was that I could pass motorists who had been passing me. They were stopped at lookouts and peering warily at their maps as if unconvinced that roads as bad as this could exist at a Tourist Destination in the United States. My quotient of dead, carbonated beverages and warm juices increased apace.

The map promised there would be bad road only from **Gul** to **Mokoea Point,** but it lasted almost to **Honokahua**. The rises and dips, whatever the road surface, continued all the way to **Napili Bay**. I averaged between four and six miles an hour through much of this terrain and in retrospect think that, for a touring rider carrying four full panniers, that was a respectable speed. Much of this road has since been improved and the surface is more reasonable, although the rolling rises and descents are the same.

Things began to improve for me in the area past **Keawalua,** and by **Kanohou Point**, it was possible to believe the worst of the road had been met. At **Honokahua Point** is a small traffic pull-off immediately recognizable by the garden of spirit figures that populate the land. Motorists always stop to see this sight where stones sit, one on top of the other, to create a garden of minimalist, memorial shapes whose figures guard the road. In other countries I've seen this type of abstract figurine with stones piled to mark a memorial spot, a Shinto shade's resting place, but never in such profusion. They serve, there, a religious function—each stone representing some spirit, memory or ghost. Perhaps that's how it started on this Maui road, but if so the meaning is long forgotten. It is now common for people to pile up stones, and the whole field of statuary has become a wonderful, strange, agnostic sight whose deeper significance, if it ever existed, has slid out of local lore and into history's abyss.

Champagne!!

Just past this point I came to **Kuaokaea Point**. The road here is wider, with a decent surface. Having climbed my 4,336th hill, it seemed a good idea to take advantage of that fact and coast into the descent. But at the Point a couple lounged in their yellow convertible, admiring the view and drinking liquid from cups. I cycled past them determined to stop scrounging, but thirst dominated pride about 20 feet down the road.

I returned to ask if they could spare anything to drink. "Oh yes," the woman said cheerfully. "We've the water from the ice in the champagne bucket. It's almost all melted."

It wasn't old silver. It was a bucket holding a bottle of chilled champagne swathed in a white hand towel to maintain uniform temperature. The woman lifted the bottle out of the bucket to show me that perhaps two water bottles of icy water were there for the taking.

As I transferred the water with shaking hands, the woman asked if I'd care for a bit of wine as well. "While cycling?" her companion asked, as if cyclists never drink. They gave me a nicely fluted plastic cup with the best champagne I've ever tasted. We sat and chatted as I tried to sip politely. What I really wanted was to drown in the stuff. I checked the label, figuring that anything that good had to be expensive. "It's Tattinger '56 for sure," I said to myself, or "maybe a '63." In the end it was Brut '88, but that's not important. Baby Duck champagne from New York State would probably have tasted as good to me at that precise moment in cycling time.

Ka'anapali

From **Kuaokea** it is only about five miles to **Napili** and **Kapalua** beach, where the road becomes a highway again. A bike path begins near here (really a highway breakdown lane) and runs all the way through **Ka'anapali** to Lahaina. This route runs past condo city, a series of huge developments, one after the other, which house an almost infinite number of transient North Americans.

The road is a slow, curving descent for several miles, and there are beaches worth visiting, should you need to rest, behind each development complex. This road empties into Lahaina's main drag of Front Street. If in doubt, stay to the right and the road will be within a block of the harbor.

Along the route, just past **Honokowai Beach Park**, is the station for a tourist-laden train which runs from Lahaina to the **Ka'anapali & Pacific Railroad Station** and back twice a day. This is a rebuilt, 1890-vintage sugarcane train, whose six miles of narrow-gauge tracks transport tourists along what was once a run between the sugar mills and the city.

The whole route from Kahului was, the map says, 38 miles, but my cyclometer registered an additional six. So I peg it at 44 miles, which included stopping at a beach or two to cool off along the way. Total rolling time was seven m.p.h. Not a great speed by anyone's count, but for someone stupid enough to set off with four panniers but neither water nor food, the wonder was that I did so well.

LAHAINA

This is perhaps the most famous of small towns in all the Hawaiian Islands. The former whaling port and one-time home of King Kamehameha I has become an upscale, glitzy bastion of what was once called the "carriage trade." Its miserably designed and too-small modern harbor hosts a whole fleet of tourist-oriented boats that offer day trips to Lanai and other local spots for diving, whale watching, snorkeling and relaxed dinner cruises.

Specialty shops along Front Street sell everything from antique scrimshaw to South Pacific native art (pieces from New Guinea, for example) at prices which, depending on your point of view or desire, range from the reasonable to the exorbitant. Lahaina has history (when he succeeded to the throne, Liholiho, later named Kamehameha II, made this the center of his government), class, good pubs, great food and, if you're lucky, inexpensive accommodations. What cyclist could seriously ask for more?

The Pioneer Inn

The only place I've ever stayed in Lahaina, except aboard a sailing boat, is **The Pioneer Inn**. I love this place, which is on the harbor, in town and a reminder of the time when Lahaina was a working sailor's port. The Inn is on Wharf Street, an old-style, wooden structure built in 1901 which, today, is filled not with seamen but with sailing memorabilia. Its front door is flanked by life-sized carvings of peg-legged, wooden sailors, the official greeters to both the hotel's front desk, the Whaler's Bar and the Harpooner's Lanai restaurant.

Sure, it all sounds too cute. But the bar is always busy and the food is good. The rooms are largely plain, practical and inexpensive (especially those directly above the noisy bar). The place is sometimes booked months in advance, so reservations are in order.

The Inn dominates the city's town square, whose giant Banyan Tree was planted in 1873 and now covers two-thirds of an acre.

The Sunrise Cafe

On the Inn's other side is the local library, and beside it on Market Street is the best food buy in town. The small **Sunrise Cafe** looks like a hole in the wall. This is a small café-restaurant that most tourists pass by because it has little to recommend it in terms of appearance or chic. Unlike the city's best restaurants (La Bretagne, Avalon, etc.) it's utensils are plastic, its plates are paper, the tables are laminated plastic and the napkins strictly disposable—no Irish linen here.

What most tourists don't know is that it is owned by the same woman who oversees the very expensive French restaurant **La Bretagne**. She's incapable of serving a bad meal, and the Sunrise is her no-frills setting where the entrées equal those at La Bretagne, but a meal (fresh fish creole, brown rice and steamed vegetables, for example) costs only $5.95. That, by the way, is less than half the price of dinner at The Pioneer Inn and a tenth the price in Lahaina's best restaurants. For anybody who cares about food but travels on a limited budget, this hole-in-the-wall is absolutely the best deal in town.

As a bonus, the cafe also opens early enough for anyone who wants to watch the dawn while sipping an espresso and eating bagels with the place's regular, daily trade. From before dawn until full light, the cafe's stools are populated by sailors who work on the area's tourist cruise boats and who stop in each day for coffee and rolls on their way to the dock.

Lahaina Complete

Guide and history books spend pages on Lahaina. The place oozes memories, each one exploited by some other writer or some commercial store. For example, one very good guide, APA's *Insight Guide to Hawaii*, mentions that sailor and whaler Herman Melville spent two weeks here in 1843 looking for a job, but left when he found none to his liking. Today, were he to visit, he'd probably find work as a deckhand on a dinner cruise ship.

Physically memorable is the *Carthaginian II*, a floating whale museum in the shape of a 93-foot long, Swedish-built sailing vessel and the only square-rigged vessel to call this port home. Near the town square is *Hale Paahao* (confinement house), the old whaler's brig built of coral block stones. The list of tourist activities and sights goes on and on.

For the cyclist, however, it is more important to know that perhaps half a mile from the Pioneer Inn is **Fun Rentals of Maui**. On Lahainaluna Road off Front Street, Fun Rentals is a full-service bicycle store with a decent repair shop. It also rents good 18-speed road bikes and mountain bikes by the day or by the week. The only condition is that rental bicycles not be ridden down Haleakala. A few trips up and down that road, an employee told me, destroy normal brakes and wheels because of the intense heat built up by the rubber brake pads gripping the metal wheel on the winding, 27-mile downhill run.

Ride Four: Lahaina to Makena Point
Skill level: Basic urban cycling skills
Connects with Rides Two and Three

There was a time, not too long ago, when riding along this leeward coast was an amble across a rural and underdeveloped coast whose major hazard was the ubiquitous cane or pineapple truck carrying produce from the plantation. It was, if not as isolated as the route from Kahului to Lahaina, a decidedly rural and coastal glide past a succession of quiet beaches and semi-rural country stores. Now the area where Makena Point protrudes into the sea has become the new Ka'anapali, with condominiums and resort areas in profusion. Traffic has grown with the tourist trade, and what was once Hawaii's best beach ride has become at times an intense piece of suburban cycling.

It remains, however, a beach lover's joy, with magnificent sandy stretches tucked behind and around the shade of low-branched trees under which you can rest and admire both the whales which cavort off coast in season and the splendor of the tropical scene.

From Lahaina

After breakfast at the Sunrise Cafe, head down Front Street in the direction away from the Ka'anapali ride. Front Street is the main drag in town, and at 505 Front Street is a shopping complex where **Cruiser Bob**'s shop can be found. His was the first and remains the best-known Haleakala cycle tour company. Less than a mile past this building, Front Street turns sharply left and ends at **Honoapi'ilani Highway**.

On the Highway there is, at first, a good breakdown lane beside the road which is ideal for cyclists. Cycling along it you almost immediately pass **Puamana** and then **Launiupoko** state beach parks. Their paved parking lots, rest rooms and even picnic tables invite you to stop and rest along the shore before going far enough to break into a sweat. These would be ideal sites for those interested in tenting around West Maui but, alas, are day parks only and camping is not permitted.

Near Launiupoko, the paved breakdown lane disappears for 2.5 miles, and cyclists are faced with the choice of riding beside the road on bad gravel or holding the edge of the road and fighting the impatient lines of traffic. Tourist cars, local commuters, local trucks and huge produce vehicles zip along at 60 miles an hour while cyclists bend over their handlebars and pedal with their eyes grimly forward. Mountain bikers may prefer the road's side, but I insist on my slice of asphalt, even when traffic is continually passing too damn close. Fortunately, the breakdown lane reappears at **Olowalu,** where an old-fashioned general store makes a convenient landmark.

Next comes **Hekili Point,** where in 1790 the trading vessel *Eleanora* blasted with cannon a group of Hawaiian canoes coming alongside the ship. Perhaps a hundred Hawaiians died in the slaughter, and in retaliation the ambitious but still-young chief, Kamehameha I, captured two *haoles*, Isaac Davis and John Young, who later became his advisors. It was a marriage made in martial heaven. Combining their and his tactical skills, Kamehameha continued his conquest of the islands, and the carnage of that consolidation grew apace—including the slaughter in Iao Valley. Now there is a nice beach where the *Eleanora* decimated the Hawaiians, and people snorkel and scuba dive where cannon-shot bodies once were pulled from the surf.

The road begins to climb just past **Kuanaokalai** and **Awalua** beaches, and for those riding this route toward Lahaina from Wailuku/Kahalui, they offer a nice resting place before the final push along trafficked roads into town. Kuanaokalai, by the way, translates from Hawaiian as "to stand firmly in the calmness of the sea."

Veiled Rocks and "Puka" Tunnels

Now, about 9.5 miles from Lahaina, the road climbs for several miles to perhaps 500 feet above the coast and offers, at roadside turnoffs, spectacular views of West Maui, East Maui, Molokai and Lanai. This is fun riding and rewarding as hell. The feel of climbing and turning and rolling with the road amid spectacular coastal scenery makes it a wonderful section of my own, personal cycle heaven.

Because the rock structure is very soft, road engineers have draped sections of the hillside with fencing in an attempt to slow, if not prevent, the erosion that occurs in wind and rain. It is strange to ride beside these fenced rock faces. It is as if there is something alive in the hills that the silver-colored metal is supposed to restrain.

There is a very short tunnel on this route with no light and no real sidewalk. My first trip through I walked, but found the walkway too narrow for my Fuji and me. The next time I waited until there was a break in traffic and then rode cautiously through. After that, I just held the lane, changed gears and climbed out of the saddle to pump through this section at 24 miles an hour. I decided, at that point, not to worry about traffic and the fact that my speed might make some car arrive at its final destination three to five seconds late. Exiting the tunnel (called on one map a *"Puka"*—Hawaiian for "hole") the road's shoulder reappears and you can simply drift back over and out of the major traffic lane. Then the road begins its descent to the isthmus. **Papawai Point** is a popular lookout from which you can often see boats about to enter or leave **Ma'alaea Harbor,** whose entrance on the road's right-hand side signals the beginning of the isthmus.

From here you can continue on Route 30 back to Wailuku (see Ride Two) or, about a mile past the Harbor, turn right onto Route 31 and head toward Kihei, Wailea and Makena Point.

Points South

After the turnoff, the road degenerates into several miles of broken and narrow pavement with too much traffic and not enough room for cyclists. The only nice thing about the next few miles is **Kealia Pond,** whose quiet marshland is a peaceful contrast to the unpleasantness of this stretch of road. This section is scheduled for an upgrade soon, so by the time this book is in print there should be both shoulder and pavement.

Nearing **Kihei,** the county rewards those whose kidneys and bikes have survived the pounding with a few miles of signed bike path. The path eventually becomes, again, a breakdown lane along the coastal highway. There are great and interesting beaches which stretch from **Mai Poina Oe Iau Beach Park**, near the Captain Vancouver Monument, down toward Makena Point. To get to them, however, you have to get off the highway and find the local roads. The highway is a shuttle for those staying at any one of the scores of condominiums and pleasure palaces that have made the Kihei-Wailea region a major resort development site. On the highway are Beach Access signs, and most of these will lead to the back roads, which serious beach hoppers prefer.

It was almost impossible to find Makena Point when I last rode this route, and after an hour's search, I gave up. A detour (temporary,

I hope) had changed the area beyond my local knowledge or map's description and the folk I stopped to ask directions were mostly visitors from Michigan, Minnesota, Calgary and New York. They knew only how to get on the major highway and drive from their rented condominium units to the airport and back.

Friends of mine in Kahului warned that the service road that used to join Makena to Ulupalakua Ranch is now off limits to visitors—cyclists included—and sometimes patrolled. To get to the ranch see Ride Seven in this chapter for the upcountry swing.

Despite the beaches that used to make this ride so worthwhile, I'm no longer a fan of the Kihei to Wailea ride. It's too busy and too built up. The highway south of Kealia Pond isolates the cyclist in a dull vista of trucks and distant landscapes while homogenizing the bends and dips of the road most of us find so interesting. Perhaps when I can again find my way to the low, coastal roads, this area will thrill me as it first did years ago. But, at least in 1989, I prefer West Maui and the region from Lahaina to Ma'alaea Harbor for scenery, good cycling and fine beaches.

For those who ride from Lahaina past Wailea Golf Course and back, the total mileage is about 60 miles, a reasonable distance for a day when you consider that, from the harbor to Haloa Point, it is mostly flat land and paved highway.

Ride Five: Kahului to Hana
Skill level: Average cycling skills
Connects with Ride Seven

This ride from Kahului down the Hana Highway to Waianapanapa campgrounds and into the general Hana area is a perfect lesson in why people bicycle for pleasure instead of renting cars. The average tourist rushes out to Hana, buys a tee shirt at **Hasegawa General Store**, and returns in time for cocktails at the hotel. The bicyclist spends a full day cycling perhaps 60 miles with frequent stops along the way. Each mile has, for us, a different attraction and a different meaning impossible to those who rush along at 50 miles an hour. The wide and well-paved highway that stretches across most of this route is a boon to tourism but not to touring. It brings millions of people (and tourist dollars) but assures that, in the rush, they'll see little but glimpses of the world through the window of a rental vehicle.

Nor are bicyclists necessarily exempt from this blindness. I have a friend who has ridden the route frequently and, each time, rides it faster than before. She brags to me about her average speed and loads down with water bottles and gorp so that nothing but a flat tire will force her to break her pace. She's strong and capable and fast—far better on a bicycle than I—but the purpose of her violent, swift attack escapes me. The point to me is not simply reaching the destination but being informed by the route, to be in the world and not blindly traversing it like a solo passenger in the tunnel of love ride at the county fair.

Kahului to Paia
I thought of all this when riding Hana Highway in 1989. Leaving town I cycled toward the airport and took the Hana cutoff onto Route 36 to H.A. Baldwin Park. Friends who were supposed to be camping there had been delayed, but I did see a cyclist with two photographers clicking away as the rider stood proudly, hand resting lightly on the handlebars of his bike.

The camera's subject made me curious and jealous in equal parts. He was a younger man with a superb physique and biceps as big as my thighs. Also, the fellow had a huge head of blond hair. Since I'm rapidly balding, that made me feel a bit inadequate as well. Thinking that he was someone famous who had set a record, perhaps up and back from Haleakala, I went over to find out why he was being immortalized on film.

"Oh great," the chief photographer said as I approached. "A cyclist. Can we borrow a water bottle?" I asked what for and he informed me that his subject did not have one and it would be great if they could shoot him drinking.

"Ah, I'm about to ride 50 miles and may need it," I replied.

"Sure, sure. Hey! You can fill up in Paia can't you?" he asked. I said yes and gave up a bottle, which the photographer examined critically. It was a bit grundgy from road dirt and he wiped it clean with a tissue from his camera bag.

Then the photographer called the cyclist over, gave him the bottle, explained how it was used, and said, "Why don't you run up and down the road to stir up some dust and get that great, tired look."

Blondie shrugged and did as he was told, puffing half-heartedly a few hundred yards up and back, up and back while scuffing his feet in the dirt.

"This guy isn't riding?" I asked in disbelief.

The photographer laughed at my naivete.

"No, he just wants a picture to send home, so he hired us to shoot him here. He'll look good, don't you think?"

I said yes, and when they were finished, collected the water bottle and rode on my way considerably cheered. Nobody will mount my picture on the wall, but damn, at least I was actually cycling.

All this happened at Baldwin Park beside the **Jodo Buddhist Mission,** which is six miles from Wailuku. From there it is another mile into the town of **Paia**. Soon this formerly quiet, rural town will be a glitzy tourist stop. The signs are there, as old clapboard wood is spruced up and trinkets fill stores where, a few years ago, hardware and canned goods once stood in rows. But it is still a good place to stock up on food and liquid supplies. It is the last major stop for quite a few miles and strategically located for those heading up Baldwin Road, which begins in town and climbs to Makawao (see Ride Seven), Kula Road and the Haleakala Highway.

Paia to Kailua
The road at this point is broad and climbing. It is a highway, and the famous bends and twists that make the road near Hana so

spectacular—"with more curves than any other road on earth" as one guidebook says—are miles away. This section of the road is a gentle climb with a good shoulder and the heavy mix of traffic (cars, jeeps and supply trucks) that is a Maui cyclist's companion.

About a mile past Paia is a trail leading to **Ho'okipa Beach Park.** The road here climbs past woods and cultivated pineapple fields to **Kapa'alalaea Reserve** near milepost 17. Just past it is **Ho'olawa Gulch,** where a short trail leads to a series of swimming pools. You'll know where they are by listening for the **Twin Falls.** The road begins now to roller-coaster through a forest filled with coconuts, bananas, breadfruit, wild ginger, bamboo, mangoes and guava. Nobody ever starved on the road to Hana.

For those who need something more than the food provided by fecund woods, basic foods (potato chips) and cold drinks can be purchased along the way in the small towns of **Huelo** and **Kailua.** In the former is a small but pleasant Congregational church with the long and beautiful name of **Hakapaupueo,** which means "owl-resting perch." In the 19th century, Congregationalist ministers established a number of churches on this island and "rode the circuit," visiting them sequentially because there were more congregations than there were preachers.

Irrigation

Perhaps the most impressive feature of this verdant coastal ride is the man-made irrigation and watering system that brings water from the wet highlands down to the island's drier regions. At mile 22.5, you can see some of the irrigation ditches, first dug by hand a hundred years ago. The system was a remarkable accomplishment carried out with the most primitive of tools, and evidence of the magnitude of this system of water transport becomes evident along the route.

Some may fault the attention paid here to local churches and the mundane public works, like irrigation, which have made modern Hawaii possible. But to understand contemporary society in these islands you must see the part western religion played in shaping towns where, before, only villages under one or another hereditary chief had been allowed. To understand settlement and life on any of these islands, the critical role played by irrigation (and drainage) has to be understood. The ability to plan and execute irrigation systems like the one seen here, on the road to Hana, made land bloom which had been barren, enabling larger communities to develop.

Farther along, down **Nahiku Road** past **Wailua** and **Pua'a Ka'a State Park,** you can see more of the incredible work done by 19th century engineers who had to transport each piece of digging equipment and all necessary materials for construction by horse or mule from the isthmus. All of that was first brought, of course, onto the island by steamships from Oahu and, before that, to Oahu from the Mainland. The logistics of supply were as difficult as the engineering feat itself. A century later it is easy to take these efforts for granted, but even with modern technologies and helicopter airlifts, the trans-island irrigation system remains an impressive feat.

Many of the bridges you will cross on the Hana Highway had their origins in that building, aggressive, 19th century age. They made the transportation of equipment by mule and horse possible, and if today the bridges are concrete, not wood, the need for them is the same.

Kaumahina State Park

About 28 miles out of Kahului you come to this state camping area where those who want a leisurely Hana trip, or who traveled down from Makawao, can spend the night. As ever, a permit is required. There are rest rooms and picnic tables as well as nicely tended grounds whose landscaping includes samples of many plants found around the island.

A few hundred yards away is **Puohokamoa Falls**, where you can have a refreshing swim. For hikers, there is the walk up the left side of the park for a spectacular view of the **Keanae Peninsula,** where at night the reason for the park's name becomes obvious. Kaumahina means "rising moon," and to see it climb, full and bright, across this craggy coast makes the idea of the illuminated and luminescent night forever synonymous with this place.

Kaumahina to Hana

After the park, the road descends to several black sand beaches and then climbs to the Keanae YMCA Camp, the island's only official youth hostel. (For hostel information, see the address in the notes to the Oahu Chapter.) About a mile past the Y Camp there is an arboretum filled with Hawaiian plants, and then, past that, is the Peninsula proper, the one that looked so ominous and lovely by the light of the moon at Kaumahina State Park.

Here the only really long hill begins, a four-mile hump from which you can see the village of **Wailua**, where stands the locally famous **Coral Miracle Church.** Its real name is St. Gabriel's, and it was built, not surprisingly, of sand and coral in the 19th century. The "miracle" was that, after the congregation decided to build their church, the beach was found littered with coral. The faithful took that as a sign that God was pleased and had provided building materials Herself.

Also visible on this ascent are taro patches that still provide what was once the starchy but basic foodstuff of these islands. Poi, the taro dish that was to ancient Hawaii what bread is to the present age, is not my idea of a decent meal, but there are devotees who still believe a real meal must include a few fingers of its slightly bitter taste.

Soon the road leads past **Pua'a Ka'a State Park,** where you can shelter from the region's frequent rains, and then **Nahiku**, site of America's first rubber plantation.

It is at this end of the highway that tourists drive more slowly. It is not simply that the narrow, bending, turning, twisting road forces the cautious to decrease their speed. Of equal importance and a better reason is that few of the visitors have ever seen anything like this terrain. The ferns, grottoes, flowers and waterfalls build to a natural aria of verdancy which, for most of us who live in cities, is simply without parallel. There are 56 one-lane bridges spanning clear pools fed by countless waterfalls along this road. As you twist and turn across them, the remnants of old villages or homes appear and then fade away behind the next bend in the road.

Some say that Hana means "rest from easy breathing," but I ride this section slowly to enjoy its curves and scenery, stopping to pick a mango, admire the ground orchids, smell the wild ginger, listen to the bamboo and consider plumeria in full bloom. This is the tropics at its idyllic best, and it is easy to understand why Charles Lindbergh, when he had less than two weeks to live, told his doctors he was returning to Hana, where he would rather live for a day than exist for a month in New York City.

On this ride I think about Lindbergh and the stunning variety of ginger plants which line the route. When I worked in Asia, candied ginger was my favorite treat, and in Hawaii ginger is my favorite flower. White, yellow and red ginger were once the most popular island flower for the stringing of leis, those garlands of blossoms worn as a necklace on Hawaiian occasions. The most common types seen today were first introduced to Hawaii in 1880. Native to the Caribbean and India, these bright and colorful plants took rapid hold and now grow in profusion on most islands. Early Polynesian immigrants introduced two other, lesser known varieties, turmeric and shampoo ginger. The former was used as a condiment and medicine; the latter's juice, stored in the stalk, was carried as a substitute for water on long journeys.

Finally, this road leads through all this verdancy to the hills and pastures of Hana itself. Past the airport is the **Waianapanapa State Park,** built on an old lava flow and popular because of its combination of hiking, swimming and camping facilities. There are tide pools, waterfalls, the sea, and beautiful trails leading out from here.

Hana

As Oahu cyclist Frank Smith wrote in an issue of the Hawaii Bicycle League's newsletter, *Spoke-n-Words:* "One of the best things about Hana is that it's a real place, not just another tourist destination." People live, work and die in the area, which has only in the last decade become a major tourist attraction. In the 1920s, it was an urban center for an estimated population of 12,000 people living in small villages along this part of the coast. When the sugar mills closed down after World War II, many left because of widespread unemployment. At that time a San Francisco entrepreneur, Paul Fagan, bought plantation land and set a herd of Hereford cows to graze in the old cane fields. His ranch is still there and so are the cows. This is where Charles Lindbergh came after the glory of his famous flight in *The Spirit of Saint Louis* turned sour with the kidnapping and murder of his child in the famous 1930s Lindbergh case. This is where he is buried.

The Road to Hana was opened in 1962, but until this decade it was largely "unimproved." Now parts of it are graded highway, and only at the Hana end—not at the beginning of the trek—do I sense the magic of this region.

In those days it was a remote retreat where travelers could always find a berth, but today finding a place to stay can be difficult. For those who do not want to camp, there is the expensive and elegant Hotel Hana-Maui, which not all of us can afford. Less expensive are Joe's Bed and Breakfast and the Hana Kai condominiums, both of which Ron Reilly of Island Bicycle Adventures recommends. You also may rent through Hana Bay Vacation Rentals.

Hasegawa General Store

Straddling the old days of isolated plantation life and the fast pace of modern tourism is the store whose name was made famous by a popular song played years ago by Paul Weston's band. Everyone who visits this region stops at **Hasegawa General Store**, usually to buy souvenirs like the tee shirt that boldly proclaims "I Survived The Hana Highway." For most of those who drive the route, that apparently means enduring perhaps 90 minutes in an air-conditioned car, but for cyclists who have come to feel—physically and intimately—each bend, curve and ascent of the way, the tee shirt might have some meaning.

Interestingly, I've never seen a cyclist who wore one. For most there is little question of surviving a highway whose miles are so rich and full. If there was a tee shirt which said "I cycled and admired the Hana Highway," it would probably sell very well.

Hasegawa is the island in miniature. When Hana was an isolated blip on the map of a distant island in the middle of a remote, mid-Pacific volcanic chain, it was a truly general, country store. Its family owners still have a large and diverse stock of tools, equipment and implements, but the call, these days, is for more tourist-oriented wares, and they cheerfully sell those as well.

Just as these islands remain a working home overlaid by the business of tourism, so too Hasegawa's place stands as a reminder that beneath the clutter of budget vacations and rental cars is a region where local folks live and build. As a friend of mine in Kahului said, "Trouble only comes when people lose respect for the island and for us. If only visitors had respect for the place, and for its people, nobody would ever have any trouble here."

Amen and lecture ended.

Seven Pools and Kipahulu

Cyclists often stay several days in the Hana area, riding out on day trips, hiking, swimming and preparing for the ride back to Kahului. While it is possible to continue from here around West Maui's southern tip, it is recommended only to the most experienced cyclists.

The road becomes very bad past **Kipahulu**, and there is a long climb that carries you past Ulupalakua Ranch and then up Kula Road to the Haleakala Highway and from there back down to town. I prefer to ride this island counterclockwise if it is going to be circumnavigated at all.

But for the majority of riders and tours, Hana is the destination, and the ride around, described here in Ride Seven, is something few people have the time or endurance for.

In the Hana area most people visit the **Seven Pools of Kipahulu,** or, in the old language, *Oheo'o.* Tourist brochures call them the Seven "Sacred" Pools, but they are not imbued by local legend with any religious significance that I know of. What is sacred these days is their value to tourists and that means that they are usually crowded. If you want a wonderful picnic, stock up in town and go past the last waterfall to a small knoll overlooking a craggy volcanic drop of the coast to the ocean itself.

Just past the pools is **Kipahulu Sugar Mill** and, past that on the makai side, the small Kipahulu Hawaiian Church, where Charles Lindbergh's mortal remains are buried.

On the way back to Waianapanapa (or the town) you'll pass the old **Hana Sugar Mill**, a remnant of the days when contract labor made the island a melting pot, with Filipino, Chinese, Japanese and Portuguese contract labor.

For those who want a feel for that time, H.O. Bushnell's *The Water of Kane* is a wonderful novel about Japanese immigrants who worked first in the plantations and then on the irrigation programs of Maui. It is the second of a two-book series, the first being *The Stone of Kannon,* which describes the hiring of Japanese workers for a Maui plantation and the problems they had in the early years of plantation labor. Both are highly recommended.

Ride Six: Kahului to Haleakala
Skill level: Expert climbing and endurance
Connects with Rides Five and Seven

The "race to the sun," a yearly climb to Haleakala State Park from Maui's coast, is a famous cycle route. The 40-mile uphill climb ends with a tortuous switchback into the park, whose landscape is best described by strings of adjectives—awesome, powerful, uniquely magnificent—which do not begin to do it justice.

Races aside, fewer people bicycle up the mountain than ride down. Many prefer to pay local tour companies to carry them to the park in travel vans and lead them back down on specially adapted, disk brake-equipped bikes.

People do ride up this mountain for the sheer pleasure and challenge of the ride. The record time for this ascent is an almost unbelievable two hours and 45 minutes, but average mortal riders cycling with a bike unburdened by panniers can expect to spend between six and eight hours on this road. Those who carry their own camping gear should anticipate a slower trip of between eight and ten hours of hard travel. If you're planning to ride this route as part of a group, a sag wagon to carry the gear is a wonderful idea.

The traditional route from Kahului is a direct ascent from near Haleakala Highway on a road shared with a constant stream of tourist and local vehicles. It can be divided into separate and roughly

©1989 TOMSA

equal parts. The first is a relatively moderate climb to and through Pukalani to the Kula Highway, which traverses the side of the mountain. The next section climbs another 1,700 feet up to the switchbacks which are the ride's most famous part, ending at Crater Road, where the final 1200-foot ascent begins.

Because the highway is so well traveled and the park such a tourist destination, I advocate another route, which begins in Paia and traverses Kula Highway for as long as possible. This ride can be combined with an upcountry and backcountry ride that takes the cyclist around the back of West Maui and down to Hana by its southern route.

Cruiser Bob's and Other Companies

There are at present three companies whose business it is to haul cyclists up to Haleakala Crater and lend them bicycles to coast down the Highway in comfort and style. The first and most famous is Cruiser Bob's, whose offices are at 505 Front Street in Lahaina. It was

Cruiser Bob who decided that more people would ride down than up and then fitted moped-style disk brakes to mountain bicycles to give clients enormous braking power for this incredible downhill ride. He also figured out that those who would not ride the mountain alone might do so in a group if it were led by experienced cyclists and followed by a support van.

Other companies compete with him now (their addresses are in this chapter's end notes). I have never been on one of these trips and cannot recommend one company over the other. The cost is around $90 for the trip, which can be made at various times of the day.

It is easy to make fun of these groups, which are shepherded by ride leaders and sag wagons as if they were returning from an expedition to Katmandu. Local folk see these lines of cyclists on rented bikes as inconvenient clutter on already too busy roads. Those who cycle up this terrain on their own also tend to sneer at groups of eight to fifteen riders ("They're not cyclists," one tourist insisted to me from the saddle of his Colnago) whizzing down hills they've never climbed. Personally, I like these groups. It is a safe way to ride and puts people on bicycles who otherwise would not have the courage or endurance to ride this incredible terrain at all. The bicycles appear to be in good repair, the support vans stocked against emergencies, and every cyclist wears a helmet to guard against a fall. Maybe the experience of riding down will convince some guests to bicycle more and, in a few years, to meet Haleakala again, riding the whole road under their own power.

Another, more practical advantage to the constant stream of downhill tours is that a lone cyclist in trouble can find help and support from experienced folk. I've talked with ride leaders for two different companies, guys met on the road one day, and both assured me that they would stop and help an individual rider as long as their own group was not endangered by the delay.

The cyclists I saw come down Haleakala rode across Kula Road and through Makawao, a route I recommend. Riding through Makawao is far quieter, prettier and more interesting than the straight Haleakala Highway ride.

Haleakala Highway

For those strong riders who are not fazed by traffic during an ascent, the direct route from Kahului to the crater and adjoining park has the advantage of simplicity. Stock up on energy food and liquid before you leave and on the road whenever possible, because there remains a scarcity of towns and stores along this ride.

Take Ka'ahumanu Avenue through town to the Hana Highway and, after a few miles, the Haleakala Highway turnoff will be well marked. Take a right at the traffic light, and for the next seven miles the ascent will be constant if not radical. This is the straight and gentle incline that leads to **Pukalani** at an altitude of about 1,700 feet. From this small, upcountry town you turn onto route 377 if Haleakala National Park is the destination, or continue across Kula Road if the destination is Poli Poli Springs Park and the round island route.

On Route 377 Haleakala riders face a steeper climb to the 2,500-foot level and a change in vegetation from the lowland sugarcane and pineapple fields to upland eucalyptus trees and highland commercial flower farms.

Maui's eucalyptus trees are in demand these days because the wood is prized in making paper for facsimile machines. The wood does not have to be bleached before the paper is made, and thus good paper costs less. This has led to a strong desire by some to clear cut large stands of wood on the island and the equal determination, by environmentalists, to prevent such insane destruction.

After about 20 miles, measured from Kahului, and just past a few restaurants catering to the tour bus trade, turn right onto Route 378. Here the relatively straight ascent becomes a series of switchbacks, a constant jogging, turning climb past the **Sunrise Protea Farm** at 3500 feet to Crater Road, which appears at almost 6,000 feet of altitude.

The protea flower is an island commercial asset, a rare and long-lived plant that these farms send as gifts all over the world. The flower's popularity lies not only in its beauty and rarity but in its longevity as well. Protea will bloom for weeks in water when sent, as they often are, as gifts on occasions ranging from Christmas to Mother's Day.

The road cuts through **Haleakala Ranch** and is dotted with cattle guards. Take a good look at these grates and remember their approximate location. As you hump up the hill at speeds of between four and six miles an hour they present little threat, but on the descent at speeds of between thirty and fifty miles per hour, these cattle grates represent a serious cycling hazard.

Finally, at the park boundary is **Hosmer Grove Campground**, where cyclists with tents can stay. It is at the edge of a beautiful, surreal, moon-like landscape, which is the crater Park itself. With the altitude, almost 7,000 feet at this point, comes a mountain cold, and those planning to ride or camp will want a heavy shirt, light jacket and perhaps a sweater as well.

The last nine miles into the park includes 3,000 more feet of elevation past magnificent overlooks into the crater. Along this route you will also find the rare and beautiful **silversword**, a plant unique to this environment. It is in fact a type of "tar weed," a cactus which has mutated until it could adapt to this alien environment.

Also up here you may see the **Spectre of Brocken**, a natural phenomenon in which your own shadow may be visible on a cloud surrounded by a rainbow-shaped halo. It is rare and occurs only in certain atmospheric conditions, but for the mystically inclined is, I'm told, an extraordinary sight. The name comes from Mount Brocken in Germany, where the effect was first noticed.

As hard as the ascent was, the descent is that fast. It may have taken all day to ride up (or two days, or three), but the trip down will take under two hours. The danger is in being caught up in the speed and thus unable to handle the unexpected. There are, for example, those cattle guards waiting to catch a racer's wheel on the descent and a decline steep enough so that fast stopping will be difficult. Ride down, especially to the Kula Road level, as if each driver were an idiot, each cow a dangerous beast and the road itself a bit slick. Having made one of the world's most famous and difficult bicycle climbs, it would be a pity to wipe out on the triumphant return.

On the descent I strongly suggest turning onto Route 400 at Pukulani and heading through Makawao. This route has far less traffic, is more scenic and is generally better in every way. Also, **Makawao** has good restaurants and food stands with which to celebrate the trip.

Ride Seven: To Poli Poli Spring State Park and Beyond
Skill Level: Strong cycling skills
Connects with Rides Five and Six

Paia to Makawao

This is the route the Race to the Sun takes for the first leg of the annual ascent on Haleakala and the one I recommend both for up-country and volcano riders. It is quiet and pretty, with minimal traffic for the first 1,800 feet of ascent. To go from Kahului, ride past the Haleakala Highway turnoff on Hana Highway, past H.A. Baldwin Park to Paia (see Ride Six). There turn up **Baldwin Avenue** for the seven-mile ascent to Makawao. The traffic almost immediately disappears as you cycle a country road where drivers who do use the route are uniformly civil and courteous. Local residents inform me that county permits are issued for overnight stays at Baldwin Avenue's little-known **Rainbow Park**, which can be found on the lower part of this road.

I prefer to head straight up to Kula Road. The ride to Makawao is a nicely defined trip in itself, a quiet, turning ascent to the 1,700-foot level whose reward is the small town which opens upcountry Maui to the cyclist.

There is a wonderful delicatessen here, **Casanova's Deli**, with excellent coffee and superb cycling food. The owner and chef is from Padua, Italy, the food relatively inexpensive and the location strategic for a rest. Cyclists should try the deli's Italian rice balls, in which cooked rice is mixed with Mozzarella cheese, rolled in egg and bread crumbs and then deep fried.

A few of these in your pannier or jersey pocket provide instant relief on the energy-depleting climb. Unfortunately, snacking and drinking espresso on the deli's porch while watching other riders zip or struggle by is so comfortable that it can end the day if your determination is not strong.

Cyclists' Rice Balls (with thanks to Casanova Deli)

Mix a half pound of cooked rice with grated mozzarella cheese. Experiment to find out how

much you want the cheese flavor to dominate. Pat
into balls and roll each first in raw egg and then in
bread crumbs (I prefer to use rye bread). Deep fry
until brown. Cool. Pack individually in wax paper
and stuff into a cycle shirt pocket until needed. One
ball is a snack, two a light lunch, and three a meal.

For those who do waver and abandon their ascent, Kaupakulua
Road leads down through Ulumalu to mile 17 on the Hana Highway.
This is one of the best descents I've ever had, with virtually no cars
and a wonderfully fast, curving, well-paved road ending not far from
Kapa'alaea Reserve (see Ride Six).

A ride to Makawao, down to the Hana Highway and out to the
Ke'ane Peninsula would be a wonderful single day on a two-day ride
to Hana.

Makawao to Kula Road

From the deli, ride through town on Route 400 to Pukalani. From
here you can either take the normal Haleakala Highway route or
continue along Kula Road for a real tour of upcountry Maui.

This area is, people say, something like the western state of
Wyoming. There are cattle ranches, the temperature is cool and the
landscape nicely green. Folks wear cowboy hats, and rail fences are
strung across the landscape. On the volcano's slopes pheasant can
be seen. Chuck Fisher, tour director for the Hawaii Bicycle League,
says there are several Bed and Breakfast homes along Kula Road in
this area. The B&B address is at the back of the Introductory Section.

In Kula you pass the octagonal **Church of the Holy Ghost**, whose
large altar was shipped in sections around Cape Horn, and the **Kula
Botanical Gardens,** which includes hundreds of plants and a rest
area for the weary. The University of Hawaii also operates an experimental agricultural station south of **Kula Elementary School**,
where roses grow amidst the more specialized research projects.

Poli Poli

This road leads to Poli Poli Spring State Recreation Area, once the
center of Haleakala visitations. I've never camped there, but local
riders tell me it is the best place to see the volcano from. Quiet, un-
crowded and largely unnoticed, **Red Hill Visitor Center**, *Pu'u
Uula'ula*, is accessible from here.

It was near this place that Mark Twain first saw Haleakala 100
years ago and wrote in his dispatches for a Mainland newspaper the
best description of sunrise in the area that I have ever read:

A growing warmth suffused the horizon, and
soon the sun emerged and looked out over the
cloud-water, flinging bars of ruddy light across it,
staining its folds and billow-caps with blues,
purpling the shaded troughs between, glorifying the
massy vapor-palaces and cathedrals with a wasteful
splendor of all blendings and combinations of rich

coloring. It was the sublimest spectacle I ever witnessed and I think the memory of it will remain with me always.

For those interested in hiking or exploring the Poli Poli Park region, I recommend Robert Smith's *Hawaii's Best Hiking Trails*. This inexpensive paperback is a good guide to hiking in the islands and, for mountain bikers, gives an idea of what to expect off the beaten trail both in this area and elsewhere in the state.

Poli Poli to Seven Pools

From Poli Poli you can either return to Kahului through Makawao, drop down to the Hana Highway or continue down past **Ulupalakua Ranch** and counterclockwise around West Maui.

Ulupalakua means "breadfruit ripening on the back." The name was a measure of time and distance in the days before bicycles or automobiles, a time when folks walked this island and these hills. If, in those non-motorized days, you carried an unripe breadfruit from Lahaina to this region, it would be ripe (and thus edible) by the time you reached the ranch. Ulupalakua was first settled by Linton Torbert, a potato farmer bankrupted when his schooner sank while carrying his crop to California gold rush miners. The plantation was later sold to Captain James Makee, who moved to these upland slopes after he gave up the sea. He had been attacked and injured on board his ship, local legends say, by a Chinese underling armed with a meat cleaver. Recovering from his attack, he decided the violence of his nautical life had been sufficient, and chose the life of a planter instead. Moving to Ulupalakua, he became enormously successful. The ranch's 1,000 acres of sugarcane yielded, in a good year, 800 tons of sugar.

Today there is a small visitors center and a local winery at the working cattle ranch whose buildings are shaded by avocado, mango, kukui and eucalyptus trees as well as the regionally popular Norfolk and Cook pines. Those thinking of camping in this area should remember that it is private land and permission should be obtained before bedding down anywhere in Ulupalakula's domain for the night.

I have not ridden the route from here around the southern tip of the island. Local riders who know it well tell me that it is for the strong and experienced rider. For mountain bike riders, it will be heaven. Sections of the road are in miserable shape, and the route is prohibited to rental vehicles because of the generally abysmal conditions. This is, in short, true backroads riding where what traffic you find is both rural (trucks and jeeps, not buses and cars) and local.

From the Ranch, the road around the leeward island is a descent to sea level occurring gradually over miles. Those considering this route need to carry sufficient water and food. The streams are suspect, and, if you plan to camp, boil local water thoroughly before use. At **Manawainui** you reach sea level again and, past **Waiopai**, pass a site with ancient petroglyphs. The trail here goes from bad to worse through the volcanic legacies and it is not until Kipahu that anything even resembling a road begins again.

For those who choose this route, Seven Pools is a perfect camping destination.

Distances

From Kahului or Paia to Hosmer Grove it is approximately 28 miles and another ten miles from there to the Crater lookout. For those riding up and back in a single day, a good speed would be five miles an hour average on the way up to the top. It is, with descent, a long day in the saddle for anyone.

From either Kahului or Paia to Keokea is about 22 miles, to Poli Poli State Park about 30 miles. From Keokea past Ulupalakua to Seven Pools it is perhaps 35 miles, but that does not tell the story of where those on touring and general bicycles will have to walk over road which is unrideable.

Addresses and Information

_____ Bicycle stores and shops_____

Cycle and Sport Shop
111 Hana Highway
Kahului, HI 96732
878-5848

Cycle and Sport Shop
West Maui Center
Lahaina, HI 96761
561-4191

The Island Biker
Kahului ShoppingCenter
Kahului, HI   96732
877-7744

Fun Bike Rentals
193 Lahainaluna Road
Lahaina, HI 96761
661-3053
(Repair and rentals)

_____ Haleakala Tour Companies_____

Cruiser Bob's
505 Front Street
Lahaina, HI 96761
667-7717

Maui Downhill
333 Dairy Road
Suite 201E
Kahului, HI 96733
871-2155

Maui Mountain Cruisers
P.O. Box 1356
Makawao, HI 96768
572-0195

_____ Camping Permits_____

County Permits (also for Molokai and Maui)
Kalana O Maui
Dept. of County Parks and Recreation
1580 Ka'ahumanu Ave.
Wailuku, HI 96793
244-4354

Superintendent of Parks
Haleakala National Park
Makawao, HI 96768
572-0306

Division of State Parks
1580 Ka'ahumanu Ave.
Wailuku, HI 96793
Tel: 244-4354

_____ Hotels, Bed and Breakfast & Hostels_____

Maui Seaside Motel
Ka'ahumanu Highway
Kahului, HI 96732
877-3311

Pioneer Inn
58 Wharf Street
Lahaina, HI 96761
661-3636

Hana
Heavenly Hana Inn (248-8442)
Hana Bay Vacation Rentals   (248-7727)
Joe's Bed and Breakfast (248-8426)

For more information, see Riegert's *Hidden Hawaii.*

_____ Books Mentioned _____

Andrew J. Berger, *Bird Life in Hawaii* (Honolulu: Island Heritage Press, 1987).

H.O. Bushnell, *The Stone of Kannon* (Honolulu: University of Hawaii Press, 1987).

H.O. Bushnell, *The Water of Kane* (Honolulu: University of Hawaii Press, 1980). A two-volume historical novel tracing the lives of Japanese immigrants to Hawaii who worked on Maui as plantation laborers.

Robert Smith, *Hawaii's Best Hiking Trails*   (Berkeley, Calif.: Wilderness Press, 1982).

Ray Riegert, *Hidden Hawaii: The Adventurer's Guide*, 5th ed. (Berkeley, Calif.: Ulysses Press,1989). This is the practical guide for places to stay and things to do.

The Essential Guide to Maui (Honolulu: Island Heritage Press, 1988). This is a general guide to beaches and places to visit on Maui.

Insight Guides Hawaii (Hong Kong: APA Productions, 1980). The Maui chapter has excellent background information and gives a sense of the island's history.

Cycling Lanai

INTRODUCTION

There is little I can say with certainty about Lanai as a cyclist's destination. Developers have discovered the Pineapple Island, and two new resort centers are scheduled to open in 1990 and 1991. While everybody involved has insisted this is a limited incursion into what, for sixty years, has been a solely agricultural island, few Hawaiians believe that any beachhead does not promise a full invasion. Maui residents, for example, are buying land for second homes and as investments on Lanai against the day when prices—very reasonable until recently—rival those in other parts of the state.

Since the 1920s this pear-shaped island has been virtually a wholly owned subsidiary of Hawaiian agriculture and land conglomerates. James Dole's Hawaiian Pineapple company purchased the island from Harry and Frank Baldwin for $1.1 million in 1922 and imported 150 foreign laborers to make his plantation work. Over 15,000 acres on the island, which is 17 miles long and 13 miles wide, were eventually cultivated, and the business of the island became a single crop.

It was Dole who believed that pineapples were the fruit of the future, and when demand decreased in the 1930s, the enterprising Dole created a market for a then new product—pineapple juice —to keep his company alive and this island's one-crop economy afloat. Eventually, the island was sold to Castle and Cooke, which now has a new vision for its island. Lanai will become, developers say, a low-density tourist site in which much of the island will remain in active cultivation while a percentage of its resources will be turned to the business of welcoming recreation and tourism.

These are the vacation isles, and it was perhaps inevitable that Lanai would eventually follow the pattern which has transformed its sister islands from Kauai to the Big Island.

That transformation is under way at present. The $35 million, 102-room Koele Lodge has just opened on a hill over Lanai City, where until now the Hotel Lanai (and one or two bed-and-breakfast homes) has been the only hotel. Then Castle & Cooke, with its partners Rockresorts, will open the 250-room Manele Bay Hotel on the island's most popular, spectacular and safest beach.

It will be the mid-1990s at the earliest before anybody knows if the plan succeeds or if the high-rise development style of Ka'anapali and Kihei will turn this island's backroad, country atmosphere into a golf/cruise/nightclub and Club Med scene.

I can tell you what the island, which until recently boasted only 25 miles of paved road, has been, but not what it will be when you arrive. Change is happening that fast.

Rather than promise what nobody can deliver—a good look at Lanai's future—here are some general descriptions of where the routes and roads are, or at least have been. You'll have to decide for yourself if it is worth visiting in the next few years.

Getting There

At present, airlines fly to Lanai from Maui and Oahu on a daily basis, but air links are not extensive. From Oahu, for example, there is a single flight in the morning on Hawaiian Airlines and a single return run at night. From Lahaina there are cruise boats that make Lanai a half-day destination, but no ferry service currently crosses the 12 miles of water that separate Lahaina from the harbor at Lanai's **Manele Bay**.

Plans are currently afoot to change that, and some charter companies are hungrily eyeing the opportunity to provide water transport between these islands. It would make good sense, but in Hawaii that does not mean it will happen or that the best charter supplier will be allowed to make daily runs in this region. When sea service is inaugurated, it could be by sail, by hydrofoil or by ferry. Hopefully, whoever gets the nod will carry bicycles as well, but at least in 1989 it was impossible to find a vessel which would carry a biker and his wheels.

Even when that service is in place, people with more money than time or aesthetic sense will probably still choose to fly to **Lanai City**. It is near the center of the island, whose altitude ranges from sea level to 3,370 feet. The first resort has been built near the harbor, but Lanai City, once the quintessential plantation town, is beginning to change as well. Soon, maybe there will even be a few hotels to house those who want to stay on the upland slopes.

Lanai City and Environs
The city was laid out as a plantation town in 1924 by Dole and Hawaiian Pineapple. It has remained a sleepy and uninspiring place ever since. Locals have liked it that way, and a Hawaii of pidgin English and country ways is still powerfully evident.

In the 1920s and 1930s plantation workers were predominantly Asian—Chinese, Japanese and Filipino. Jim Dole paid good wages, and those who came to work for him have stayed. The descendants of those immigrant workers are still on the land and in the city whose population was, until recently, a stable 2,500 citizens.

From the city you can travel the **Shipwreck Trail**, which runs to the Island's eastern shore, descend to the **Manele Bay** area, favored by Island sailors who need supplies, or (and I've never done this) travel from the city to **Kaumalapau Harbor** on the eastern shore. That's about it—three rides on an island less than 20 miles wide and, at least until recently, all of them including roads in terrible shape.

The typical rental vehicle here has been a four-wheel drive jeep which can chug and rock over almost anything. For the bicyclist, this means a mountain bike has been the order of the island in recent years.

In past years, cyclists were well advised to carry spare inner tubes and tires as well as a patch kit. The kiawe tree's thorns which littered some trails would decimate both tube and tire until only full replacement could repair the damage.

Kiawe is Island mesquite, an extremely hard wood that for generations has been used in local cooking fires. Now it is used in fancy restaurants as a flavorful charcoal and fuel. What is important to cyclists, however, is that thorns from the kiawe are rock hard and needle sharp. The most I've ever seen in one tire was 35 punctures when an unlucky and unobservant mountain bike rider cruised over a whole kiawe branch. His tire was damaged virtually beyond repair, the tube ruined and his cycle holiday ended.

GENERAL RIDE DESCRIPTIONS

The following routes are described in general terms and in the belief that they will be improved or rideable within the next few years. I suspect they will remain, for some time, terrain better suited to fat-tired all-terrain or mountain bikes than to slim and speedy touring-style tubes.

In fact, if those who are pouring millions of dollars into developing this forgotten island had as much sense as cash, they'd prohibit any type of non-agricultural, motorized vehicle and dedicate the whole to bicycle travel. What is a half-hour trip in a noisy jeep would be, by bicycle, a nice, morning's trail ride, and what presently is a quick car trip would be a decent cycle tour. It would limit high-density tourism and assure that the feel of this place, its quietness and peace, was not interrupted by endless rental cars charging up and down a tiny island.

But it is unlikely these suggestions will be heeded. The likelihood is that roads will be put in to make it possible for vacationing tourists to drive everywhere they need to go, and another nice, quiet preserve will be taken from the sensible cyclist's future and ruined by the car.

Lanai City to Manele Bay

This is an eight-mile trip from the city center to the island's only campground. It is a decent place to pitch a tent, but is operated by the Keole Company, which charges the exorbitant price of $10 a day for the privilege. I have never camped in this area, preferring to sail in and out and thus stay aboard a vessel swinging free in the harbor, but I know others who think the camping fee worthwhile.

From the city, turn left onto **Manele Road** into a fast downhill on surface so bad there is never anything to do but brake the whole way if you hope to stay upright and keep the bicycle in some repair. After that descent the road briefly levels out through pineapple fields until another downhill appears and runs for about four miles.

The road is no better than near the city and is definitely mountain bike terrain. Total descent is about 1600 feet, and for masochists who like bad roads with steady climbs on a bad surface, returning to town from city is a terrific ride.

Manele Bay, which will be strongly affected by new development, has always been a sailor's place, and the kitschy tourist stuff sold to the island's few visitors never really detracted from the beauty and quiet of this low and protected harbor area.

From Lanai you can, I'm told, go west on Route 44 toward **Kumalapau Harbor**, where fifty years ago a million pineapples a day were loaded during the summer season. Three miles from there is **Kaunolu Bay** (the road was, for my old touring Schwinn, unpassable when I first tried it years ago). King Kamehameha once had a summer residence here, and its remains have been thoroughly studied by archaeologists.

Returning to Lanai City from Manele Bay is what you would expect, a slogging climb in which the hump is made worse (1800 feet in eight miles is, after the Haleakela Crater rides, nothing special) by the miserable road surface.

Lanai to Shipwreck Beach

This is a 14-mile trip which does have superior views to recommend it (I did it in a jeep, ok?). Take **Keomuku Road** out of the city and, where it forks, stay to the left. You can see Maui from its dry, eastern foothills to the pineapple fields and the new growth crop of Ka'anapali condominiums. You can see, as well, the island of Molokai with its dry leeward side, the green of Kaunakakai and the verdant Halawa Valley side.

Finally, **Mokuho'oniki** is also visible, an open, volcanic crater whose lip alone remains above water like a ship just nibbling at the air. This has been a favorite destination for snorkeling tours and day sails from Maui for years. At present, however, there is a movement to regulate its use as anchor site because the volume of visitors may be damaging Mokuho'oniki's fragile ecology.

On Lanai there is also **Keomuku Village**, abandoned after the collapse of the Maunalei Sugar Company in 1901, and I suspect parts of it might be restored if a new tourist attraction is needed by the impresarios orchestrating the new island business.

Also on the windward side is the "**Garden of the Gods**," which is along **Awalua Highway**. I've never camped in this region, but those who have insist it is a fascinating if spooky overnight adventure. About seven miles out of Lanai City, boulders are scattered in disfigured lava formations and, at night under the full canopy of stars, seem to take on an eerie life. It is supposed to be a ghostly sight at sunrise or sunset.

There are other roads which I've seen on the map but cannot speak of with any authority. From Lanai, jeep enthusiasts head up **Munro Trail** to circle the island's highest spot, **Lanaihale**, from which you can see, on a clear day, Oahu, Molokai, Maui and the Big Island. I suspect that if anything is improved besides the Manele Bay-Lanai City route it will be this trip to the island's summit.

The Norfolk pines you'll find here were planted by George C. Munro, a New Zealander hired around 1910 to manage an island ranch. He was in the habit of riding horseback and sowing seeds from his saddlebags, a la Johnny Appleseed.

Conclusion

At this writing, improvement has already begun on the Manele Bay access. I suspect that the Lanaihale access will be upgraded and that Shipwreck Trail will, in the course of time, be cleaned up and the beach itself eventually seeded with resort-style inns.

Nobody ever went broke betting on the venality of developers. Certainly underdeveloped land in Hawaii is at a stupendous premium, and many who live elsewhere in the state have wondered how long it would be before Lanai fell from grace as well. But perhaps owners and islanders alike will keep the changes to a minimum and let Lanai remain a working, quiet island with a low if lucrative tourist profile.

That would be good for bicyclists who seek a not too arduous, two- or three-day amble. The island is small, the altitude not extreme, and it could become, like Molokai, a place that welcomes the scale and attitude bicyclists bring.

Cycling Kauai

Riding Kauai means to cycle with a continual sense of déja vu. Pedalling against the trade winds or up a hill, so much seems so familiar because this small, benign, volcanic island's landscape has contributed memorable scene after unforgettable vista to the world's cinematic consciousness. Two generations of movie buffs have gained their first visual images of a tropical idyl from films shot on this island. Movie makers have come here again and again to shoot films in which the languid, steamy, romantic tropics co-starred with actresses and actors ranging in caliber and fame from former Mouseketeer Annette Funicello to the great John Wayne. Kauai—coast, canyon and valley—has been the setting for *Pagan Love Song*, *Birds of Paradise*, *Miss Sadie Thompson*, *Blue Hawaii* and *Donovan's Reef*. In the 1970s, *King Kong* walked the Na Pali's trails. Later, the Vietnam War was refought on this island in *Uncommon Valor*, and in *Raiders of the Lost Ark* Indiana Jones searched for a sacred artifact. Kauai's drier regions were the background for a television version of *The Thornbirds*, whose storyline is set in Australia.

But the island's most famous film role was in *South Pacific*, filmed in the **Hanalei** region. It was there, at **Lumahai Beach** that a young, innocent Navy female first decided to "wash that man right out of [her] hair" and then lost her heart to a French planter. A peak behind the beach is still called by some **Bali Hai**, because in its shadow Juanita Hall sang the song which promised that for each of us the islands called, and if we answered, love and not isolation, fulfillment and not separation would be the reward.

There is still a hint of mystery to Kauai which neither development nor tourism has touched. From **Hanapepe**, whose roadside
sign proclaims it the "Biggest Little Town on Kauai," to **Hanalei**,
where residents have fought the incursion of large scale tourism,
Kauai has a sense of being not so much timeless as, even better, al-
lowing each of us time for ourselves. The landscape is so memorable
and the associations it evokes so powerful that you remember, for
example, when Elvis Presley was an avant garde and sexy singer;
when surfing was believed to be a radical, mysterious sport. Those
were the days when a girl named Gidget became a figure of national
acclaim.

Although contemporary Kauai faces the intrusion of condominiums and development, increasing traffic congestion and urban
unemployment, it simultaneously remains an island of sugarcane,
back roads and gorgeous coastline. It is the perfect place for
mountain bike rides on cane roads and country lanes going, really,
nowhere. Kauai is large enough to allow exploring and small enough
to be known with some intimacy. It is, in short, ideally suited to those
who wish to see slowly and be calmly in a single place. Singer and
activist Buffy St. Marie came here over 20 years ago when, harassed
for her support of causes like the American Indian Movement, she
needed a home where she could raise a family in peace. Kauai still
offers a spectacular landscape without the deficits of urban pressure
or glitz.

It is not a big island, and those seeking long rides with incredible
climbs should take their manic obsessions elsewhere. Like Molokai,
Kauai will disappoint those who wish to ride centuries every day.
From the city of Lihue, near the principal airport, it is less than sixty
miles north and west to road's end, past Hanalei to the Na Pali hiking
trail and forests. To the south and west it is less than fifty miles until
the road ends near quiet beaches from which the still-restricted
island of Niihau can be seen. In between stands the Koke'e range, a
4,000-foot climb from the shore, and, beside it, the glorious Waimea
Canyon. Excepting cane roads and detours—that's it. Two directions,
one mountain and a canyon so beautiful and and deep it is almost
beyond belief.

"There are not too many places to go," Oahu rider Betsi Timm said
to me of Kauai. "But there's plenty there to do." Strong riders will
hump up Koke'e, and mountain bike aficionados will glory in the
trails and paths that run through Koke'e State Park to the edge of
Waimea Canyon or through the maze of trails that run along its outer
side. Others will glory in the miles of semi-paved cane road on which
the wind is hushed by tall stalks rising over a bicyclist's head. On
Kauai one cycles to and through: to Hanalei and its incredible coastline; Salt Ponds Park and its adjacent glider field; the Kilauea
Lighthouse, a federal bird sanctuary; or the North Shore's lowlands
wildlife conservation district; through cane fields and taro patches,
upland forests or coastal beach sand. Kealia Beach is built for body-
surfing, Hanalei for swimming and the whole for those who love to
bicycle without caring about going too far.

Traffic is becoming an imposition here, but Kauai residents are

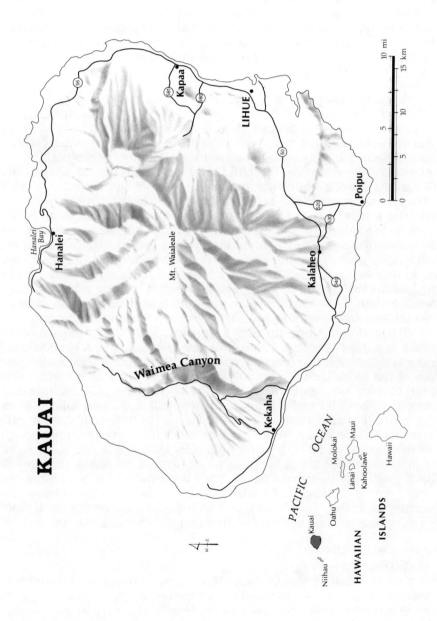

KAUAI

56

Kapaa

581

580

LIHUE

50

Poipu

520

530

Hanalei
Bay

Hanalei

Mt. Waialeale

540

Kalaheo

Waimea Canyon

Kekaha

10 mi

15 km

PACIFIC OCEAN

Niihau

Kauai

Oahu

Molokai

Lanai

Maui

Kahoolawe

Hawaii

HAWAIIAN ISLANDS

N
W • E
S

fighting it. With the crowding of Maui's Hana Highway and Oahu's freeways as cautionary examples, Kauai officials are experimenting with the idea of "controlled growth," which they hope will result in the best of all worlds. As on other islands, there is no good shoulder on many important roads, and cyclists sometimes are pressed by trucks, buses and tourists' cars whizzing along the main highway. Kauai is something of a compromise that works: busier than Molokai but easier to ride than Maui. It is the intermediate rider's island par excellence and one, clearly, I have affection for.

Island Bicycle Adventures

I last rode Kauai in October of 1989 with a small, Oahu-based bicycle tour company, **Island Bicycle Adventures**, run by Ron Reilly and Roberta Baker. I rode with them in part out of curiosity about how cycle touring companies introduce Mainland riders both to the intricacies of distance bicycling and to the ways of island life. Organized bicycle tours are becoming increasingly popular, and it seemed important that I see the islands not only from my own perspective but from that of group-oriented visitors as well. In addition, I wanted to ride with Ron on a tour in which time was measured not in hours but in days. In Honolulu we had cycled together on short club rides and in cycling classes, but to see him on the road over several days was something I looked forward to. Among Oahu cyclists he has the reputation of being one of the best touring riders around, a tall, balding, 47-year-old rider who sets a sensible pace as soon as he climbs into the saddle and then can keep it going all day long.

"He isn't fast," one mutual friend warned. "You'll pass him 15 times in a day." But that is the style I needed to learn. A good touring rider is consistent day after day after day. Sprinters will race along for five or ten miles before stopping for a rest, and just about when it is time to race off again the touring rider appears. A moderate but consistent pace for eight or ten hours--up hill and down valley-- gives the touring cyclist time to see and be in the landscape while still covering the necessary miles and, as a bonus, leaves energy enough for the next day's 50- 60- or 80-mile ride. I wanted to break my habit of jamming at 20 miles an hour in city traffic, or along 10 miles of back road, only to have to pause, wipe my brow and rest for a minute until I jammed on again. I wanted what Ron Reilly had and has—real touring expertise. This book's research was an excuse to get it from him on an island no sane individual can do anything but love.

Getting There

You can sail to Kauai, and if southerly, Kona-style winds are blowing, as they do sometimes in the winter, it is a downwind sleigh ride from Oahu. Following seas lift the boat and push it along, helping the wind as if urging the sailboat across open water to Kauai. Some people do this, those who have boats large enough to carry a bicycle tied securely to the aft safety rail, and it is the most glorious way to travel yet devised by ingenious man. But when the winds are prevailing trades, blowing north by east, then the voyage is a long, long slog of pushing close-hauled into the wind and rising seas, until landfall at **Nawiliwili Harbor** near Lihue seems a failed hope and steady, stable land an almost forgotten dream. The distance may be minimal by modern measure—a half-hour's plane trip takes passengers from Honolulu to Lihue on the hour, 12 times every day— but sailors know what cyclists learn: distance is relative to the means of travel and, either on the sea or in the bicycle's saddle, wind, wave or hilly terrain can make even short trips into marathons.

For those with neither the time, energy, inclination, or equipment to make the passage, there are an enormous number of prosaic but efficient airline flights each day. **Aloha** and **Hawaiian** Airlines both fly from Oahu to Lihue on the hour or half-hour. In addition, both airlines have a series of scheduled flights that can carry travelers from Maui or, usually with a connecting stop, from the island of Hawaii. Interisland travel is relatively inexpensive (at present the cost is under $50), and even with surcharges for carrying the bicycle ($20 fee for the bicycle one way), the cost of visiting this piece of Paradise is, from Oahu, about $64 no matter which carrier you choose. Here as elsewhere in the islands, cyclists do not have to box their machines but are requested to turn the handlebars and kick off the pedals before handing the bicycle to the baggage folk.

From the Airport

Cycling from the airport into Lihue, the island's principal town, is a breeze. Those seeking camping permits must take a left at the first traffic light when exiting the airport onto Highway 51 and then a right at Rice Street about a half mile down the road. This is Lihue's main drag, a narrow street without a shoulder in a city beginning to feel the press of traffic congestion. The county building is off Rice on Eiwa Street, while the campground nearest to the airport is just north of town at **Hanama'ulu Bay**.

For those who wrote ahead to secure their permits or for those staying six miles away on "hotel row" in Kapa'a, the route is almost as simple. Exit the airport and take a right at the light onto the well-paved shoulder and signed Bike Route of Route 56, **Kuhio Highway**. Past the subdivision of Kapaia, campers will take a right at **Hanama'ulu Road**, which becomes **Hehi Road** just before the park. Fifteen minutes from the airport and you begin pitching a tent at the campground on **Hanama'ulu Bay**. Island Bicycle Adventure guests stay, as do most first-time tourists, in the **Kapa'a** hotel and condominium subdivision. From the airport it is a six-mile ride on Route 56, past the camper's cutoff, past **Wailua Golf Course** and over a bridge spanning the narrow **Wailua River**. Just past a sign for the turnoff to **Opa'aeka Falls** there is a new Shell station and convenience store where a right-hand bend leads past Papaloa Road condominiums to the hotel, where I found Island Bicycle Adventures' Ron and Roberta ensconced in the lounge, deep into the trip's briefing with their 10 other guests.

There are a variety of other places to stay in this area, but I recommend, as do Baker and Reilly, the locally owned **Kauai Sands.** This hotel is part of Sand and Seaside Hotels, the small, island hotel chain which includes the **Maui Seaside**, which housed me on Maui. My preference is partly chauvinism, a belief in supporting local businesses and local owners against the incursion of anonymous, offshore corporate hotel chains. As importantly, however, these hotels have always been supportive of bicycles and bicycling. No Sand and Seaside desk clerk has ever sneered at my bicycle. Some hotels complain when a bicyclist appears out of the rain, wheeling a muddy machine. On Kauai, when that happened, the desk clerk just laughed, gave me a cup of coffee from the employees' urn and tossed a few towels my way (two for the bicycle and one for me) so I could clean up before wheeling through their lobby. Fancier hostelers do not want cyclists to carry their machines to their rooms, insisting they be thrown into a baggage storage room or, worse, left outside unattended. Sand and Seaside clerks throughout the islands seem to welcome tourists who prefer to wheel and have been uniformly happy to engage in long discourses on differing routes and roads.

The Kauai Sands is very near the famous **Coconut Palms Hotel**, where Elvis Presley made *Blue Hawaii.* Its name comes from the acres of coconut trees which were once a royal preserve. In those days this was the playground of Kauai's ruling families, and it was here that the last great Kauaiian king, Kaumualii, played by the ocean and prepared, as his ancestors had for generations, to rule. In those days when lineage was everything, it seemed a reasonable assumption. After all, Kaumualii's father was Maui's high chief, Kaeo, and his mother, Kamakahelei, was of almost equally high lineage and a powerful priestess in her own right. Kaumualii's birth at Holoholoku—the Birthing Stones—(see Ride 3) carried auspicious signs, and the sacred bells of the area rang to welcome his entry to the kingdom. It was his bad luck, however, to come of age during the unifying reign of the violent, warlike unifier of the islands Kamehameha the Great.

Made ruler of Kauai at the age of 16, Kaumualii fought Kamehameha's attempts to annex Kauai. In 1796, for example, The Unifier attacked with a fair-sized fleet, which capsized in the waters between Oahu and Kauai. The battle thus ended even before it began. A few warriors did wash up on southern beaches near Poipu. The Hawaiian name for this coastal area, *Mahaulepu,* ("falling together") may refer to their fate. When Kamehameha tried again in 1804, his armada was struck down by a typhoid-like fever. Kaumualii began to think that, perhaps, the gods were indeed on his side. By then he was married to a woman who history says was beautiful, powerful and the love of his life—Queen Deborah Kapale. Kamehameha The Great died in 1818 and his successor, Liholiho, visited Kauai in 1821, as a gesture of friendly relations between related kings. Kamehameha The Great's successor, the ruler of five islands, invited his cousin to dine on the royal yacht and weighed anchor for Oahu before the meal was finished. Kaumualii was thus made a prisoner and Kamehameha II became ruler of six islands. Kauai's king died several years later, a lonely exile on Oahu in the area which is now Honolulu.

ISLAND BICYCLE ADVENTURES

Ron Reilly is from New Zealand and Roberta Baker is from Nebraska. They met while working at a Kauai medical laboratory twenty years ago, fell in love, and have been together ever since. What they're trying to achieve is quixotic and almost impossible to do economically: Island Bicycle Adventures' dream is to fulfill a mission: to introduce visitors to the islands at the scale of the bicycle. This means they limit the size of any single tour to between twelve and fourteen guests and design each ride to include the greatest diversity of sights, plants and landmarks on any part of all the islands they visit. Briefings before each day's ride include, in a low key fashion, background material on the history, botany and animal life which guests might see on any particular day.

Riding with either of them can be an irksome adventure because, as you absentmindedly tool down a cane road or back lane, your ride companion will suddenly disappear. Ron, for example, who has the madness of all bird watchers, will suddenly stop to exclaim at a rare flower (favored by this or that bird) or a rare yellow breasted warbler. Riding back, you find him crouched over the object of his curiosity, his mouth a wide oval of smiling, hushed surprise. His hands flap indecisively as he first waves other riders away ("Don't startle it!") and then, changing his mind, beckons them closer to see his find ("Look, Look here!"). Roberta's passions are slightly different, but the results are the same. On a twisting road near Hanalei, first she was on my wheel and then, suddenly, she was gone. I doubled back a mile or two to where she stood beside her bike at a coastal vision of late afternoon and she said, almost apologetically, "I just had to stop and enjoy it." And so I stopped with her to accept the beauty my preoccupation with cycling as motion had kept me from seeing. Then she named the plants which surrounded us, as if gently introducing me to old friends.

Theirs is not a pushy, evangelical passion, but an environmental knowledge transmitted by story and in person, a stance that comes from the way they ride and plan routes. So it is available for guests who want to know the name of a river, the history of a plant, a legend about a waterfall or the type of ship in a harbor. Those who want to ride on and through are welcome to do so uninhibited by the stories ride leaders like to tell.

Almost of equal importance to this posture of place is a belief in bicycles and bicycle touring. Their trips and routes are a rolling week of cycling indoctrination in which guests are taught to spot mechanical problems on their machines and to ride—whatever the road—with maximum safety. Part of what they offer is a miniature bicycle safety course which includes tips on riding across varied terrain, riding in groups and riding safely in different types of traffic.

Riders unused to 18-speed bicycles can be coached up hill and down on when, where and why gears should be shifted. This advice is not pushed, and stronger riders who prefer to jam all day in the wrong gear or who simply want to blast along a route are free to do so. Every day begins with a safety check in which guests examine their bicycles from front tire to rear derailleur, looking for loose nuts or potential breakdown points. The basic drill is led by Ron as he goes over his own machine and asks guests to check their own as he explains each point. Check the handle bar for stem bolt looseness; spin the front wheel to make sure it is aligned; is the chain dry or too loose? Squeeze the brake handles to make sure the pads are correctly aligned and sufficiently tight; spin the pedals— do they need grease? Is the derailleur sticky or a tire underinflated?

Minor problems are inevitably found and corrected (brakes need tightening, a pedal is working loose), while the other guests watch as if the tour were a beginning bicycle mechanic's course. The safety check, riding instruction and local teaching combine to equip new touring cyclists with enough knowledge and experience to ride other islands—or other places—on their own. "Oh God, I hope not," Reilly said when I mentioned this to him. "We want them to come back with us."

RIDES

A Caution

In both this chapter and the next, which describes a trip with Backroads Bicycle Touring, I've not necessarily followed the precise routes the individual tours will follow. Instead I've tried to incorporate the best of what these professional tour companies suggest and, where different destinations are available, to add them to my ride list. This is more important on the Big Island, where the total land mass is larger and possible route variations more numerous, than on Kauai. But those who ride with either group should not be surprised if some rides outlined in these chapters are not found in the company's itinerary or if, while destinations remain the same, changes have been made in the route directions.

Ride One: Kapa'a to Salt Pond Park

Skill level: Basic cycling skills
Connects with Rides One through Four

Kapa'a to Lihue

Oh, the first day of a bicycle tour when everything is potential! There is energy to burn and excitement to spare because these are roads you've never ridden before and, certainly, there will be new things to see. Aches and pains come later, as do the inevitable mechanical problems—a bad derailleur, a punctured tire or the brake pad that shifts out of alignment five times in an hour. With a group there are all sorts of people, each of whom will ride differently and look at different things, and before the last mile, I will have ridden with each of them. The night before any new tour I'm beside myself with excitement.

IBA's first day is an easy 35-mile ride, largely on back roads, from Kapa'a to the south coast's **Salt Pond Park**. Because it is the first day, people are dubious about the need for a bicycle safety check until someone discovers a bicycle whose bearings need a little grease. The errant wheel is promptly removed from the bicycle ("See, this is the quick release") and passed around so everybody can feel the roughness, the drag in the less than freely spinning wheel. Then the bearings are exposed in the hub and regreased. Everyone watches like surgical residents in their first day of real-life surgery. "I never knew how to get in there," one person said as the wheel lay dismembered before us. "I thought it was hard," someone sniffed, "but even I could do that at home." Pleased, Ron smiles, nods and says, "Exactly." He wants us to learn that anybody can do bicycle maintenance at home. After the bicycles are judged to be in tip-top shape, everyone is given a route map containing detailed directions for the day's ride (turn left at this sign, right at that landmark—go straight 1.1 miles at the intersection: here is a hill and traffic is bad for a half mile. . .), mounts up and rides away from the hotel.

About five minutes after the last rider leaves, Ron mounts his bicycle and pedals slowly after them. He is the sweep and will stay near the back of the pack throughout the morning, helping when problems occur and riding with those who wish for company or instruction. Roberta is in the van and, after paying the hotel bill, drives past us all to set up a snack stop at Rice Monument, thirteen miles down the road.

The route is simplicity itself. Leaving Kapa'a you return toward the airport on **Route 56**, following the signs toward Lihue. There is a nice, easy, mile-long hill four miles into the ride that ends a mile before the airport. Filled with enthusiasm, I started with Ron but in my excitement forgot my purpose was to learn a touring pace and attacked this hill like a madman. Here was a nice road, a mild climb and a good shoulder—who could ask for more? Old Ron could dawdle at the rear. I was for the lead. Clicking through the gears I climbed at

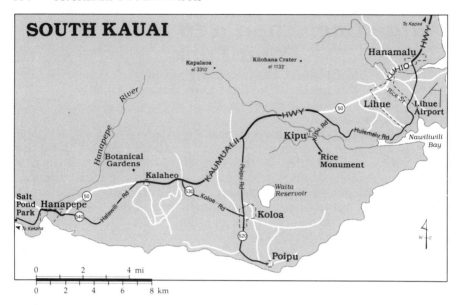

19 miles an hour, glorying in the sun, the road and perhaps in the act of passing other riders who waved at me as I chugged along.

The Fuji's steel frame bucked a bit, bending to my weight as I placed my hands on the brake hoods and pushed for all I was worth. A horse will sometimes bend its knees and shake when, carrying a heavy load, it is forced up a very steep incline, and that is how my bicycle feels: like an animate creature feeling the load. Fancy modern bicycles made from aluminum or titanium or carbon fiber may be lighter, but good steel frames have a flexibility that makes them almost a living thing, bending to the stress of a rider's weight as he or she climbs out of the saddle to hump up a hill. While a part of me knows the bicycle is inanimate, another thinks of it as a living thing, and whenever it bucks I worry that the poor beast is being pushed too far.

At a T intersection just past the airport, following directions on our route map, I turned left at the sign for **Nawiliwili Harbor** and let my momentum carry me onto a moderately steep, shoulderless downhill past the **Westin Kauai Hotel** and **Kalapaki Beach,** past the pleasant **Garden Island Inn** to the harbor wharf where sailors from Oahu regularly dock. Quiet in the morning but riotous at night is the **Jetty Club** where, Ron later reminisced, he sometimes had closed the bar in his younger years. At **Nawiliwili Road** I heard a loud report as my back wheel sank to a sorry, deflated state and my spirits drooped as well. Damn. Had I been on my own I would have taken it as a sign and turned onto Nawiliwili and visited **Menehune Gardens**. But I was with a group and anxious to blast along, so the flat was vexing.

Nawiliwili to Menehune Fish Pond

I dismounted, pulled my spare tube out of the pack and popped the rear tire as other riders whom I had passed a few minutes before

cheerfully rode by chortling "Bad luck," "See you later" or an in-
sincere "Do you need help?" Certainly not. Examining the tire I found
a good-sized shard of glass, which had pushed deep through the tire
and into the tube. Just as I was setting the new tube in place, Ron
rode up, cool and relaxed, dismounted, and offered to help. "While I
set this new tube on, you could patch the old," I suggested. "Just in
case I have another flat." He patched and, as I pumped, the new tube
refused to inflate. Its valve was defective and let air out almost as fast
as I could pump it in. So the new tube came off and the old one, now
patched by Ron, was put on the wheel once again. Roberta then drove
by on her first sweep of the crew, and Ron flagged her down to pick up
another spare from their supply so I'd have a fresh tube in my kit.

   "The record number of flats in a day was set by Roberta when we
were riding across America," Ron said as we remounted and prepared
to head out. "I'm not sure I want to hear this," I replied, but Roberta,
climbing into her van, laughed and said there was little danger that I
could equal her record. "Eleven. I had eleven flats and went through
two tires in one day. It was all very discouraging." I said something
flippant like "Ah well, bicycling at its best" and rode off with Ron to
find the back road he'd mapped out for us all.

   You can get to Salt Pond Park by simply bypassing Nawiliwili
Harbor and taking route 56 from the hotel directly to Kaumuali'i
Highway, Route 50, near Lihue and then heading straight down to the
coast. But that means bypassing a lot of lovely scenery accessible to
cyclists who wheel to the harbor and turn right at Piers One and Two
before riding between Matson Containers and the large oil tanks that
dominate the back area of Nawiliwili Harbor. Often there is a large
cruise or cargo vessel at dock here and signs are posted suggesting
you should not drive through, but cyclists can calmly wheel along
this area and, bending left at a one-lane bridge, turn right onto
Hulemalu Road at **Niumalu Park**.

   Hulemalu Road doesn't seem like much, and in places the ride
gets bumpy and rough, but I wouldn't have missed it for all the
asphalt in Honolulu because this back road is virtually bereft of
traffic and noise. It is a quite lovely, scenic road which runs behind
the Hoary Head Mountains, a collection of low hills whose outline is
supposed to suggest that of a reclining old giant. After turning onto
the road, there is a short, half-mile climb to an overlook of **Menehune
Pond**. The Menehune were Hawaii's little people, a race of ever-
industrious, always shy, and extremely helpful leprechaun-like
Hawaiians who, legends say, would do a prodigious amount of work
for deserving humans and accept only token payment in return. For a
night's harvest help a single prawn from the farmer was payment
enough for them. Fanciful folk aside, the working fish pond's overlook
is quiet and serene.

   I had followed Ron to the pond and sat with him as we admired
the scenery and he told his own stories of the place, most of which
focused not on magical people but, more personally, on its value as a
trysting place in the days when he was courting Roberta. Just as he
was warming up to his tales, extemporaneously embroidered to
include both mysterious flashing lights (Menehune!) and a glimpse of

Hawaii's powerful fire goddess, Pele ("Now, I know this sounds crazy, but. . ."), Roberta drove by. Why, she asked, was Ron dawdling? There were riders he should be checking, she reminded her partner, and then drove the van away. "Romance," Ron sighed and dutifully mounted up. She need not have worried. It is hard to get lost once you turn onto **Hulemalu Road,** where we pounded along hard-packed earth through Kauai's sugarcane fields.

Cane Roads
The whole purpose of this back road route was to place people in the fields of sugarcane whose planting, harvesting and processing have been for generations the lifeblood of Kauai's agricultural production. "What would Kauai be without cane?" a Kauai politician once asked rhetorically. The answer is that it would be a very different place. The air is sometimes filled with the smell of burning cane fields when harvesting is ready to begin, and, at other times, tall cane growth blocks the wind and only a field's tallest, highest leaves can be heard to rustle as we ride through seemingly endless fields.

Some areas of Kauai have had cane in production for over a hundred years, a fact botanists find hard to believe, especially since the crops are not treated with tons of pesticides. Such additives are not needed here where Hawaii's isolation has kept infestation to a minimum. Local agriculturalists say it is not only the richness of Kauai but the frugality of local production that has made sugar so permanent a crop. Each year the mature cane is burned before it is harvested so that leaves and shoots are incinerated by the flames and drop to the ground as fertilizer. Then the stalks themselves are harvested and squeezed for their juice, which, finally, is boiled into a syrup that is eventually shipped to the Mainland to be refined. Spent husks are saved and eventually burned for fuel, and then the whole cycle is begun again.

At a Y intersection we turned right (a left would have meant riding a dead end road) and then continued straight past a private cane haul lane until coming to a stop sign where a left-hand turn carried us to **Rice Monument.** A right at the sign would have led directly to Kaumuali'i Highway—Route 50. At Rice Monument, 13.3 miles from the hotel, Roberta had set out a snack of bread, meats and cheeses, fruits, juice and water for the morning snack. Ron and I were last to arrive. Everyone else was merely enjoying the day and exploring the local scenery. Off the road and almost hidden by plants and undergrowth was the stone monument and marker dedicated in the 1920s to a plantation owner by his Japanese immigrant workers.

Rice Monument to Poipu Cutoff (Malunia Road)
Highway 50 is the major road that cuts from Lihue along the island's South Coast and ends at **Barking Sands Beach**. It is not nearly as interesting or as quiet as the cane roads. The highway's shoulder, in this section, is ever present if often rather rough. Most of us cycled on the road itself, pulling to the shoulder when a large truck came by or, at bridges, where the road narrowed. Somewhere in this area I had my second flat of the day. Spinning the rear wheel, I found

a small nail imbedded firmly in my rear tire to create a puncture about three inches from its most recent patch. At least it was neither raining nor dark, I sighed, as I pulled out the patch kit and slung the bicycle on its side after pulling its rear wheel off to repair it again.

Island Bicycle Adventures' next rest stop was **Salt Pond Beach Park,** but independent cyclists may prefer to take a detour onto **Maluhia Road** and travel down through Kola toward the Poipu region. This is a well-marked road because Poipu has become a significant tourist destination where each year more hotels, condominiums and specialty tourist shops sprout up. It was virtually leveled in 1982 when Hurricane Iwa slammed into Kauai, but has been rebuilt and expanded since then. Once it was a quiet, backroads Kauai community, but now the old out-of-the-way beaches front large developments. Snorkeling and diving have become economically viable adjuncts to the tourist trade, which brings people to Kauai for a few days or a week. It is not an area I know well but seems to be popular among those who wish a day or two in relative luxury.

The road itself is worth exploring, however, at least in its early parts. On Maluhia Road you go through a magnificent and justly famous "Tunnel of Trees," an enormous stand of eucalyptus lining the road, which is shaded and covered by its branches and leaves. A little farther south the road passes through Koloa on the way to Poipu and, here, you can turn right onto route 530 for the less traveled road to **Lawa'i** and its prestigious **Pacific Tropical Botanical Garden**. Created under Congressional Charter and designed and landscaped by Chicago millionaire Robert Allerton in the 1960's, the Garden is a botanist's paradise. Its purpose is to locate and study plants of potential medical or economic importance and to save tropical plant varieties which are, for one or another reason (feral pigs, development, etc.) endangered. Tours of the grounds are available most mornings. Don't be surprised if the garden looks familiar. Garden grounds, pools and waterfall have been used as a setting for various movies as well as for scenes from television's *Fantasy Island*.

Heading west again on Route 50, there is a nice mile-long climb to the town of **Kalaheo**. Here the highway begins a descent to Hanapepe, but my recommendation is to follow Island Bicycle Adventures' route, which includes a left-hand turn—follow the signs toward McBride Hill—onto **Halewili Road** toward **Numila**. Just before this turnoff I had another flat as I raced downhill at 25 miles an hour, a powerful blow-out which sounded like a rifle's report. Another piece of glass had found the same tire and punctured the same, poor patched tube again. I debated putting another patch in place, but the damn thing was now so spotted with repairs it looked diseased, so I retired the tube with honor and used the new one Roberta had given me hours before. Then I took the long, gradual, graceful Halewili Road descent toward the sea and, after four miles, turned left back onto Route 50. In a half mile, a right-hand turn led into **Hanapepe Town.**

Hanapepe's History

The name means, literally, crushed ("pepe") bay ("hana") and refers to the eroded lava rock that is carried from the mountains down to the shore by the Hanapepe River. It could also refer to the ruling ali'i of Kauai who were crushed near here in their last battle against Kamehameha the Great's family. This was the last rear guard, futile battle anywhere in the islands against subjugation by the Kamehameha dynasty, and Kauaians are proud that they were the last to hold to independent rule against the onslaught of the violent, unifying king. Kaumualii, the island's last independent ruler and by all reports an excellent king, had been tricked, captured and imprisoned by Kamehameha years before this battle occurred. His son, Humehume, who had been schooled in New England and returned to Kauai an alcoholic and a malcontent, wanted to regain Kauai's independence and in 1824 attacked **Fort Elizabeth** (just past Salt Pond on the road to Waimea), where Hawaiian troops were stationed.

Humehume never had a chance. For all his New England schooling he lacked the requisite military experience to lead an army. Just as important, his men were inexperienced and had few modern weapons. Repulsed from the fort and in retreat, Humehume took his stand in Hanapepe Valley with a ragtag army of warriors largely armed with spears and one cannon with which he could fire downhill. Maui governor, Kamehameha royalist and experienced tactician Hoapili led loyalist troops against the insurgents. Whenever the Kauaian's cannon fired, Hoapili's well-trained men fell flat to the ground to avoid its shot and then returned a rather deadly volley of rifle fire. The fight for independence quickly became a rout, with Humehume and his men in rapid and disorganized retreat. Several weeks later he was captured in the Kauai highlands and shipped to exile on Oahu, where he died a few years later in disgrace.

Hanapepe Today

Today the town shows few signs of high tragedy. For the tourist it boasts a single business street of plantation-style, wood architecture which looks like the set for a Clint Eastwood western. Hanapepe is not a tourist mecca but, rather, the center of a rich agricultural valley, fed by the river, where taro grows on the plains and flowering bougainvillea paint the surrounding cliffs in themes of brilliant color. Passing through you'll find the Green Garden restaurant, famous for its lilikoi chiffon pies, Shimonishi Orchids and Feeds, a general store, James Hoyle's art studio and a dry cleaners. "If only there were a place to stay, I'd love to keep the group here," Ron said, a sentiment shared by many who pass through and love this quiet backroad town. And that, I suspect, is precisely how area residents like it. Folk heading to Koke'e State Park or on day trips from the Poipu area can go through, visit, shop and eat, but there is no place for anyone to stay between **Waimea Plantation Cottages** on Route 50, a few miles down the road, and Poipu in the other direction.

You can, of course, camp nearby at Salt Pond Park, and that is where we were heading. Heading through town, I thought about the lilikoi chiffon pie but steeled myself, rode to **Lele Road** and hung a left toward the sea. After turning there I followed signs saying Kauai Humane Society, then passed the Veterans Cemetery on the right until exiting at Salt Pond Park. From Lihue on back roads the whole trip was about 26 miles, and, had we taken Route 50 straight through, the distance would have been nearer to 20 miles of sometimes rolling but not too difficult terrain.

Salt Pond Park

I could have camped at this county park for days. It stands directly on the sea and next to the old salt pond from which Humehume's ancestors gathered the sea's salt on the tended and managed flats. Next to the park is a huge field for gliders, and, as we lunched on food Roberta had set out (including the lilikoi chiffon pie I had dreamed of for two miles), large, engineless planes descended out of the sky in silence, ghosting to rest on the runway by the sea.

I sat for a good 20 minutes in wonder as these gliders, which appeared with no audible warning, soared, turned, banked and then seemed simply to fade to rest on the tarmac.

Challenged, I took my kite from the bike's bag and flew it into the 20 mile-an-hour trade wind which had set whitecaps running across the waves. The parafoil flew almost eagerly up to the sky and I played out string very rapidly. Flying almost directly into the noon sun, I had ·to shade my eyes against the glare while maneuvering the kite, which turned, dove, danced and sang to the air. Looking up, I forgot to glance down and tripped on a rock, dropping the kite's string in the fall. Delighted, the kite immediately took charge and began to take itself out to sea as, liberated from my control, it played out the string itself. I ran into the waves grabbing for the reel, shouting rather stupidly, "Stop, stop I say," until I grasped the kite's reel as it bobbed up a rock ledge. Waist deep in water, I began to reel the kite in again and set it at a lower level. But the wind's drag was strong and snap! The kite was gone. The string had broken and, like a hawk finally tired of its trainer, my parafoil had decided it was time to be free.

Ride Two: Salt Pond Park to Polihale State Park

Skill Level: Basic riding skills
Connects with Rides One and Three

After lunch, Island Bicycle Adventures rides or sags up 4,000 feet on a twenty-mile climb to Koke'e State Park. Touring riders would be well advised to do this trip in the morning when the heat is not so extreme and they have the leisure to take their time on the harder parts of the road. That would mean camping at Salt Pond, staying in the Waimea area or abandoning the climb altogether and riding to road's end at Polihale State Park about 22 miles down the road.

From Salt Pond, return to Route 50 and turn left for the road to **Waimea**. This is two lane with a minimal shoulder, but traffic is not too fierce, and you will see cyclists along here with some frequency. In about 6.4 miles (who really trusts a cyclometer's reading?) Fort Elizabeth, a trace of Russia's failed attempt at a foothold in this part of the Pacific, appears on the left, just before the Waimea River crossing. Construction on the fort (named after the Emperor Alexander's consort) began in September, 1816, but its permanence proved more passing than Alexander and Elizabeth's relationship. In 1817 the Russians were driven out of their mid-Pacific base by, among others, a young and feisty American government concerned with competition in the then bustling sandlewood trade with China. I've stopped here and found little but a few crumbling foundations and the broken dreams of Russian imperialism in the Pacific. Really, the Russian czars had very bad luck with their conquests. They sold Alaska, ignored Southeast Asia and, in the mid-Pacific, have only the nearly obliterated traces of this early-18th century fort to remind them of a time when the world was ruled by sailing ships, and royalty tried but failed to hold the world in check.

Past the river you are in **Waimea** (where there are shops for those who need supplies). Here is where Captain Cook made landfall (there is a statue with a plaque that says so), **Lucy Wright Beach Park**, where many cyclists camp before climbing Koke'e, and **Waimea Plantation Cottages**. I've never stayed there but Ray Riegert praises them in his **Hidden Hawaii** guidebook:

> Here in a spectacular coconut grove, fronting a salt-and-pepper beach, is a cluster of 1920s-era plantation cottages. Each has been carefully restored and many are furnished with period pieces. One-, two-, and multi-bedroom houses, with full kitchens, rent for moderate and deluxe prices; maid service is every fifth day.

Campers seeking even more seclusion can continue on route 50 to its end, take a right at Mana Road and a left toward **Barking Sands** and **Polihale State Park**. Up past the park are sacred springs, a heiau, beaches littered with shells, and hiking trails galore. This is road's end, and it would be nice indeed if all roads ended in so spectacular a location.

Ride Three: Salt Pond Park to Waimea Canyon State Park
Skill level: Strong climbing skills
Connects with Rides One and Two

From Salt Pond Park or Hanapepe, go west on Route 50 to

Waimea, where the climb to **Koke'e Lodge** and **Waimea Canyon State Park** begins. Backroad aficionados and mountain bike riders may wish to climb via Waimea Canyon Drive, a steeper, secondary road with a mediocre surface, which joins the better paved and better graded Koke'e Road after about eight miles. Koke'e Road is recommended for those intending to make the climb, which is hot and has several fairly steep, straight sections of incline in the 4,000-foot ascent. There is challenge enough here to make even hill happy Coloradoan or British Columbian riders happy, especially if it is attempted immediately after an early morning start in Lihue.

The first few miles is a fairly consistent but not overly difficult incline which then gets serious on a straight stretch of road that seems like forever but, Ron Reilly says, is only a mile or two. Then the road takes a jog and shoots up again for another mile or two of real ascent. The majority of the altitude gain occurs between mile 3 and mile 12. No convenience stores litter the road. No country stores break the monotony or offer a chance to stock up on liquids. During the day the heat can be ferocious, and extra water bottles (as well as energy food) are highly recommended.

The whole ride is only 20 miles in length from the coast and, after the first 3,100 feet of altitude gain, the worst is definitely over. The landscape by then has become green and not brown, the air relatively crisp and almost cool. Winds come through the mountains as if to welcome those with the foolish temerity to ride this high and far alone. The last five to eight miles are positively a delight, with winding roads and only a relatively slight incline, which, after the real hump, seems like nothing.

Along the latter half of the route are overlooks where you can stop and contemplate the depths of Waimea Canyon. This is a view that would be ample repayment even if the uphill occurred in sleet and snow. To the right, through woods and bush, are the depths and space of the deep and wide region that has been saddled with the silly nickname of "Hawaii's Grand Canyon." There is no comparison. The Grand Canyon is bigger, and, for those who rank their love in quantity and size, I suppose Waimea must fail. But for the rest of us who know that beauty insists upon its own rules, comparisons do no justice to either. Mountain goats climb, birds fly and rivers run through this eroded, volcanic landscape of crumbling, crimson hills. Across the day the colors change as the sun first lights the canyon's western wall at dawn, fills the canyon with shadowless light at noon and then signals late afternoon with shadows growing up Waimea's eastern face. My notebooks have bad sketches and strings of adjectives attempting to describe it all. One page notes how the misted, almost frosted dawn light changes to deep shadows and rich autumnal colors in the late afternoon sun. Never mind. It is as impossible to catch full reality in words as it is to hold the moment in a photograph, but that futility does not stop thousands of tourists from expending millions of frames of film each year. I'll not sneer at your blurred images if you don't laugh at my overwrought words.

Koke'e State Park

If Waimea Canyon is this island's spectacular fissure, Koke'e State Park is the companion, uplands preserve and a touring cyclist's (or hiker's) delight. It is a park, with rangers and rules designed to preserve rather than develop an extraordinary section of this subtropical, volcanic world. Here also are good campgrounds and a limited number of cabins, which can be rented through the park's central offices at **Koke'e Lodge**. These rustic, six-person cabins are one of Hawaii's great buys. The $25-a-day fee includes beds and linen, a stove, pots, pans, dishes, and a wood-burning fireplace. **Island Bicycle Adventures** books its lodgings far in advance, as must anyone who wants to stay here.

Koke'e is riddled with hiking trails, and in 1989 a bicycle rental company, **Koke'e Mountain Bikes**, opened its doors and now offers two bicycle tours of the area each day. Those who ride up on their own two wheels are still allowed to explore, although it would be wise to check with park personnel to see if specific trails or areas have been designated off limits to bicycle riders. There is concern that mountain bikers might damage the trails, although I don't think it is a serious worry myself. Those with the skill and desire to climb almost 4,000 feet for the privilege of camping on a hill near one of the world's most spectacular ditches will, presumably, also have the sense to ride responsibly through these woods.

Near the cabins and campgrounds is Koke'e Lodge, whose nice bar (with a wood-burning fireplace) and restaurant, are the commercial choices in the park. If you wish to camp, you should bring supplies, because there is not even a convenience store until you return to sea level and its towns. Inundating the area and a temptation to the hungry are gaggles of protected Hawaiian *moa*— native chickens and roosters—which tourists feed throughout the day with popcorn purchased from the Lodge. You would think that the almost constantly fed moa would sleep through the night, but instead they begin crowing at three in the morning and keep it up all day. When they are munching they are silent—even these loud, colorful birds cannot gobble and crow simultaneously. Perhaps people feed them so frequently in hopes of a few minutes of silence.

The moa's presence signals this island's freedom from the violent mongoose, introduced to Hawaii in the early 19th century to battle a then burgeoning rat population. As so often happens with introductions of this kind, the mongoose did not affect the rat population at all but found other indigenous and welcome species—like the moa—very palatable, attacking them instead. Rats are nocturnal and the mongoose a day creature, so the two just never had a chance to meet, but these Hawaiian chicken were easy pickings and, on most other islands, have virtually disappeared as the mongoose population has grown over the years.

Kauai's freedom from the mongoose is said to be due to a Nawiliwili dockworker on shift in 1833 when a load of mongooses was delivered. The curious dockworker got too close to the animals' cage and was bitten by a mongoose apparently angered at the human species which had trapped, caged and transported it to Kauai.

Angered and injured, the dockworker kicked the animals' crate in retaliation, knocking it into the sea, drowning the mongooses and thus saving moa from extinction.

Canyon Trails

There is little I can say about the more spectacular trails that lead from the park down and through the Canyon's sides. Roberta speaks lovingly about a trout fishing spot accessible only to those who hike along a dense, overgrown track and then rope down a small cliff to the hidden stream overstocked with lovely fish. These are specially stocked streams, of course. Rainbow trout are considered a delicacy in Hawaii, but the climate is too hot, in general, for the fish to breed, so, each year, state officials restock the streams for folk willing to endure such insane effort for the privilege of sitting in seclusion and casting a line into isolated, wooded water. Ron babbles on about the mountain goats he loves to watch jumping along high, crumbling inclines with the whole canyon as their backdrop and knows each bird flying within fifty miles by genus, species and personal name. He can even imitate their calls. None of these things did I see, although both Ron and Roberta did their best to take me, with other group members, on a hike down Cliff Trail into Halemalu Canyon, a section of the greater Waimea Ditch.

I wanted to stay at the cabin and hike or cycle along wooded trails, but they—and other group members—insisted I take this little four-hour-long jaunt. "Bicycling isn't everything," one guest said to encourage my participation. "Of course it is," I insisted, shocked at such blatant heresy. "This will be interesting," a Texan in our group cajoled, and, finally, I acquiesced. Slightly ashamed of a discomfort with heights, I decided that it had been a childhood fear, which now, in middle age, I could easily control. So I scampered with the others down a nicely covered, tree shaded trail. But as it began to open, I began moving more cautiously, falling behind the others who ran happily ahead. My eyes were on the ground, cautiously surveying where my feet would next fall, when Ron, who was with me, shouted "Tom, look! Look there!" Like an idiot, I obeyed without thinking and saw that the whole trail opened onto the miles wide Canyon which our path was about to enter.

No rails. No walls. Nothing but vast, open space that seemed to erode the crumbling dirt beneath my feet. I knew that the ground was disappearing and felt myself freefalling into space. A part of me knew this was nonsense, that the land was firm and that I could walk along this yard-wide canyon trail without danger. But my heart went into overdrive, my stomach began to heave and, as I dropped to my hands and knees in a futile fight for stability, all I could do was try to find something solid, firm and close to focus on to keep the world from spinning. "Oh look, a mountain goat!" Ron exclaimed, the cretin, as I slowly crawled on hands and knees away from that terrifying site and sight.

If only I could have breathed normally, I might have been able to stand, and, if I had been able to do that, then certainly I could have run away. As it was, Ron finally tore his eyes from the vision of mountain goats to see me hopping slowly backwards like a rather confused frog, because, somehow, I couldn't look away from that floating, seductive, and miserably open Canyon space. "Are you all right?" he asked. I didn't bother to answer and finally achieved enough distance to obliterate the view of the Canyon. Then I stood and stumbled away.

Horrible as it was for me, everyone else seemed quite comfortable with the hike and later told me in nauseating detail what a wonderful time they had gamboling around and swimming in a water hole deep in the nowhere abyss. One guest had the temerity to offer to send me photographs of this expedition. "You'll see, and, next time, it will be easy," Ann said. I didn't bother to reply. For me, beauty and ease were the upland trails away from the canyon. This whole area was very hard hit in 1982 when Hurricane Iwa slammed into Kauai, wreaking terrible damage. Developers were able to turn Poipu around quickly, but nature's regeneration takes more time. A number of trees in these upland woods were stripped of their leaves by the storm and died. Others, of course survived with little damage. So in the verdancy of forest vegetation, of flowering arbor and bush, stand naked, white, sun-bleached skeletons of dead trees with only the major branches articulated against the greater green and brown of the forest that surrounds them. The scene looks like an almost-finished painting, as if an artist had brushed everything except these slivers of white branch and trunk which were left the color of untouched canvas.

Koke'e to Lihue

The downhill ride from the park is really quite magnificent, a route designed for a full paceline of careful cyclists willing, occasionally, to pull off and let impatient traffic by. There is a good road surface and 20 miles of nonstop, winding descent as the hard-won gains of the long ascent become a flying ride downhill whose only real danger is too much speed on a curving, winding road.

Ron and Roberta's guests had heard about a festival in Waimea everyone else wanted to see, but I was determined to blast back to Lihue to a kite store which, I hoped, would carry parafoils to replace the one which had broken free. I left the others and rode out from Hanapepe in late afternoon, sure I had enough time to reach Lihue before dark. The others thought I was crazy (they were going to sag back in the evening), but, frankly, I was relieved to be alone and riding without a scheduled group rendezvous or the chatter of other people. It was nice to cruise in solitude, alone except for the sporadic traffic and an occasional, local bicycle rider with whom I would chat for a minute or two as we passed on the road. Route 50 took me all the way and I was making good time when a violent tropical storm slammed in with torrential rains that lowered visibility from miles to yards. This happened in an area of road construction where, of course, the shoulder disappeared and traffic zoomed perilously close as I doggedly peddled on. In several areas where the construction work had littered the road with gravel, cars came within inches of my bicycle, so, thoroughly terrified, I dismounted and walked.

In retrospect it was an adventure, but in the living of it I was wet and miserable. Also I wanted to get back to Lihue before night fell because, like an fool, I'd not brought my bicycle lamp on this ride. I'd forgotten my cardinal touring rule: delays occur and day rides sometimes extend beyond dusk so always carry a light. Finally the rain let up and I was making good time when, as I turned past the airport in the gathering dusk, my rear tube blew again. I threw my hands up in despair as a police car traveled by in the opposite direction, and, as I popped the rear wheel off and started to change the tube in the almost dark, the officer drove up and asked what the trouble was. Never was I so happy to see an automobile as when his headlight gave light to my braille tire-changing.

The cop asked if I was all right (pop in the tire irons and pry at the wheel) and I started to ramble on about all my flats as he stood politely listening. I asked if he had a flashlight (check for glass or metal in the tube. Ah! there's the little bugger that did this tube in) and, when he said no, asked if the officer wanted to hold the wheel while (new tire in place) I grabbed the pump. "Too dirty," he said and turned toward his car whose headlamps were the only light around. "Wait! Wait" I cried, and as he turned asked, inanely, if he liked to bicycle. He shrugged and said he really had to go, but by then it didn't matter. I'd pushed enough air into the new tube to get me back to Kapa'a and the hotel.

The last five miles I rode in the dark, and what had been a lark of a ride on the first day was now slow work. There are no street lamps along this stretch, and without a headlamp I had to cruise blindly until traffic whizzed by and, in that flash of automobile headlight, memorize the next twenty or so yards of road. I rode at perhaps six miles an hour where, in the day, I'd averaged three times that.

Arriving at the hotel, I was caked with mud and my cycle shoes oozed water as I walked in. The desk clerks never batted an eye and gave me coffee, a towel for my body and another for my bicycle, thus earning my gratitude for ever. At the shopping center next door to the hotel I found the kite store still open, bought a new parafoil, three beers, two hamburgers and a postcard to send to my aunt: "All's well," I wrote on it. "Having a wonderful time."

Ride Four: Kapa'a to Hanalei
Skill level: Average urban skills
Connects with Ride One

This is another ride made longer by sightseeing detours. Rather than taking Route 56 directly to Hanalei, we first turned south from Kapa'a, back toward town, as far as the **Opaeka'a Falls** turnoff— Route 580—just before the Wailua River Bridge. This right-hand turn carries the early cyclist out of the morning's rush hour traffic. As development encroaches on Kauai, rush hour traffic in the Lihue to Kapa'a corridor has slowed to a crawl. Riding on the wide shoulder in this area you see tourists and local commuters sitting disgruntled in their cars, slowly inching forward. It is probably discourteous and

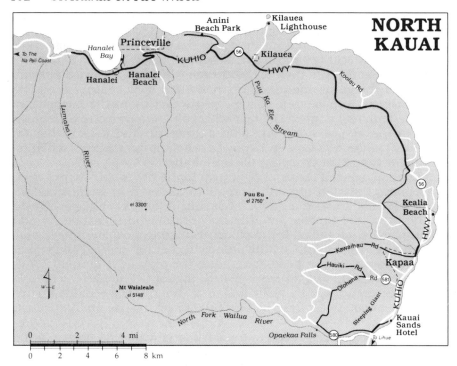

provocative but, for me, an almost irresistible compulsion in such situations is to smile and wave merrily as I wheel past the traffic-bound automobile driver. Only two people shook their fists at me. On Oahu during rush hour, I normally get at least two dozen glares and a few raised middle fingers in response to a friendly wave and grin.

Traffic becomes light at the turnoff and immediately I relaxed into a gentle 1.5-mile climb through an area rich with local history. On the River's south bank, near its mouth where you turn uphill, the ruins of an old heiau lie in a coconut grove, and near it is **Hau'ola Pu'uhonua,** an ancient place of refuge for those who had broken traditional *kapu* —cultural prohibitions—or for warriors fleeing defeat in battle. Those who reached a *pu'uhonua* (place of peace; each island had its own) were allowed to live and, after a period of exile in the safe quarters, eventually to return to their communal world. It sounds childish, like a child touching home turf when pursued by bullies and then turning from safety (with a parent nearby) to taunt his tormentors. But I've often longed for a modern version of the Pu'uhonua while cycling in heavy traffic or after some particularly taxing battle at work.

Just past this area and still near the roadside is the **Pohaku Ho'ohanau**, the Royal Birthing Stones, where generations of royal women gave birth to the island's future ali'i and heirs. Farther uphill and just before the Falls is a dirt road turnoff to **Poli'ahu Heiau,** and near there are the bellstones, whose ringing is said to have signaled the birth of a male ali'i at the **Pohaku Ho'ohanau**. Ron's group did not stop here and that's too bad. He said it was because there were so many other things to see, but perhaps it is a matter of disciplined conservation. It is very hard to achieve a ringing, clear tone on the bellstones, and clumsy attempts by visitors to hit the old bells just right have caused serious damage and deterioration to the artifacts.

Opaeka'a Falls is a lovely, open view with the falls in the background, and across the road you can see in a valley below a reconstructed traditional Hawaiian village that has become a tourist site. I've never been there, just looked at it from the falls while thinking that someday I should take the time to go down and see the show. But thinking this I know that good sense and not the miles I plan to ride have kept me from acting on this sense of history's obligation. From the Falls it looks real and gives a glimpse of what early travelers may have seen, but up close and in the presence of a gaggle of tourists the illusion would undoubtedly disappear, and ever after the view from these falls would be robbed of its power for me.

From Opaeka'a Falls, we followed the "Kauai Loves You Marathon" route through quiet back areas leading eventually to **Kawaihau Road** and, eventually, to **Kealia Beach** next to the main Kuhio Highway. It is a nice trip which jogs and runs in a big loop whose purpose is no more than the pleasure of being on the bicycle, away from traffic and riding through semi-rural streets and the omnipresent sugarcane. From the falls, we turned right onto Highway 581 (**Kamalu Road**), rode along to Hauiki Road for almost two miles (including one early right-hand jog) to **Waipoli Road,** where we turned right for another tenth of a mile. Then there is a turn onto **Kainahola** and, almost immediately, another onto **Kawaihau Road,** whose gentle mile-and-a-half descent empties onto **Kealia Beach**, whose north end has a sheltered cove safe enough to swim in.

Route 56 runs from here directly and without much of special interest (except glorious views and a number of beaches) all the way to **Kilauea** town. There is a shoulder along much of this rolling terrain, but it tends to disappear at the most inopportune times—at the bottom of a hill where a narrower bridge appears and a large truck decides to pass, for instance. It would be so easy, so sensible for the state to assure that a consistent and well-paved breakdown lane rimmed this and other islands. It would provide both an added measure of safety for automobiles and bring cyclists out in droves.

One person attempting to bring sense to the roads of Kauai—and to achieve a balanced development for Kauai— is activist county mayor and cyclist JoAnn Yukimura. She is at this writing a new, reform mayor who, as a young lawyer a decade ago, commuted on her bicycle. Now, as the county's mayor she has announced her interest in making this place the bicycle haven of Hawaii and is working to fulfill the pledge as part of a total plan for "controlled" development. Cyclists on Oahu have contributed to her campaign fund in hope that she will not only be successful on Kauai but, as importantly, that her success will serve as an example to the officials who approve ever more road construction on Oahu and other more populated islands.

Kilauea Lighthouse

This is a side trip not to be missed, especially for dedicated bird watchers. A right turn onto **Olo Road**, just past a Shell gas station and food market, sends the cyclist past a lovely and distinctive Episcopal church built of stone and then down a mile of ill-paved **Kilauea Road** to the Lighthouse.

The road ends with a steep, quarter-mile descent to the **Lighthouse and National Wildlife Sanctuary**, which sits on a thin wedge of volcanic outcropping that commands a magnificent view of the coast. Were this nothing but an isolated lighthouse, the sight of miles of twisting volcanic shoreline would be recompense enough for the detour. But in addition this is a federal sanctuary (admission is charged: $2 a visit) where you can see fly the Great Frigate birds (*'Iwa* in Hawaiian). Their seven-foot-long wingspan and colored breasts (red for males and white for females) offset black bodies that float and glide high above the lighthouse, like wood smoke or smoldering ash pushed into the sky by the air currents that rise from a smoldering campfire. Adults breed after five to seven years, with only a single egg in each clutch. They are not, really, very polite birds for all their grace and beauty. They gather food by diving down on other fishing birds, startling them into dropping their catches, and then leaving off the attack to grab the other bird's lost catch.

They are perhaps the most spectacular of several species that make this sanctuary their base. Red-footed boobies (*'a* in Hawaiian) can be seen here by the sharp-eyed and patient birder. Also using this haven is the Laysan albatross (*moli* in Hawaiian), better known as the gooney bird, a name which is quite undeserved. They may look cumbersome and drunk (i.e. "gooney") when seen trying to walk on land, but in the air these large birds are lovely. They soar with effortless power, banking with only the tip of a wing, or hang suspended on air currents for what seems like hours. I had the impression one was imitating a kite I used to own. It stood almost immobile in the air 70 feet above my head, correcting for minute changes in the wind by simply dipping one wing or the other, ruffling a tail feather or wagging its head to hold the air currents in place.

Kilauea to Hanalei

From Kilauea to Hanalei is about 15 miles on Route 56, whose shoulder disappears on the outskirts of the Princeville region. This is a large commercial development above Hanalei, owned by Australian interests, which has been the site of several local battles over development, tourism and the area's crowded roads. There is at present a lovely row of Eucalyptus trees bordering the highway in the Princeville region, which developers want to take down so they can widen the road. Auwe! Sensible residents are againšt the plan, but it is possible that by the time this book appears in print the conservationists will have lost another round and the trees will be just another trace of history and misdirected progress.

A bit farther on there is a roadside pull off just before the descent begins to the town of Hanalei. From here you can see the whole valley, which has become a federal wetlands conservancy district. Taro and other lowlands crops have been planted in an attempt to maintain a wetlands environment that will support a number of endangered species whose habitat has been progressively eroded by increasing development and the changes which greater urban density brings.

Hanalei residents have done their part to keep massive tourism at bay by refusing to approve the widening of a narrow, single-lane bridge at the bottom of a mile-long descent that separates Princeville from what some believe is the most beautiful coastal spot in all Hawaii. There is no shoulder on this drop, and I rode down it with great care as impatient tourists, windsurfers in old cars, and local folk hurrying home all wound around the narrow road behind me. This is the first and largest of the area's several, one-lane bridges, which are all too narrow and fragile for large tour buses to cross. So the endless loads of Greyhound-style buses are, thankfully, barred from here.

Cycling through this region of narrow bridges and lowland crops, you may hear a bellow that sounds something like a cow, but is louder, deeper and more authoritative. It is a buffalo, a new animal to the islands, kept on a ranch on the outskirts of this region. In 1981, Bill Mowry imported 13 bison to his **Hanalei Garden Farms** from Denver, later adding to his stock with 38 more. Today the herd numbers almost 200 animals. In addition to Bill's buffalos, his farm raises grass carp in an ancient fish pond as an experiment in aquaculture, as well as native plants, flowers, papayas, bananas and plums.

Cycling along Hanalei's beach roads is almost as good as cycling can get. There are hills to climb (but none too high), one-lane bridges where cyclists, like cars, must yield if someone coming from the other direction has arrived first; incredible vistas, wonderful beaches and an absence of the large buses and vans that make some other island roads an endurance test. There is Hanalei Beach Park, where *South Pacific's* heroine vowed to "wash that man right out of [her] hair." It is one of a score of sandy beaches that dot the coastline to the Na Pali trailhead. There is even some sandalwood in the surrounding country, which, after its depletion in the 19th century, is testimony to the resilience of the land if not to man's stewardship of it.

Kauai was once the center of the sandalwood trade, in which American ships carried sandalwood to China, where its fragrance was much admired. These ships returned, in due time, with their holds filled by goods offered in trade. It was an enormously profitable business for the ship owners whose vessels sailed the Pacific route as well as for for the Hawaiian ali'i who owned the land and trees. To harvest the wood and raise foreign capital (for palaces, clothes, military expenditures and, of course, his own trading fleet), the boy king Kaumualii instituted a sandalwood tax on his subjects, requiring all citizens to contribute either one Spanish dollar to the royal treasury or 133 pounds of sandalwood. Since almost nobody had that much money, a fortune in Kaumualii's day, most Kauaians had to spend a part of the year cutting sandalwood from the forest. The number of workers taken from agriculture and their normal tasks to satisfy the trade's insatiable demands wreaked havoc with the traditional economy, and the whole enterprise ended only when the forests of the sweet-smelling wood were depleted. Like some more

modern entrepreneurs, the ali'i and their trading partners presumed that natural resources were infinite and found, much to their dismay, that even whole forests could be depleted by greed and rampant trade.

Hanalei and Na Pali

Surprisingly, for an area so famous and beautiful, there are not a lot of places to stay for non-campers. **Island Bicycle Adventures** stays at the Hanalei Colony Resort on Route 56, which is a nice condominium setup. Other possibilities are listed in the notes at the end of this chapter and in Ray Riegert's *Hidden Hawaii.*

On weekends and holidays, camping is allowed at **Hanalei Beach Park, Hanalei Pavilion** and **Waioli Beach Park. Haeina Beach Park,** another county campground closer to the Na Pali, allows camping on weekdays as well. Most have good fishing as well as a place to pitch your tent.

This area is a controlled tourist destination, which means that those who will travel without the aide of large buses and vans can find everything from snorkeling to rubber raft, coastal trips to spend their money on. There used to be good crabbing off Hanalei Pier, and perhaps there still is. I'm not sure since I've not dropped a crab trap in years (they're cumbersome to carry on the bicycle).

But I do ride here and love these roads and this region. Certainly, the **Na Pali** ("the cliffs" in Hawaiian) is a part of Hanalei's mystique. Magazine articles and books have been written about this amazing 11-mile trail along windswept cliffs and through a dense rain forest filled with wild orchids and fruit. This wilderness region, which begins where Route 56 ends, flows from the coast up to the Kalalau valley in a riot of tropical verdancy I've only known, elsewhere, in Peru and Equador. Many people make it a day trip, a hike, while others disappear into the region for a week or more.

It is inland from here that Kalalau the Leper made his stand when officials in the 19th century attempted to separate him from his family and send him to Kalaupapa with other Hansen's disease victims. He was willing to go if his wife and child could accompany him, and officials gave their word that they could, but as he was about to enter exile, he found that the officials lied and he was to go alone.

No way. Of all those who accepted segregation because of a disease no one then understood, Kalalau is the most famous of deserters from the disease's enforced exile. He headed into the woods of Northern Kauai, his wife and child with him. Officials hunted for him with determination, and, at each turn, he alluded them. They lived here for years. His son contracted Hansen's disease and died of it.

Sheriffs who hunted him were shot at for their troubles.

Kalalau died in the woods, eventually a victim of leprosy. But he died free after becoming a folk hero whose resistance to exile and fight against authority exercised without compassion was honored by everyone but the officials who had tried and failed to catch him. Jack London wrote a short story called "Kalalau the Leper," which was circulated on the Mainland and received with indignation in Hawaii. Nabobs from Honolulu to Lihue did not appreciate his telling of The Leper's tale or the sympathetic treatment of a man whose independent stance and love of the land had become a threat to authority.

Something of that sentiment of independence and defiance has stayed in the region to the present day. It is not only the local refusal to change their bridges and thus the rhythm of life to accommodate tourism. The feeling is more general. One story from Ron Reilly will perhaps give a flavor of the place.

The Hippie Days

In the 1960s greater Hanalei was a haven for the so-called "counterculture," and those who sought a simpler existence believed the land in this area near the Na Pali trail was something akin to Paradise. With a bit of plastic sheeting strung overhead against the rain, life's other necessities were easily met by the land. There were fish in the ocean, food on the trees, and nobody needed much clothing in a climate so benign. A tattered shirt and cut-off jeans were considered winter wear. Those seeking a simpler existence could ask for little more.

There was, for a period, even a hippie industry during the puka shell craze of that period. They say actress Elizabeth Taylor started it when she was photographed for a mass circulation magazine wearing a local shell necklace. Suddenly, everyone on the Mainland wanted one too. Since they sold at that time for $25 and more a string, collecting and stringing puka shells, which at the time littered Hanalei area beaches, became a full-time job for those who had nothing more industrious to do. Soon the sand was covered with crawling entrepreneurs, each scouring the sand for usable shells. It became an almost obscene sight, like something out of a 19th century British pornographic print. The beach was covered with hundreds of shell hunters, moving side by side with their rumps in the air, crawling along the sand in search of more and more saleable puka shells.

Auwe! It might have gone on forever, but the very demand that sparked the business proved to be its undoing. Not only were shells becoming scarce (and thus more expensive) on Kauai, but a brilliant entrepreneur discovered that beaches in the Philippines were covered with the necessary product as well. Locals were organized on that island, and a new cottage industry was briefly born. But the Philippine contingent glutted the market, and, with availability, not only did prices drop but new fads superseded the puka craze and the bottom fell out of the market. Finally, somewhere around the time of the Tet offensive, life returned to normal here and the shell hunters retired to simply enjoying themselves on the beaches of the Hanalei region.

Quite a congregation camped in this area during the period, and the region's older citizens looked on with growing discomfort. Sanitation conditions ranged from primitive to nonexistent, and officials eventually ordered the campers to disperse because they were believed to constitute a health hazard.Those who remember the 1960s will assume, as I do, that the hazard was less important to those officials than a lifestyle whose battle cry was: "tune in, turn on, and drop out." As Ron Reilly tells the story, Harold Taylor, actress Liz Taylor's brother, then came to the hippies' rescue. He owned a number of acres in this area and offered camping rights to the hippies, who moved happily from their makeshift camps to the sanctuary of Taylor's private land.

This was seen by the powers that be as an unacceptable challenge to their authority. They eventually retaliated and announced their decision to expropriate Taylor's land and turn it into a park. It was so ordered and once again the band of hippie warriors was ordered to move on. What officials had forgotten was that many of the so-called hippies were individuals who had chosen to live lightly upon the land. Like Kalalau the Leper a hundred years before, they were attached to their environment and willing, when pushed, to fight for the privlege of continuance upon it.

Their weapons were a little different and in the end even more effective than his. Before coming to Kauai, a number of the so-called hippies had gone to college and some came from families with money and clout. Representatives of the group (and, presumably, Taylor himself, who, the story goes, was not pleased with the expropriation) decided to fight back. They searched the law books and local ordinances, discovering a county regulation which said that if a resident of at least five years' tenure was evicted, the expropriating government had to provide alternate accommodations free of charge.

Since many of the hippies could prove they had been in situ for the required period, the government had to provide them with accommodations in town. Many live here still, Reilly says, and their lifestyle has become that of model citizens as they have grown to be middle-aged and often middle-class entrepreneurs. Now they can worry about their own children's penchant to waste days at the beach rather than do homework just as, in the 1960s, their parents insisted they stop loafing, apply themselves and Get A Job. Perhaps these former irritants in the official eye even lecture their offspring on the evils of smoking the marijuana which, as children, they themselves first planted here a generation ago.

_____**Addresses**_____

Island Bicycle Adventures
569 Kapahulu Ave.
Honolulu, HI 96815
(800) 233-2226
(808) 734-0700

Bike Shops

Outfitters Kauai
2360 Kiahana Plantation Dr.
Poipu Beach, HI 96756
742-9667
(tours/rentals)

Pedal and Paddle
Hanalei, HI 96714
967-9069
(rental)

Dan's Sportshop
4393 Rice
Lihue, HI 96766
246-0151

Outfitters Kauai
P. O. Box 763
Lawai, HI 96765
332-9283

North Shore Bike
Cruise & Snorkel, Inc.
P. O. Box 1191
Kapa'a, HI 96746
822-1582

Bicycle Kauai
1379 Kuhio
Kapa'a, HI 96746
822-3315

S. Shore Activities
2230 Kapili Rd.
Poipu, HI 96756
742-6873

Bicycle John
4028 B Rice
Lihue, HI 96766
245-7579

Koke'e Mountain Bikes
2360 Kiahuna Plantation
Poipu, HI 96756
742-9667

Parks

Parks Office
Department of County Parks
  and Recreation
4396 Rice St.
Lihue, HI 96766
245-8821

Division of State Parks
3060 Eiwa St.
P. O. Box 1671
Lihue, HI 96766
245-4444

Hotels, Motels, Hostels, Camps

Garden Island Inn
3445 Wilcox Rd.
Lihue, HI 96766
245-7227

Kauai Inn
Hulemalu Road
Lihue, HI 96766
245-2720

Kapa'a Sands
380 Papaloa Rd.
Kapa'a, HI 96746
822-4901

Hanalei Colony Resort
P. O. Box 206
Hanalei, HI 96714
826-9333

YMCA Camp Naue
P. O. Box 1786
Lihue, HI 96766
246-9090
(dormitory accommodations)

Waimea Plantation Cottages
Route 50
Waimea, HI 96796
338-1625

Hanalei Apartment Hotel
Route 56
Hanalei, HI 96714
826-6235

Cycling the Big Island

Most Hawaiian cyclists see this island as a series of two-, four-, or six-day jaunts. Sometimes they ride the Hilo coast, camping at small, unknown parks and jamming along from its funky, principal town to road's end at Waipio Bay. Another time local riders may focus on the Kailua-Kona side, where the Ironman Triathlon occurs each year, bringing thousands of cyclists and spectators to what is the premier endurance event. On this leeward side, where the coast is mostly new lava unadorned by much plant life, the miles click by across a harsh, black, lava rock landscape to the relative greenery of North Kahala and the verdancy of Upolu Point at the island's extreme north tip. But between and above both Hilo and Kailua-Kona—and visible from both sides of the island—is the Hawaiian upcountry, where huge cattle ranches stand quietly and cowboys ride the range.

That is my favorite Hawaii, a place where you can cycle for miles along the island's spine past stands of ohia trees and clusters of ohelo bushes ripe with berries. All this, wonderful as it may be, is only preparation for and preamble to the island's volcanic theme, because most importantly, most magnificently, there is new Hawaii. At the island's southern tip is Volcanoes National Park and the glorious spectacle of Kilauea's ongoing eruption. Cycling to and through the park is a trip through time to the beginning. Here new lava pours into the sea or over a mountain ridge, changing and creating and burning each day as new plant life grows in the eruption's wake. Volcanoes National Park is like nothing else I have ever seen, and even repeated visits do not lessen the wonder of this continuing creation within an inhabited, forested but ever changing volcanic island chain.

Routes

One can speak of Molokai as a single community because its population is so small and so integrated that it functions as an extended family, and folk from its leeward side will know and help friends living in Kaunakakai. It makes sense to discuss Oahu as a single, thematic whole not only because Honolulu dominates and sets the tenor for the island but because, from Waianae to Kaneohe, the physical differences are just not that extreme. Riding around Oahu there is little sense of radical differences in climate or more than the usual diversity in the ways of life pursued by its inhabitants. It is all a variation on a theme.

But the island of Hawaii is at least four distinct geographies. There are two coastal environments, windward and leeward, whose geographies and economies are clearly distinct. On the Hilo side, where trade winds dominate, the landscape is tropical and lush enough for orchids to grow, while Kailua-Kona residents live in an arid climate whose geography is dominated by relatively new volcanic flows. Distinct from the coastal folk are upcountry ranchers who wear jackets in the chilly mornings while herding cattle across range land greater in size than the island of Lanai itself. Finally, there is the active volcanic life, the erupting, steaming ever-present **Kilauea** and its older sisters, **Mauna Loa** and **Mauna Kea,** which dominate the whole.

Campers delight in this diversity, and more attention is given here than in previous chapters to potential camping sites. This is simply a function of Hawaii's size—a bigger place has more places to stay. Trips require longer distances, and those who wish to ride in leisure may choose to break their day at one or another park rather than pushing on along the road to an urban center. To facilitate such travel, visitors can buy an all-parks island camping permit which gives the holder permission to stop at any county campground for a week or two.

The island is serviced by two principal airports, one in Hilo and the other in Kailua-Kona. **Aloha** and **Hawaiian** Airlines flights arrive at and depart them both on an hourly basis from Honolulu, and service is available as well to and from the other Hawaiian islands. Mainland tourists interested in cycling to **Volcanoes National Park** will prefer to begin their trip on the Hilo side, while triathletes interested in the Ironman route will fly immediately to Kona. Backroads Bicycle Tours, with whom I rode in late 1989, and Island Bicycle Adventures—which also visits here—both begin their trips in Hilo, and for the average cyclist this makes sense. It is only thirty miles to Volcanoes National Park, and, for those riding in a counterclockwise direction, the route north to Honoka'a includes a good shoulder on the island's eastern shore.

Airport to Hilo

There is a dense row of hotels and motels an easy, two-mile ride from the airport. To get there, turn right out of the airport onto **Kanoelehua Avenue** (Route 11) and go straight through the first traffic light onto Banyan Drive. In the 1930s young banyan trees were

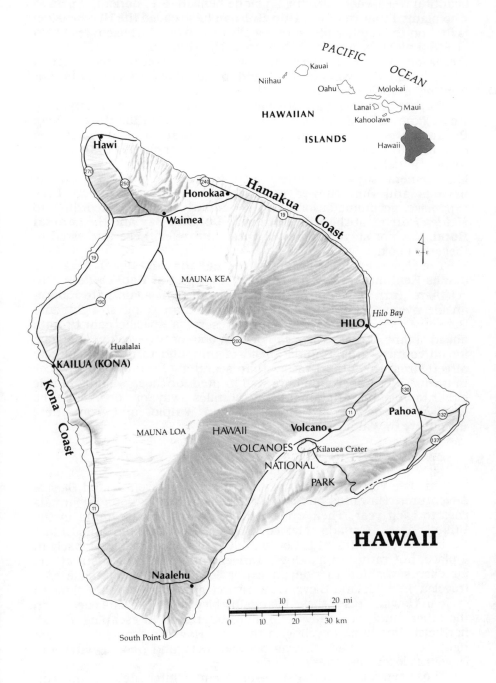

PACIFIC OCEAN

Niihau Kauai

Oahu Molokai

Lanai Maui
Kahoolawe

HAWAIIAN

ISLANDS Hawaii

Hawi

270

250

240

Honokaa

Hamakua

Waimea

19

Coast

MAUNA KEA

19

190

200

Hilo Bay

HILO

Hualalai

KAILUA (KONA)

130

Pahoa 132

MAUNA LOA HAWAII

VOLCANOES Volcano 137

11

NATIONAL Kilauea Crater

PARK

11

HAWAII

Naalehu

0 10 20 mi

0 10 20 30 km

South Point

planted by important people of the day and now they have matured to beautiful trees, each carrying a plaque beneath it to honor the person who planted that tree. The **Hilo Hukilau** (also called the Hilo Seaside) is first on the right, a pleasant, locally owned hotel whose rates begin at $48 a night for a room with a lanai. The Hukilau is not on but near the beach. Across the street from its entrance is a protected lagoon where local kids swim and play, and beside it is a small boat harbor fronting on a pleasant beach at the southern end of Hilo Bay.

Farther down Banyan Drive among other hotels are the **Hilo Bay Hotel** (known locally as "Uncle Billy's") and the **Naniloa Hotel**, where Backroads guests stay. In late 1989 the Naniloa would not allow bicyclists to take their bicycles through the lobby and to their own rooms, a policy which wipes them off my list of places to stay. Management says they know bicyclists are a growing group of patrons and that they're going to reconsider the policy. Less expensive accommodations can be found in town, according to *Hidden Hawaii,* at the **Hilo Hotel,** the **Dolphin Bay** and the **Lanikai Hotel.** I've not stayed at any of these and refer those interested to Riegert's book.

The closest camping grounds are **Onekahakaha Beach Park** and **James Kealoha Park**, right behind the airport at **Keokea Point**. To get there, turn right out of the airport and right again onto Kalani-anaole Avenue at the traffic light rather than going straight onto Banyan Drive. Because you cannot reserve a specific campground ahead of time, it makes sense to order a one- or two-week permit good for all county campgrounds ahead of time and to head to the site directly from the airport rather than searching for the county offices in town. The campgrounds are well located for those wishing to ride either to Volcanoes National Park, 32 miles away, or north along the windward coast toward Honoka'a and Waipio, and from there upcountry to Waimea.

BACKROADS BICYCLE TOURING

This is a very different type of tour company from Island Bicycle Adventures. Hawaii is one of only dozens of destinations Backroads goes to each year. Their cycle touring groups can be found in the United States, Canada, Mexico, Europe, New Zealand and China. Backroads' commitment is not to cycling Hawaii, to being intensely in a place, but rather to making arrangements and giving instructions for clients wishing to ride an exotic location. Most of those who traveled in my Island Bicycle Adventures group told me they came to cycle in Hawaii, to see these islands by bicycle. Backroads clients, on the other hand, generally were more interested in escaping a cold, northern climate and cycling in the sun. Hawaii's "[tour] dates were right," one guest said. "It was between here and New Zealand and Hawaii's closer," another explained.

Those who were interested—or became interested as the trip progressed—in learning more about Hawaii from the tour leaders were sadly out of luck. Backroads ride leader Chris Sibley told me that it is company policy not to have ride leaders who specialize in one region. In a normal season, for example, he'll lead groups in France, Ireland, Hawaii, California and New England. Because ride leaders are rotated every few weeks, they do not build up a store of local knowledge or experience. On my trip with them, made in November, neither Chris nor his partner, Alan Jay, were at all familiar with Hawaiian history, plant life, animals or—most importantly—local road conditions or problems. Each handles this destination once or twice a year at most and then moves on, so they, like guests, must work from route maps prepared by Backroads' California office. Each route map contains two or three options of varying length to get between the starting point and the destination.

Another difference between both tour groups is that, while Backroads' ride leaders are able mechanics who can fix a flat, replace a busted cable or grease a hub, they are not teachers. Guests are not taught how to keep a bicycle safe or coached in better cycle techniques, and the full onus is thus on the rider to bring any problems to a group leader's attention. There are no daily safety checks, and, as happened, even those guests riding Backroads-rented bicycles may cycle with badly adjusted brakes or derailleurs because they just don't know any better and nobody has shown them what to look for. Unlike Island Bicycle Adventures, Backroads is not committed to teaching its people better riding techniques or the history and lay of this land. Riding with them is rather like riding a half-century route with reservations booked for a nice hotel at the day route's end.

Interestingly, many of the guests on my tour were returnees who had ridden with the company before in either Baja, the California wine country or New England. Some were disappointed in the lack of local knowledge on the ride leaders' part and others in the fact that, contrary to their assumptions, bicycles were not automatically checked by ride leaders before each day's ride. But, on the whole, most of the 20 guests seemed satisfied both with their trip and with the Backroads package.

Rides

It is a strange fact that the larger the area covered, the less there is to say about a trip. The minute description possible on, say, Molokai or Kauai is simply lost in miles logged here. On sixty- or eighty-mile days you ride more and stop less as the rhythm of cycling rather than seeing takes over. This is why frequent local visitors tend to specialize in a region, returning again and again to Kailua-Kona, Waimea or Hilo.

Backroads circumnavigates the island in a ten-day tour that includes two rest days for sightseeing. Island Bicycle Adventures spends six days going from Hilo to Kailua-Kona via Volcanoes National Park, with a sightseeing day thrown in. My friend Karen Cisney spent six days going from park to park on her way from **Hilo** to **Hawi** at the island's north tip; another acquaintance, George Fisher, spent a week just exploring **Waipio Valley**. To give a sense of the potential of this island and to describe a single ride, I've had to reduce some possibilities to a paragraph's mention or a sentence's aside to show where the basic route can be expanded into a long-term ride.

The windward side of Hawaii is known, locally, as the **Hamakua Coast**. It is a wonderful and not too difficult ride which can stop after perhaps 40 miles at the town of **Honoka'a** or continue a few miles farther into the **Waipio Valley**. Some people stop and camp along the route, taking several days in leisure for what others may do in half a day. At the coast's northern tip, you turn inward and ride up toward a very different environment, where ranching is the principal business and Waimea the region's cultural and tourist center. With each few hundred feet of elevation the vegetation changes, first gradually and then markedly, as lowland fruits and flowers give way to grassland, bush, and stands of ohia tree.

Hilo

Past the hotels on Banyan Drive is **Liliuokalani Gardens**, a large park-like area with Japanese bridges, lions and lanterns stretching back to the sea. At the intersection where the park ends, a left-hand turn past **Suisan Dock** (and a local retail fish store), where local fishing boats bring their catch to auction each day, and then an immediate right at the **Hilo Iron Works** puts you on what will become the round island road, Route 19. The Iron Works is a clearly industrial structure which signals everything I like about Hilo. It refuses to get too clever or too pretty and remains, for all the island's tourism and tourist business, a homey, working place.

On the Highway, where a good shoulder exists, you ride along flats near the bay and over what used to be the "Crescent City." Until a large tidal wave swept half the town off its pilings in 1946, that was Hilo's nickname, and the city did indeed rim the crescent-shaped bay along which cyclists now ride out of town over the Wailuku River Bridge and up to Hawaii's northern regions. After the 1946 destruction, locals rebuilt their city and added a long stone breakwater across Hilo Bay to prevent a similar disaster in the future. The breakwater is still there and is an aid to sailors seeking safe harbor but, alas, is no guarantee against destruction. After a second tidal wave struck in 1960, city leaders gave up on the coastal construction, drained the lowland for a park and moved the city back to where it is today.

The buildings are still largely of wood, and, cycling by, you can see **The Bicycle Shop**, where visitors are welcomed with answers to questions about island roads and, of course, encouraged to buy whatever cycling supplies they may have forgotten in their rush to leave distant homes. On the bulletin board in the shop is notice of an annual, local mountain bike race which runs from the summit of **Mauna Kea**—at 13,000 feet—down and across the Saddle Road (at 6,000 feet) and then back up to the 13,000-foot-high summit of **Mauna Loa**. This is so clear an example of obsessive, fanatic behavior that I am surprised it has not been made into an international event to be filmed by the television networks and used as a training ride for triathletes. Up the hill (a small one, to be sure) from The Bicycle Shop is **Kaiko'o**, the government and commercial center for the island.

Ride One: Hilo to Puna Region
Skill level: Moderate—some traffic and climbing
Connects with Rides Six and Seven

This is the one Big Island ride in this book compiled largely from secondhand information rather than from on-road experience. It is not disinterest but, rather, a lack of time and resources that has kept me from making a detailed study of this area. The description will therefore be rudimentary. This is for most people a side trip, a detour on the route to or from Volcanoes National Park, although, from the Puna region's western end, the actions of Kilauea's continuing eruption may also be visible. In fact, the whole ride down to and around this district is a trip to and through a new geologic region where the effects of recent volcanic activity are evident.

The Puna region was, in late 1989, the center of a major controversy pitting state energy officials against local activists concerned with the state of the region's rain forests. State officials want to build a geothermal power-generating facility in this area to lessen reliance on imported fuels. While all Hawaiian citizens would be delighted to have alternate sources of inexpensive power, some are worried that such a project would dangerously and permanently affect the region's ecology. Nothing, they say, is worth that.

Further, the idea of tapping the earth for geothermal power strikes some Hawaiian activists as sacrilege. If Pele lives—and the fire goddess has shown her continued presence through the continuing eruptions at Kilauea—then to sink holes for geothermal power is a physical invasion of her body. That is something Pele's followers are adamantly opposed to on religious grounds.

Some local residents are also concerned for similar reasons about plans to put a spaceport suitable for launching or landing orbital craft in the southern area of this island. The spaceport would mean jobs and money for an area that could use both, but critics are concerned about the potential damage to the land.

Some have tried to paint the protestors as flaky Luddites guarding the fire goddess Madam Pele's home against the intrusion of rational, necessary technology. I try not to judge another's religious belief, preferring to accept honest faith in others on the principle that I have no corner on revealed truths. Certainly many residents take the idea of the Hawaiian goddess seriously; living so close to an erupting volcano it would be hard not to personify such power. But religion aside, the issues of conservation and preservation are real ones being weighed and debated seriously by residents whose long-range concern is a precious and fragile ecosystem they believe to be at risk. The potential effect emissions from a geothermal plant would have on the area's rain forest is not known, and I, at least, share some of the protestors' concern.

So, should you travel in this area, my suggestion is to respect the local folks' concern and the complexity of the issues. Jokes about Pele and flippant comments about environmentalism are neither asked for nor likely to be welcomed.

178 • Six Islands on Two Wheels

Backroads inserts the Puna triangle into its ride back from Volcanoes National Park as a 60-mile detour that adds miles to their ride but leaves neither time nor energy for sightseeing along the way. Island Bicycle Adventures does not travel through this area, preferring to concentrate its Hawaii time on the park region nearer Kilauea Caldera itself. For those who camp and tour simultaneously, this is a wonderful one- to three-night trip to the coast with campgrounds at **Harry K. Brown County Beach Park** and **McKenzie State Park**.

A left-hand turn upon leaving the Hilo Airport access road and you're on Route 11, heading toward Volcano Village, in the midst of heavy traffic. Traffic is often fierce in the first eight miles of this trip, and the shoulder, although present along most of the route, is rough. I've both cycled the highway along this road, straddling its white line, and taken the shoulder. Neither is ideal. On the white line, traffic whizzes too close for my comfort while the shoulder is more suited to a mountain than a touring bike. Fortunately, things improve as the distance from Hilo increases and the road climbs toward the Pahoa cutoff. About six miles from the airport, on the divided highway's opposite side, is the **Mauna Loa Macadamia Nut Factory**, which offers free daily tours.

The rate of ascent is minimal but constant along the eight miles from town to the Route 130 cutoff, which requires a 90-degree turn to the left off the main route and down through Pahoa to the sea. Here you can also just continue straight, climbing constantly for another 22 miles until Volcanoes National Park appears. This is always tempting because, past this intersection, the traffic lessens markedly and the idea of a gentle, constant upgrade past woods and into the cool of 4,000 feet altitude is almost irresistible. It is not a hard climb, just a long one with a constant but not too difficult rate of ascent which any moderately able cyclist can do.

A left-hand turn, however, runs through **Keaau**, whose Hongwanji Buddhist Mission's gold shrine is said to be a worthwhile stop. Around this island and, in fact, throughout the state, there are scores of Buddhist missions of several sects. Jodo and Hongwanji are the most popular, and for those new to Hawaii this might be reason enough to detour toward a good example of the exotic, which will, after time in the islands, become familiar. About a mile southeast of Keaau on Route 130 is the old Puna Sugar Plantation. Here a 19th century plantation manager's house has been converted into the **Banyan House Bed and Breakfast**, with nice views of the ocean.

About ten miles down Route 130 is the town of **Pahoa**, reached after riding through an area of orchid and anthurium farms. This was, until recently, a quiet, rural ride, but in late 1989 the traffic had transformed it into an urban trip in which too many cars inhabited too little road for a cyclist to doze and daydream through the woods. Pahoa itself is also changing. Once it was a lumber camp that exported the wood used to make the ohia-wood ties for the old Santa Fe Railroad. Now it's a place to stock up on food and water for a trip to the coast, and along the town's long shopping strip corridor are Dairy Queens, a 7-11, Pahoa Natural Groceries, a coffee shop, a craft

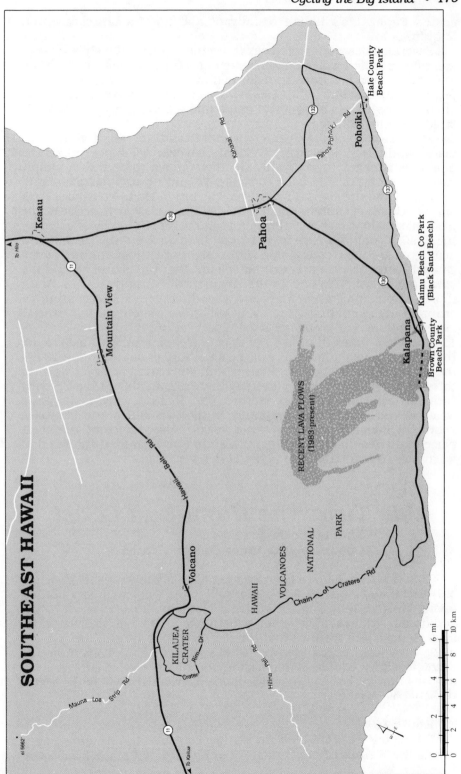

SOUTHEAST HAWAII

Keaau

To Hilo

Mountain View

Volcano

KILAUEA CRATER

Crater Rim Dr

Mauna Loa Strip Rd

el 5662'

To Kailua

Hawaii Belt Rd

Hilina Pali Rd

HAWAII VOLCANOES NATIONAL PARK

Chain of Craters Rd

RECENT LAVA FLOWS (1983-present)

Kalapana

Brown County Beach Park

Kaimu Beach Co Park (Black Sand Beach)

Pahoa

Kahakai Rd

Pahoa-Pohoiki Rd

Pohoiki

Hale County Beach Park

N
W E
S

0   2   4   6 mi
0   2   4   6   8   10 km

center, Papa Aldo's Italian restaurant and its Mexican competitor, Luquin's.

Several miles south of town is a small crater, which one book identifies as the former cucumber patch of a local man named Nii. This whole area has been transformed by recent volcanic events. Repeated eruptions since the 1950s have cut roads, burned forest and changed more than a vegetable patch into a miniature of the island's large, erupting Kilauea.

From Pahoa the road runs downhill toward the sea and Kaimu's black-sand beach. It is a nice destination where riders pouring on the miles might want to stop and sip their guava juice before simply turning around to ride back to Route 11 and up to Volcanoes Park. Until recently, the coastal route from the beach led to Volcanoes Park and the Chain of Craters Road. This was the ideal way to arrive at the park, along the coast and through the area most directly affected by the 1950s eruptions. Now more recent flows have cut the road, which dead ends on the western side within sight of large plumes of steam caused by molten magma exiting coastal lava tubes and setting the surrounding water to boil as the lava almost instantly cooled. Since this is happening every day and the direction of the continuing eruption remains uncertain, you will have to check the precise location of the road's end yourself.

There are other things to see in this area and other things to do. Here, for example, about six miles east of Kalapana on Route 137 is the **Kalani Honua Culture Center and Retreat.** I've never been to this eclectic place. Its brochures say there is something for everybody with lectures on Hawaiian culture and history, classes in hula, weaving and lei making, programs in modern dance and aerobics, sports facilities, hiking trails— the works. Also, the coast is a great place to do absolutely nothing but camp, swim, stare at the sea and learn how to relax from the rigors of the world.

Ride Two: The Hamakua Coast
Skill level: Basic skills
Connects with Rides One and Three

This ride from Hilo to Honoka'a is one of my favorites. If you ride only as far as Honoka'a or Waipio Valley, the whole trip is a not too taxing 45- to 55-mile day. If you're seeking more exercise, it is an additional sixteen miles (and a perhaps 2,200-foot altitude gain) from Honoka'a to Waimea and the Parker Ranch range. The scenery along the route ranges from pretty to spectacular, and, even though there is some traffic, a nice shoulder along the coastal section assures that all but the most idiotically driven cars will be kept at a reasonable distance.

Route 19
Riding out past Hilo, I walk my bicycle when the traffic is heavy across the **Wailuku River** bridge, about a mile and a half from town.

Climbing a bit after the bridge and still not four miles along the route, you'll see a wonderful graveyard on the road's left. Some people argue that cemeteries are wasted land taken foolishly from the world's agricultural bank, while others grumble about the pagan foolishness of burying the deceased. It may be a socio-religious rite, and certainly the land could be used for other things, but these criticisms miss the point. Nothing says more about a community than the graveyards it keeps alive on the land. As you walk through one, the history and current state of the supporting community is quickly and clearly revealed.

If most graves are dated before, say, 1950, and there is still land available for new internees, then it is obvious the community has been shrinking as folks moved to other locations. Some places lost population during and after World War II, for example, and never recovered their drive or momentum. Are the more newly dated graves kept in good repair and the older ones rather unkempt? Then be assured that a major shift in ethnic or religious background occurred sometime between the first settlers and those who have come in the last fifty years. Ancestors who have no attendents are distinguished from newer arrivals whose daughters or grandchildren visit and remember. I am always suspicious of graveyards with huge memorial structures festooned with gaudy flying angels and large sculptures. As a rule these are always a bit unkempt and almost never decorated with hand picked flowers or hand-strung leis. It is as if, having paid a fortune for the final memorial, families have forgotten their own.

This graveyard, whose residents are primarily Japanese, has no large, unsightly pieces of funereal architecture. Instead there are rows of well-kept, low gravestones, each adorned with fresh flowers to show that someone remembers and cares. The names are carved into most with Chinese characters but use English for the inevitable dates: born 1920 - died 1946. The place speaks clearly to a strong, stable, local Japanese community, a group of fishermen, agricultural workers and shopkeepers who probably came to Hawaii first for plantation work and then stayed for the freedom and island life. Judging by the headstone dates, the families interred here have been on Hawaii for several generations, and the living, who place flowers on each grave, still honor those great-grandparents who left their original, familial sites to venture into this then strange land. Ties remain to that migration, links of language and culture and family tradition. The care this graveyard shows is, in fact, time's trust, a recognition of past sacrifice and, perhaps, a promise to the future. Why else would people care so lovingly for the memories of the departed if they did not hope that, someday, others would remember them?

Onomea Bay

Leaving the cemetery, I came to a right-hand turnoff less than three miles later marked "Scenic Route," which bends away from the highway and toward the bay. It is really quite wonderful, a back road only a few miles long, but one which bends and curves through a forest of shaded trees that have littered the road with fresh mangoes and passion fruit. At Onomea Bay is the **Hawaii Tropical Botanical Garden,** whose 1600 species of flowers, palms and other plant species (not all Hawaiian) make it a horticulturist's delight. This is, after all, the "Orchid Isle" and for those who have been too thrilled with the cycling to notice that these flowers grow wild, perhaps a refresher course in their many types is called for at the Garden.

The scenic route ends at a sign ordering a left-hand turn at the intersection past the next corner store, just after a large playing field appears on the right. The road then climbs up, turns right and back onto Route 19.

Ten miles outside of Hilo there is a turnoff on the road's left side up Route 220 to **Akaka Falls State Park**. It is only a short detour, albeit one including a sharp uphill ride (or walk) of about a mile. On the left, as you head toward the Falls, there is a market for those who neglected to buy juices or soda in town and, a little farther on, a general store in the tiny community of **Honomu**. The park itself offers spectacular, verdant, lush tropical scenery and, yes, a beautiful waterfall. It is well worth a half hour or so for those who count touring days as more than miles gained in the training log.

Only the truly fanatic cyclist or somnambulist motorist would not stop for a moment at a bridge across Route 19, just north of the Falls. It is the first of many along this route which carry the road across deep streams running from the hills down to the nearby sea. Like the Akaka Falls Park, these bridges give glimpses on small valleys so dense in their vegetation that each becomes a study of light upon darker green. There is a smell of ripe fruit and a whisper of water coming from each, and from it all rises a vision of the undiluted tropics. Here I can remember the power of the tropics as ideal, and understand how it evoked the images of innocence and Eden in the then industrializing world. We forget that the lure of the tropics— lush, innocent, virginal—propelled 19th century painters and writers from civilized Paris and London to the ends of the world. Here are glimpses of how seductive and tantalizing the tropics must have been to Captain Bligh's impressionable Mr. Christian, to a young Herman Melville whose years on ship created a series of South Pacific adventures like *Omoo* and *Typee*. Mostly, the feeling is gone, lost to the condominiums, convenience stores, and resort developments which have taken over the state, but along this road and in its secluded parks the dreams of those days still whisper as trade winds blow through the trees.

Laupahoehoe

These thoughts carried me past a number of small, weathered wooden churches, which looked like studies from a Walker Evans photographic essay, to the town of Laupahoehoe. A sign marks the right-hand turnoff to **Laupahoehoe Point**. After that there is another right whose road curves down a steep, narrow hill, past a Jodo Buddhist mission to the beach, where camping is permitted for those with a county permit.

It is a wonderful beach, although fully exposed to the prevailing winds, which whip along this coast most days from the northeast. In a tidal pool along the lava rock-littered beach was what appeared to be a perfect, natural bonsai tree, a small if slightly shaggy example of how the wind can bend and mute a growing plant by pushing forever on one side. It was all of perhaps three feet in length, and I ate lunch in its company. Then I dawdled while flying my kite, unwilling to leave the park's beauty and thrilling to the strong winds that made the parafoil dance and twirl in every shift of the wind.

Riding back uphill to Route 19, I stopped at a turnoff to admire the woods, where tall koa trees and shorter stands of the ohia tree grow. Koa is a premier island wood traditionally used for everything from old-style, mammoth surf boards to modern, island-style furniture. There is selective logging in this area. The lumber is taken back to Hilo and then turned into veneer or sold to furniture makers. Also present is bluegum eucalyptus, first planted as a windbreak earlier in this century and now a wood valued as a commercial asset in its own right when turned into wood chip, which, in turn, is transformed into paper and wallboard.

Honoka'a

From the beach it is about 18 miles of rolling, slightly steeper road to Honoka'a. For some reason, Backroads recommends a detour at **Ookala,** a six-mile ride down a back country lane which is less traveled but no more interesting than the round island road itself. Indeed, both ride leaders seemed to have forgotten this detour existed and did not sweep or sag the detour, and in the process they temporarily lost a rider who, feeling the effects of tropical heat and jet lag, waited patiently if in vain for a ride. Others also thought the ride was getting a bit onerous as afternoon traffic became heavier and the roads went from gentle to rolling terrain. Since this was the first day, I suspect it was the heat and jet lag that made this part of the road a trial for some of Backroads' guests, because they cycled harder inclines and longer miles with alacrity by the end of the tour's week.

Campers may wish to consider the **Kalopa State Park** cutoff to the right of Route 19 a few miles before Honoka'a. This is a little-known area with a very steep ascent, where my friend and fellow Oahu cyclist Karen Cisney stayed on a recent tour. The road to the park is not particularly well marked but, for those carrying a good island map, easy enough to find, she says. It is a little-known and little-used camping area and, for those who wish to be in solitude among the trees, a park Karen recommends. All but the very strongest riders will have to walk their bikes up at least a part of the way. Karen said that she might have been able to ride it if her bicycle had not been handicapped by 40 pounds of touring gear. Most riders will prefer, as I do, to go on to Honoka'a, Waipio Valley or blast up the hill to Waimea and the excellent facilities there.

In town, on the road's right, is the **Hotel Honoka'a Club**, a local bar, restaurant and hostelry whose rates range from $28 for a single room to $43 for a four-person room suitable for a couple with two children. Club officials said they always try to put cyclists in first floor rooms so they don't have to lug their bicycles and gear up flights of stairs. It is not The Grand but it is clean, simple and superbly located for those who wish to break their ride to upcountry with an overnight stay in inexpensive digs after a relatively easy approximately 45-mile day. The bar is furnished in 1950s decor—not a choice of trendy elegance but simply because little has changed in forty years. There is a large, faded Smirnoff vodka sign, and drink choices range from beer (two types), to soda (three varieties) to hard liquor. One of Backroads' guests rolled in to ask the bartender if she could make a mixed drink and the woman nodded, shyly, yes. He then asked for a Mai Tai, assuming, perhaps, it was something of a national Hawaiian beverage and not merely a tourist's drink. She stared at him as if he were out of his mind. A Mai Tai? "You do make mixed drinks?" he asked again, and again she nodded agreeably, giving the Smirnoff advertisement a signficant glance. He took the hint and asked for a Bloody Mary. This, I knew, was my type of bar. Beer comes in bottles, and no drink requiring more than two containers (juice and vodka; coke and rum) is ever served.

Honoka'a to Waimea

Those wishing to head upcountry immediately can bypass the Honoka'a Club and continue through town to where Route 19 makes a left-hand turn and then heads up to Waimea—also called Kamuela—and, ultimately, over to the leeward side and the town of Kawaihae. It is perhaps a 2,200-foot climb from Honoka'a to the uplands, and the traffic for this cross-island route is often very heavy and impolite. This is a commuting route for people living on one side of the island but working on the other, and, like people everywhere who drive long distances between work and home each day, motorists here get cranky. To make things worse, there is little shoulder along the road for this 13-mile ascent..

Hawaii Bicycle League touring director Chuck Fisher says there is a badly marked but very usable side road, which begins just before the major route and ends near Waimea. It is not as well graded, but the traffic is far less fierce and it is, he argues, preferable for cyclists going either to or from the upcountry road. I've not taken it, although it is well marked on island maps. Chuck suggests those interested ask for directions in Honoka'a to assure they don't miss the turnoff. My recommendation is simply to stay overnight in Honoka'a or Waipio Valley rather than blasting up Route 19 during rush hour or in early morning commuting traffic.

The 2,500-foot altitude in Waimea means nights will seem cooler to those who have been in the islands for a while, and in the winter a windbreaker and long pants are a must. On this route the vegetation changes, mile by mile, from lowland lush into upcountry grassland dotted with scattered stands of trees. It is a pattern that defines the island and, indeed, the tropics in general. Altitude from sea level and proximity to prevailing winds create major changes in the plant life. This side of the island from the coast to Waimea is in the path of daily trade winds, but, on the Kona side, those winds (and their rains) are usually blocked by the high volcanic mountain spine that divides the island.

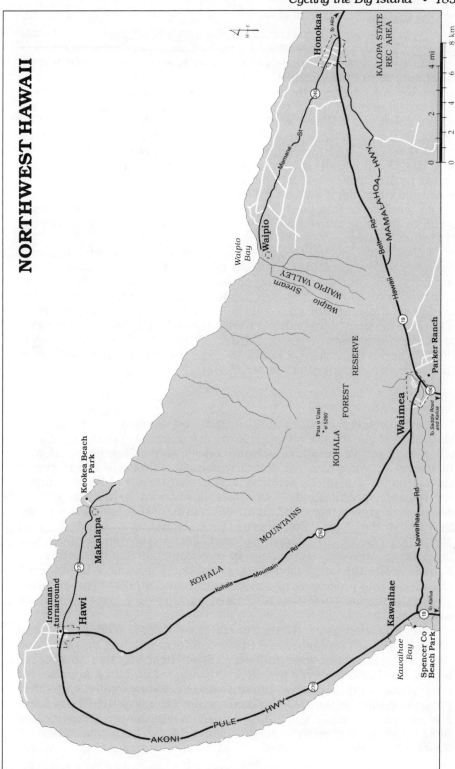

NORTHWEST HAWAII

To Waipio

Cycling straight from the Hotel Honoka'a Club past the upcountry cutoff means overnighting in a lush, hidden tropical valley that is Hawaii's perhaps least visited tropical delight. At the **Waipio Valley Lookout,** eight miles from Honoka'a, a right-hand turn leads down to a region which, in the century before Europeans and North Americans arrived, was a center of island cultural and political life. In the valley are **Hiilawe** waterfalls, which feed a river once stocked with fish that local men and women caught with their hands; a black alluvial beach; and fertile taro fields where Hawaii's dietary staple, poi, is still cultivated. It was here in the 1960s that the U. S. Peace Corps built Borneo-style longhouses and Filipino-style huts in which to train its Mainland volunteers for two years of service in rural Asia. Today some folks just pitch a tent where the Peace Corps village was, swim in the waters bellow Hiilawe Falls or hike contentedly through **Waimanu Valley**.

Fellow Oahu cyclist George Fisher recommends the secluded and inexpensive **Waipio Hotel**, a retreat that sits deep in the valley. There are no tennis courts, swimming pools or day charter companies here. Nor are there a lot of amenities (for instance no meal service or electricity), so those interested in this valley detour to a backroads retreat will need to carry some supplies with them. There are, however, two kitchens for guests' use, orchards, waterfalls, cliffs, wild ginger, orchids and a night whose sky is so clear and air so pure it will seem like a moment on another, better planet.

Waimea

Early western visitors first introduced domesticated cattle to Hawaii as a gift for the ali'i, stock to raise and eat. What they didn't teach local people was how to build fences, so the Hawaiians allowed their new animals to roam. Not surprisingly, wild herds of sheep and cattle quickly became a scourge in the countryside. Range animals are held to specific fields, but these newly wild herds ran at will, decimating young trees and plant life as they scrounged for a meal. New Englander John Palmer Parker took the matter in hand when, in 1809, he offered to round up and pen these pesky and now unwelcome western intrusions in exchange for homestead land. Kamehameha the Great gave Parker two acres, and thus began what has grown into an empire of 225,000 acres and 50,000 head of cattle. Today the Parker Ranch is advertised as America's largest privately-owned ranch.

What started as an attempt to end the decimation caused by feral animals on open range became first a locally sustaining business and then a major island-wide industry. From beef supplier to the Big Island, the Parkers developed their growing ranch into a supplier for the territory and, of course, purveyor to the square-rigged ships that provisioned in the Sandwich Islands while sailing in the China trade and across the Pacific's whaling routes. When the business became more than a homestead, cattle were driven from the ranch to **Kawaiahae** on the leeward coast and shipped to the Parker slaughterhouse in Honolulu, providing beef and lamb for the groaning tables of the territory's elite.

Parker hired Latin American cowboys to work the range, and thus the legend of the *paniolo* (a Hawaiian corruption of the word "espanol") began. This was the local cowboy, a combination of Texas cowhand and Latin American *vaquero*. These days it is hard to find a trace of the Spanish language that was the original paniolo's tongue. Like most of the island's 19th century immigrants, these cowhands intermarried with local women, as did Parker himself, who married *Kelikipikaneokaolokaha* (also known as Rachel Kipikane), a granddaughter of Kamehameha the Great. Later immigration by Chinese, Japanese, Filipino, and American workers has made the paniolo a local hybrid who is more likely to sing a Gabby Pahanui song in Hawaiian than one in Spanish by Latin America's contemporary singer Rafael. Yes, they play the guitar, albeit in the local slack key style, and many still learn the highly portable ukulele, which was introduced by Portugese sailors and workers along with the cattle.

The Parker dynasty survives and changes. In the 1960s a descendant of John Palmer Parker sold large tracts of land to resort developers and then turned over active management of the ranch to modern, state-of-the-art ranching professionals. But the whole up-country region still is filled with Parker this and Parker that (Parker Ranch Shopping Center, Parker Family Cemetery and Mana Hale— the old Parker house, etc.) and the family's history has become communal, local lore, although it is still young enough to be oral history as well. At the **Kamuela Museum**, for example, a Backroads' guest spent hours viewing the eccentric collection of Hawaiian, American and Asian artifacts that are a part of this polyglot culture. Its curator, now in his 80s, happily reminisced for hours about how it was "back then" when he was a boy and about the changes the last half century has wrought. Then and now, before and today: it is a recurring Hawaiian theme, but here the two exist so closely that it is personal history and not simply a nostalgic wish for a simpler, older way.

Ride Three: KamuelaTriangle
Skill level: Moderate, some climbing
Connects with Rides Two and Four

Parker Ranch is becoming a "destination" in its own right, a place where weekend cowboys rent horses to ride for a morning, mount helicopters for flying tours in the afternoon or simply walk through museums and take guided tours of the land. Those interested in spending the night in this region usually try to stay at **The Lodge** or the **Kamuela Inn**. Cyclists sometimes ride in and then, almost immediately, blast out of town and down to the Kona Coast, thereby missing not only local museums but one of the most beautiful days I've ever known in the saddle. The triangle ride is not offered by any tour groups, but is one I recommend for any who wish to see this island in all its incredible diversity.

After filling water bottles and stocking up on snacks, I headed west on route Route 19 from Waimea toward the intersection with Lindsey Road. At the junction with Route 250, which heads down coast to Kawaihae, however, I turned right toward **Hawi**. Here the traffic almost disappears and a six-mile climb begins. On this uphill and to the left, the Kona coast is visible far below, but to the right is quiet ranch land covered with grass and beautiful ohia trees. Along the way are lots of lovely flowers whose names I do not know but always think I should. It is not a bad climb, merely constant, and the views at each turn—coast far below and quiet range nearby—more than repaid any effort expended as I humped up the spine of this north Kohala island tip.

Soon the road begins to roll, and then the rolling becomes a gentle descent past other ranches (Kohala Ranch is a prominent landmark), which will end only when you reach Hawi and the sea. This is a spooky ride. There is no sound but the wind through the trees, a whisper of spinning wheel against well-aged road, and the rustle of cattle which canter away with a reproachful, backward glare at cyclists gliding through their world. How do cattle know what it is, silently rushing by? It is as if they sense me as an imposition, a new bug on the landscape which has, after all these years, become their own. Each time a herd or group turned from me, I felt as if I'd been shunned by some strict, religious community.

Some people take this route at high speed, and it is easy to build up momentum to 35 or 40 miles an hour, although the winds that twist down this road can be a problem. I cycled at perhaps a third that speed, stopping every two or three miles to rest and admire the world.

At the town of Hawi the sleigh ride ends, and there are country stores where you can stock up. Here the upland cool has become tropical heat, and it was with a shock that I knew, again, how fast things change with altitude in the tropics. A right-hand turn onto the **Akoni Pule Highway** leads up to the island's tip and **Mahukoa**, which, in early days, was the terminus of a narrow-gauge railway built to carry sugar headed for Oahu and the markets. Another 19th century immigrant entrepreneur, Samuel G. Wilder, settled in what then must have seemed to be forgotten lowlands and started a sugar plantation. He built the railroad in the 19th century with, of course, Chinese labor, although within a few generations trucks had replaced this more sensible, civilized form of travel and the railroad was dismantled.

Past here, near road's end at the island's tip, is a famous statue of Kamehameha I, which is something of a tourist attraction although I've never been sure why. It has, to my mind, neither grace, dignity nor beauty and seems to serve only as a route marker where I know I'll turn around and head back through Hawi toward Kawaihae. This is a gentle, benign and excellent stretch of slightly rolling road with a good shoulder that must be welcome to Ironman triathletes who ride it in their annual race (see Ride 4). The triathlon's bicycle route begins in Kailua-Kona and turns around at the 50-mile marker in Hawi before returning to where it began for a full century ride. Most of this coast is a terribly hot, dry, volcanic landscape on a road with no shoulder and not much to see. But this section, as far as Kawaihae, is more temperate (remember that sugar was grown nearby not too long ago) and divides the coast environment from that of the upland ranges, which stretch uphill to the east.

On the way south toward Kawaihae, along Kohala's Highway 27, campers can stay at either Kapaa Beach Park or Mahukona Beach Park. Also on this route several miles from Kawaihae is **Lapakahi State Historical Park,** which, unlike the religious heiaus which dot the coast with memorials of the ceremonial tradition, is designed to give the visitor a feeling for the commoner's daily life. Here are exhibits designed for self-guided tours of traditional life when Hawaiians lived by farming and fishing. Just above Kawaihae is the largest restored Hawaiian religious site in the state, **Pu'u Kohola,** which Kamehameha I built in honor of his war god Kukailimoku. Now the heiau is totally land based, but once it extended from its current location down to the sea, where sharks swam hungrily before it.

There is a small shopping plaza in Kawaihae where you can stop for shave ice, soda or other, more substantial refreshments. From here you can continue down coast toward Waikoloa or Kailua-Kona, a trip I do not necessarily recommend. The shoulder disappears just past town and, excepting several parks, there is little but heat and traffic until you reach the finish marker for the Ironman race (see Ride Four). There is, past Kawaihae but before Waikoloa, a campground at Spencer Beach Park and another at Hapuna State Park, where you can also rent cabins. What I prefer is to ride from Kawaihae back onto Route 250 and climb again to Waimea for drinks in town in the late afternoon. There is a more interesting route to Kailua-Kona, which runs through the mountain cool and away from the coast's heavy commuter traffic and shoulderless roads.

The nine-mile climb back to upcountry would be pleasant if it were not for the traffic and minimal shoulder on the road, but, as long as you do not ride during the island's rush hour (early morning and late afternoon), it is manageable. As a bonus, **Kamuela Museum,** on the right as you approach town, is a good place to stop, rest and enjoy the world before plunging in for a history lesson in the world just ridden through.

The whole triangle is, perhaps, a 30-mile day, although it seems longer because of the climbing that begins and ends the route. But nowhere else do I know a trip so short that contains such a diversity of landscapes and multiplicity of interests as this one.

Ride Four: Waimea to Kailua-Kona

Skill level: Experienced; long rolling hills
Connects with Rides Two, Three and Five

This is a spectacular ride. It is not overly long, perhaps 40 miles.

Nor is it dangerously taxing. Total altitude gained is only 1,000 feet from Waimea, although the long, rolling hills that make it so interesting also mean the total amount of climbing is far more than the altitude gained. For a moderately experienced rider this is a full day of fairly strenuous cycling. Because there is no place to stop for food or water until the outskirts of Kailua, it is important to carry liquids (at least three bottles) and purchase good cycle food before hitting the road. Traffic is minimal along this route, but the winds can be fierce throughout the ride, and any who have not endured miles of turning road and long descent with a thirty-mile-an-hour crosswind pushing at the side will find it a wild experience. The secret of surviving bad crosswinds (in fact the secret for most things on the bicycle) is to slow up a bit until control seems absolute.

The ride requires almost no directions, because there is almost nowhere else to go but down to Kailua-Kona, and the road heads unerringly in that direction. Head south on Route 190 out of Waimea and stay on that same road until it terminates on the leeward coast. A few miles out of town there is a left-hand cutoff onto the **Saddle Road**, which carries riders up to and around Mauna Kea's slopes and back down to Hilo. This is a harder ride, which campers may wish to break at **Mauna Kea State Park**. Those wishing to hike to Mauna Kea's summit should be warned it is not an easy climb.

To Kailua-Kona the road is clear and quiet after the Saddle Road turnoff, rolling up and down, up and down toward the leeward coast. There is a decent shoulder most of the way and, about a third of the way down, a huge sign marking the turnoff to Waikoloa, which is due east and about seven miles away from Route 119. This is a major coastal resort facility, where the Hilton Waikoloa and Sheraton Waikoloa have carved full-service, upscale destination facilities out of bare lava rock. From there to Kailua by the coast is about 22 miles on the low road, and cycling sybarites might want to take the detour and rest for a day.

Waikoloa

Both hotels are the type of place where people go who want to be nowhere else. They can swim, snorkel, parasail, play golf and do a thousand other things without meeting anyone from Hawaii but resort employees. The Hilton looks like a 1930s-style Busby Berkeley set, with large pillars and an opulence that calls for dancing girls prancing down wide, large stairs. The Sheraton Waikoloa, where Backroads Bicycle Tour clients stay, is slightly less grand but no less luxurious. The entire population of the Cook Islands could be fed for a week on the food set out each day in their buffet brunch/lunch. My recommendation is to give it a pass. This is not my idea of a holiday, and those who want to see the area can make it an easy, day's exploration while cycling out of Kailua (see Ride 5).

Besides, I cannot conceive of anyone who has ridden this far on Route 119 wanting to break cadence for anything but a rest stop to gaze in wonder at the island history which unfolds around this road. Here the whole botany and geology of island formation is written in large letters across the land. Here are notes from my workbook, which give a quick description of what you'll see:

> Far away, along the coast, there is the deep black of naked lava rock, which looks like a charcoal drawing. Moving upcountry from there one first sees thin, wispy tufts of dry land grass and, closer, grasslands with a few bushes interspersed. It is as if the land were bald and God had decided it needed a hair transplant. There, at the front, is black forehead. Then a few newly planted hairs can be seen but here, near the road on which I stand, the whole growth is straw-colored, thick and rich. Indeed it is so thick that the grass becomes bush and, finally, upland from me toward the Mauna Kea side there are ohia trees in full flower with hints of red against the straw-yellow and leaf green. Wow!

Even better is what this whole process shows and says about the lava flows that for centuries have transformed the island. The University of Hawaii Press map of Hawaii has marked on it the dates on which major flows occurred. Looking at the map along the route you can see where the 19th century lava has become cultivated by tree, grass and bush. More recent flow areas remain quite bare and give the land from this uplands perspective the appearance of a landscape over which a cup of dark coffee with all its dregs (Kona blend of course) has been recently poured by a local giant.

We think of eruptions and the resulting outpouring of magma as an ending, as a destroyer. It burns away trees, covers grass, destroys homes and makes the land unfit for habitation. Traditional Hawaiians knew better. Pele, the fire goddess said by some still to be living in Hawaiian volcanoes, was not simply a capricious villainess. The land itself is fertile and grows from these destructive eruptions. The way the land builds upon hot rock is shown clearly along Route 119 from Waimea to Kailua. Wherever fire ravages grassland and wood, the process of regeneration—grass to brush to trees—is the same, but here, in volcanic Hawaii, it is not regeneration but. rather, generation occuring for the first time. The process starts when moss or grass first roots in lava rock to begin the process that will end not in stone or pebble but with soil. The grass itself is a storehouse of nutrients and moisture which, over time, creates conditions suitable for more grass until a field is created in which bushes take root and from which trees will grow. In each stage, the roots make the rock crumble into soil, nutrients are held and water stored until the whole is range land or perhaps, someday, full forest.

All this becomes manifest as you ride up and down the never ending, undulating hills, always a bit more down than up. There are sharp bends in the route where you must exercise caution. There are neither convenience stores nor police stations where someone who has dumped can go for help, although, in an emergency, the truckers and local folk who drive this way usually will lend a hand.

Most of the descent is found in the 12 miles nearest to Kailua as, mile by mile, traffic picks up as civilization reappears. In the seven miles nearest to town where a road shoulder would be most useful, there is nothing but the narrow two-lane road and what is becoming each year a more constant stream of traffic. The last four miles is no pleasure at all, and I frequently pull over to let the large trucks go by. Heading down from Waimea, civilization announces itself with developers' signs, each promising a new townhouse or condominium project. All guarantee scenic vistas for those willing to pay the project's price. Even a generation ago, the idea that someone would build big buck palaces along Route 119 more than a mile out of town would have been greeted with a hearty laugh. Now land has become precious even over ' 're as folks tired of other tourist traps seek to create new retreats ɪn Hawaii's leeward side.

Kailua-Kona

Finally, coming into town, it is urban cycling again. Straight down the street is the **King Kamehameha Hotel** and the **Kona Seaside**, both of which welcome bicyclists. Indeed, the town at large accepts cycling as part of the local economy and riders are generally seen as more than a simple nuisance. This is clearest in the little things. The King Kamehameha, for example, has in every room a small packet of clean rags wrapped with paper for cyclists to use rather than normal towels when they need to clean their bikes. So simple a courtesy but so rare!

The Ironman Triathlon

The reason for this acceptance is the Ironman Triathlon, which brings more than $7 million to the local economy each year.

Marathons began in ancient Greece as a military messenger service, but the Triathlon is an idea that began as a dare in Kailua-Kona in the 1970s. Retired Navy Captain John Collin came up with the idea of combining three separate sports races—swimming, running and cycling—into a single one-day marathon event. In its first experimental year, 15 people started the race and twelve people finished it. More incredibly, participants and the handful of

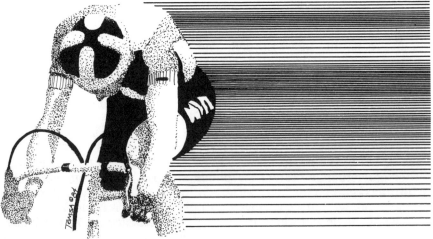

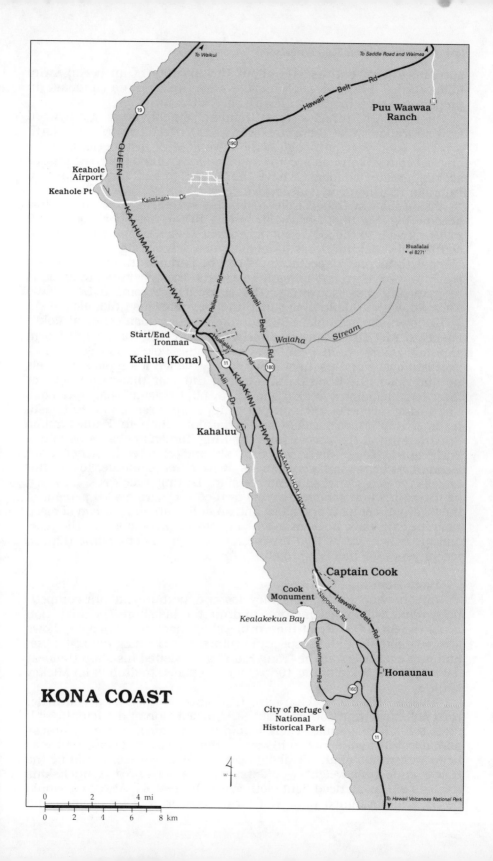

To Waikui

To Saddle Road and Waimea

19

Hawaii Belt Rd

Puu Waawaa Ranch

QUEEN

190

Keahole Airport

Keahole Pt

Kaiminani Dr

KAAHUMANU HWY

Hualalai
• el 8271'

Pailani Rd

Hawaii Belt Rd

Start/End Ironman

Hualalai Rd

Waiaha Stream

Kailua (Kona)

11

180

KUAKINI HWY

Alii Dr

Kahaluu

MAMALAHOA HWY

Captain Cook

Cook Monument

Napoopoo Rd

Hawaii Belt Rd

Kealakekua Bay

Puuhonua Rd

Honaunau

KONA COAST

160

City of Refuge National Historical Park

11

W—E

To Hawaii Volcanoes National Park

0   2   4 mi

0   2   4   6   8 km

spectators were enthusiastic about the insanity of an ocean swim followed by 112 miles of bicycle race up and down coast in preparation for a marathon-length run in the heat.

In 1980 ABC tuned in and "Ironman" quickly became a byword for endurance. Now there are over 1,000 triathlons held in North America each year (although some have shorter distances), and the original competiton has become so taken for granted that true crazies seeking greater challenges have the "Ultra" to look forward to—two Ironman triathlons on consecutive days.

Along the way to becoming a sporting spectacle, the Ironman has become big, big business, contributing in the neighborhood of $8 million a year to the local economy. Race week sees more than 1,000 contestants and hundreds of media types descending on the region, along with as many spectators as can be jammed in. Triathletes are ready to race, everyone is ready to eat and most visitors are anxious to party and buy souvenirs. The event has become a Sao Paulo Carnival, with athletic rites substituted for religious rationale.

In town, for example, I like to take my afternoon coffee at Poki's Pasta on Ali'i Drive almost directly opposite the harbor-front sign showing where, each year, the race ends. Poki's has good food, excellent coffee and pasta of every variety, which it supplies to hotels up and down the Kona coast. Most of the year that means two or three large batches a week (rigatoni, ravioli, fettucine, spaghetti, etc.), but during race week their output is upped to three or four full pasta loads a day. Dave's Bikes and Triathlon Shop in Kamehameha Square, around the corner from the King Kamehameha, is usually a fairly quiet place where you can sit and chat with owner Dave Bending as he repairs a customer's bicycle, rents another to a visitor or sells the occasional souvenir tee shirt. During race week, however, he maintains and services, by his own count, perhaps 70 percent of the triathlon competitors' bikes and snatches an hour or two of sleep when he can. This, he says, is when he makes his money for the year, and his only regret is that business has been so demanding that, in recent years, he has been too busy to race.

Dave Bending

Anyone who cares about bicycles and, certainly, about competition cycling will take some time to drop into his shop. The attraction is not the $8,000 state-of-the-art bicycling machine, which he shows favored customers and respectful visitors, but Bending himself. I met him first over beers at the "King Kam'" and visited his shop the next day. I felt like a kid of the 1950s who happened to drop in on Mickey Mantle.

Imagine the movie character Crocodile Dundee as a triathlete. He'd still have that leathery, fair, sunburned skin and a fetching, almost self-effacing smile. There would be the same sense of fitness and absolute confidence in his walk, that same air of competence as he slouched in a chair, drinking beer. Gone, of course, would be the Bowie knife (the weight would be intolerable) and the buckskins (cyclists in Hawaii need light clothes which breathe). Also gone would be the wide-brimmed bush hat (brim hats are not for cycling) and perhaps 20 pounds of body weight, useful when wrestling crocodiles in the Australian Outback, but in a bicycle endurance race nothing but a handicap. Picture Crocodile Dundee as a triathlete and you know Dave Bending. He has the same slow smile, sandy hair and easy familiarity as the fictional Dundee, but the frame and accoutrements are built to a bicycle racer and triathlete's specifications.

He is clearly a man who has found his niche. Born in California, he lived in both Europe and Canada, but rooted in Kailua-Kona where he is now as native as the ohia trees which prosper in the upland or the bougainvilleas that color sections of the triathlete's route. He doesn't ride Oahu ("too much traffic!"), Maui ("too crowded!") or Molokai ("too small!"). The Big Island, however, he cycles again and again. This is his native habitat, which he has circumnavigated, at last count, 18 times. Often he rides to Volcano House in a day (it took me two) and then back around to Kailua-Kona on the next. "No problem," he says. "Nice trip." Once, when there was a full moon, he and friends just kept riding all night and circumnavigated the whole island in a single day. "The cops weren't pleased at all," he remembers with a puzzled frown. Their displeasure at cyclists racing downhill on narrow, night roads was something incomprehensible to Dave. "Good fun that was!" I asked if he rode from Kailua up to Waimea on the uphill road. "Sure. No problem! It's a pleasant afternoon," he says while drinking a beer after work at the King Kam'. "Great fun."

This is a man born to the exquisite madness of ferocious, distance cycling, and his fame has spread around the world not as a racer or competitor, although he is both, but as a master mechanic. His shop is the center of triathletes' cycling concerns and, during race week, a magnet for serious competitors. Failed bicycles with big cogs and small clusters come into his shop and race wagon to be, almost miraculously, healed and returned as good as (some say better than) new.

I had heard the tales and was worried that he might sneer at my aging Fuji Touring V. After all, it is not a racer's bike, and high-tech triathletes sometimes show as much distaste for touring bikes as they do for cars. I need not have worried, because Bending's attitude was my own. Each bicycle, to him, serves its master, and it is the mix of man and machine on road which he finds so intriguing. I asked him to look over my touring machine and see what he thought of it. As long as I was not looking for speed, he said, the frame was a very nice one. His fingers whispered over the spokes and found three out of tune. "You might want to rebuild that wheel, though," he said. "Spokes are getting old and out of true." The next month two of them popped. His hand on the handlebars sat like a blessing when he suggested it would steer a bit better if I changed the headset. Then he looked at the gearing and suggested I might change my front cogs a bit for a better gear spread. Dubiously, I looked it up in another shop's table and found, of course, that he was right.

The Ironman Triathlon Route

For those in Kailua who want to try the course themselves, the directions are really very simple. Very early in the morning swim a distance of 100 yards out and back from the pier in front of the King Kamehameha Hotel. Swim it as quickly as you can and then, returning to the pier, get onto the bicycle.

Climb Hualalai Road, take a left on Kuakini Highway, a right on Lalani Road and the next left at Queen Kaahumanu Highway, named after the favorite queen of (who else?) King Kamehameha. The road here is asphalt over lava and runs straight north to Hawi. About 12 miles out of town is the Keahole Airport, where the marathon race will turn around, but cyclists keep on riding. And riding. And riding. I do not know if racers see anything or feel anything during this 112 miles of endurance riding. Nor have I ever asked if they notice the graffiti of white stones placed to create letters on the road's black lava sides along a good part of this highway. "The Three Caballeros," "Kane loves Kevi," "The Class of '89" are all spelled out carefully in the white rocks that were left over from the building of the roadbed.

At Hawi, turn around and ride back the way you came to the Kailua pier. Then jump off the bicycle, exchange riding shoes for runners and retrace the bicycle route to a mile past the airport, turn around and race back to Ali'i drive. If there is any hope in being a winner, you've completed this madness in under eight hours.

"No problem!" Dave Bending says happily, thinking of all the fun. "No way," I whisper under my breath; not for this touring cyclist.

Winners and Finishers

I have a strong prejudice against this type of race, because

triathletes do not see the landscape as more than a series of obstacles (a hill here, strong wind there). I doubt if most have any more interest in the environment than a greyhound has in the dog track. The event is a test, a struggle against physical limits and one's fellow professionals which closes off the sense of place, of relation to the environment. Race in Honolulu, race in Australia, try the Penticton triathlon—the glories of specifc environments become inter-changeable.

The Ironman, people tell me, is different. It is the grandfather triathlon, the place where it all began and a symbol not only of excellence but of rejuvenation as well. Every year there are contestants who wish not to win but to finish, mothers of four children, middle-aged men recovering from an illness, folk who decide they need some outrageous goal to give their life new meaning. I understand their need for challenge, but lament its taking a form which isolates the body in the spirit of a race and doesn't make swimming, cycling or even walking a challenge in itself.

Maybe what I miss are the days when such races were individual tests run by a group of amateurs, a friendly challenge between friends who lived and worked together. Maybe it is prize money which has made the event a commercial, franchised business where the name is all and the place almost nothing. Ironman is a name, now, not a local event, and what was special to this region has become as unique as a McDonald's franchise. That, I think, is a pity.

Old Kailua
A half-mile east of the Triathlon's finish point stand two traces of a time when cycling was an unknown sport and the *ali'i* reigned supreme. On Ali'i Drive stands **Mokuaikaua**, Hawaii's first church, built in 1837, and, across from it, **Hulihe'e Palace**. Both are constructed of lava rock and coral, and both were designed by then island governor John Adams Kuakini, the brother-in-law of King Kamehameha I. Kuakini was considered an unworthy Christian (today's mild behavior was yesterday's mortal sin) and prohibited from attending the dedication of the church he had designed. Its interior is koa wood paneling over an ohia wood structure, originally crafted by deserters from the 19th century sailing ships who constantly jumped ship in the Islands to try their hand at life ashore.

The governor's palace is even nicer and has been restored by the Daughters of Hawaii, descendents of early residents, who, before admission, have to trace their ancestry back to the early 1800s. I like the palace, an eclectic place that borrowed a bit from everyone. There are Victorian arches, New England architectural lines and a floor plan which suggests in its broad spaces something of the American South. Kuakini died in 1844 and the building passed on to his son, whose wife, Princess Ruth Keelikolani, inherited it when the son died a few years later. She was six feet tall and weighed 400 ponds, size being considered, among the ruling families of those days, a symbol of prosperity and dignity. The furniture in the house is built to her size, although she was large even by the standards of the day and race. A chair made for her remains, as do beds, and in them both one feels again like a little child squirming in a huge, adult-sized room. There is a giant hat box carved for Princess Ruth out of a coconut tree and a wooden clothing trunk which is larger than any home dining table I've ever eaten on. It would seat a family of six very easily.

Hulihe'e is also called the summer palace, because for years Hawaii's royalty and reigning monarchs came here in the summer to escape Oahu's heat. King David Kalakaua, the Merrie Monarch, Princess Ruth, Bernice Bishop, King Alexander Liholiho (a.k.a. Kamehameha IV) all slept and dined and lived here.

Admission to the palace is $4, and the spectacle is, in its own way, as grand as that of the yearly triathlon. It is a place filled with ghosts and traces of that strange, 19th century crew who found much to like in the new, strange western ways but never really gave up their own traditions. Princess Ruth, for example, was never comfortable sleeping in her mammoth bed and tended to spend the night on the floor of a grass house built behind the palace where she could recline on a bed of maile leaves covered with a velvet blanket.

Ride Five: Kailua-Captain Cook
Skill level: Intermediate; some traffic and climbing
Connects with Rides Four and Six

Hawaii is not well designed for casual, short-range bicycle touring. It should be easy to slip in a day from Kailua-Kona to Volcanoes National Park, but for all except the Dave Bendings of the world, the distance is just a bit too great. You can ride in a long day to Shirakawa's Hotel in **Waiohinu** near **Na'alehu** and **South Point** or the beach parks near **Punaluu,** but to cover those miles—at least a century ride in the heat—you would miss so much of interest that most touring riders break the trip into two days, with first a 30-mile ride to **Captain Cook** via **Kealakekua Bay**.

From Kailua, I rode south on Ali'i Drive past the church and palace, past the hotels, shops and condominiums that are springing up each year along the route. About six miles out of town and just before **Disappearing Sands Beach** (known for its good snorkeling) is the tiny Saint Peters By-The-Sea church. Built in 1880 and moved to its present location in 1912, it has an etched glass window behind the altar which looks out onto the sea. It has the feel of the best religious sites I know, one of reverence without pretense in simple, unadorned lines. You can imagine fishermen stopping for a moment of prayer before heading out into strong Kona winds to fight for a day's catch offshore.

A left-hand turn onto Kamehameha III Road at the Keauhou Shopping Center sign starts a 1,500-foot climb made more difficult by heat and wind but aided by a decent shoulder along the modern road. At the intersection with Route 11, take a right (the road continues to climb for a few miles more) and stop in **Honalo** at the Aloha Theater for a cup of coffee. This restored, wooden theater, built in 1932, has a spectacular view of the fields that spread below it to the sea and a nice cafe section. The ohia wood posts that support the front porch are really quite spectacular, as is the lattice work above the theater's front doors.

The road's shoulder disappears in this area, although traffic is usually fairly polite. You roll along until a sign appears for Kealakekua Bay, where a right-hand turn leads onto Napoopoo Road, which heads down to the coast after veering right at Middle Keei Road. On the right a little farther on is the **Royal Kona Coffee Mill Museum**, where I cadged free samples of Kona brew (given in tiny cups you can refill indefinitely). There are pictures of old coffee plantations in the store, whose real specialty is not education but the sale of coffee by mail to visitors' friends back home. Behind it is the Kona Farmers Co-Op, where the real work is done and the beans from the crops of 400 small farmers is turned into the famous Kona brew.

This is coffee country. From Keahu to just past Honauna, 630 farms on 2300 acres along a 20-mile stretch of road raise America's only commercial indigenous coffee, which some say ranks among the best beans in the world. The crop was introduced to the Islands in 1825 by the British ship *H.M.S. Blonde*, which carried several coffee plants from Rio de Janeiro. First planted on Oahu, slips were transplanted to Captain Cook in 1828, and a new industry was born as the young plants thrived in what is, for the coffee plant, an almost perfect environment. The region is cool and dry in the winter, and the afternoon clouds which roll in most days shade the coffee plant's tender leaves during the sun's hottest hours.

The beans ripen as cherries, which are picked from the trees and taken to a plant where the red skin and a layer of mucilage are removed, leaving the bean exposed in splendid solitude. These clean beans, called parchment in the trade, are first dried and then milled until the green coffee is exposed beneath the remaining skin and the processing—grading, roasting and packaging— is begun.

Down the hill from here, almost at the coast, is a T intersection whose right-hand turn leads almost immediately onto the exceedingly beautiful Kealakekua Bay, where cruising sailboats lie at anchor. It was here, in this bay, that Captain Cook dropped anchor and was first mistaken by the natives for the returning god Lono. Later, after discovering he was just a man, they killed Cook and battled with his crew. A plaque on the rock near the bay marks the spot where the first Christian service was ever performed in Hawaii, when Cook himself read the burial service over the mortal remains of crewman William Whatman in January of 1775. Visible across the bay is a monument to Cook himself, supposedly on the spot where he was felled by local warriors, a tale told very well by H.O. Bushnell in *The Return of Lono*.

There is also a plaque here in memory of Henry Opukaha'ia, a Hawaiian boy who, upon conversion to Christianity, was sent to New England for schooling and, eventually, was expected to return as an exemplar of the faith. He died in 1806, however, in New England at 26 years of age, a victim of typhus fever. This presumably saddened but certainly did not deter the religious zealots who decided the young man's faith was an example to them all and that his mission would be carried out by others. New England missionaries began to arrive by the boatload and, appalled by the islanders' sinful habits (sloth, gluttony, sexuality), set out to transform the native peoples into their own image.

It is easy to look back and blame those righteous women in whalebone corsets and humorless men in black coats and stove pipe hats as narrow-minded provincial hypocrites. We have forgotten how powerful faith once was—to missionaries and natives alike—and how pervasive a force God and gods once were in everybody's life. Kamehameha used these people well as builders and adjuncts to the state. Royalty thrilled in the baubles of the emerging, industrial age and the goods that came to Hawaii from around the world. Things changed forever, but looking back, I find it hard to mourn a time when places were named for the rivers of blood which flowed from conquest's battles, when women were not allowed to eat with the men and a kapu system of prohibitions insured that the ali'i would live their lives on the labor of hereditary commoners.

Puuhonua o Honaunau National Park

All this went through my mind as I left Kealakekua Bay and headed to Hawaii's most famous Place of Refuge. You reach the federal park and historic site along a long, almost deserted, bumpy dirt road. There are huge, six-foot-thick walls and an immense stone platform for traditional rites, because it was here that those who had lost in battle or broken a tribe's prohibition—both offenses punishable by death—were granted first sanctuary and then absolution. Had those warriors been cyclists who raced along the hot, dry road, they certainly would have deserved both. Some people find it a spooky place, and, for Hawaiians, it has the type of significance we invest in our greatest cathedrals: Chartres, Canterbury and perhaps Saint Peter's in Rome.

To me it is merely sad to think of the labor spent to build so large and lavish a place to house those who, fleeing for their lives, were required to run and hide through the lands I cycle now with such relative ease. I tried to imagine what it must have been like to run down the hill from the Aloha Theater, along the highlands by night (to hide) and then down to the plains and, finally, across through the heat to this place. I'm glad to have made the ride, and if camping were allowed I would have spent the night in hopes of recapturing the spirit of awe and majesty this place once held. Instead I mounted up and rode away without a backward glance.

Captain Cook

Leaving the refuge, I turned right onto Route 16 and a full 1500-foot climb back up to the hills above the coffee plantations. In the first few miles I passed a sign indicating Wakefield Botanical Gardens on my right and another promising Saint Benedict's Painted Church to the left, but I stopped for nothing except exhaustion. It was mid-afternoon and the heat was so intense that, even after my rest, I was immediately depleted of all energy. There were wonderful flowers and beautiful scenes, but I remember nothing until reaching a T intersection where Route 11 returned (left toward Kona and right toward South Point) except the way the paved road leered at me as I inched along.

I turned left and felt a breeze as altitude and shaded trees brought the heat under control and a steady but not too difficult climb became not endurance but pleasure. Each downhill sped the bike along, and uphill I could carry the pace when, in the heat, I could barely spin my pedals. Rushing along, I began to regret that my night's reservation was nearby and that I'd not turned south at the intersection and ridden on, as Dave Bending would have, to Volcanoes National Park (80 miles distant) or Shirakawa's Hotel a mere 45 miles down the way.

Instead I stopped that night in Captain Cook and stayed at the rather forgettable **Manago Hotel**, which does not allow cyclists to bring their machines into the wooden hotel's small rooms. Unfortunately, there is no competition to speak of in this area. There are other inns farther back, up the road in Honalo, but not in Captain Cook. Nor is there a great selection of places to eat and drink. Manago's again. Dinner is served early, and those riding to the hotel should be aware that once the restaurant closes they're almost without resources for the night, so people coming this way should plan on eating at, say, 6 p.m.

Ride Six: Captain Cook to Volcanoes

Skill level: Experienced; climbing and traffic
Connects with Rides One and Five

Were it not for a lack of shoulder and heavy traffic on sections of this ride it would be among the island's most magnificent. From Captain Cook the route rolls down to sea level at South Point, the south tip of the island, and then climbs for perhaps 30 miles up 4,000 feet to **Volcanoes National Park**. It travels across a landscape replete with trees and shade past coffee plantations and macadamia nut groves to the coast and then climbs past dry range to the Ka'u Desert on the slopes of Kilauea. Really, who could ask for more?

From Captain Cook, head south on Route 16, back toward the City of Refuge's cutoff, past it and through the coffee growing region of Kona. After perhaps five miles the road narrows and begins to twist, a fact apparently lost on motorists, who rush through the bends with little thought to slower cyclists or other vehicles. Folks along this route drive just too damn fast and with unsafe abandon in either direction. Stopping near the Milolii turnoff, I was compelled by the beauty of the region and horrified by my conversation with a local man who pointed out as points of scenic interest the sites of recent car crashes. Nor are drivers on this road very polite. They will sometimes honk their horns (very rare in Hawaii), shake their fists and whiz by in their rush to get to work. If you leave very early in the morning, just as the sun comes up, you can avoid some of this.

Fortunately, this dangerous area is only perhaps 15 miles in length, and then the road's shoulder returns and the worst of traffic's hazard is safely past. The landscape along this whole long ride from Captain Cook to the coast is ever newer, with lava flows transforming the land not in 1750, 1890, or 1910, but as recently as the 1950s. Where the rains have been sufficient, the black rock has been covered by lichens, moss, hardy grass and, finally, with stands of the sturdy ohia tree. The University of Hawaii Press series of island maps includes, in its Big Island version, the dates of major flows inked in along the coast, and while the map is woefully out of date—there is no mention of course of the most recent flows—it remains an invaluable aid along this coast. The relation between the dates of lava flows and the landscape is evident, mile after mile.

After about 28 miles a sign announces departure from the Kona District and entrance to the *Ka'u* region, the first-settled and now least populated of Hawaiian districts. In the 1950s, swindlers sold tracts of this area's barren, lava-covered land to Mainlanders looking for a piece of paradise on which to retire. Those who had grown weary of buying uninhabitable plots in the Arizona desert purchased, instead, almost equally arid and inhospitable tracts in the Ka'u region. Eventually, of course, it became a scandal and the adver-tisements ceased. Today it remains a part of Hawaii distinguished by dryness and sparse population, although, with the press fo. habitable land growing more fierce each day, sooner or later the onslaught of homesteading and tourism will come here too.

None of this bothers me as I cycle through, and, indeed, I like the silence, the absence of tourist glitz and the sound of my wheels on the road. Soon irrigated stands of macadamia trees line the sides of the road. This is, as another sign proclaims, The Largest Macadamia Nut Grove in the world. Most people assume these nuts are native to Hawaii but, in fact, they were a late introduction brought from Aus-tralia in the 19th century. Slinking beneath each row of trees is a network of irrigation lines, an addition to the landscape which makes this crop possible in the Ka'u region's arid land. They always remind me of intravenous lines set in the arms or neck of the hospitalized ill and it always seems strange that, with a life system so similarly fragile here, that the land and its orchard always look so healthy.

Manuka State Park, on the left just past the groves, is a nice place to stop and rest. Near its parking lot is a long, low stone marker that says, simply, "Hawaiian Grave." Draped over it on the day I passed was a single, yellow ginger lei. You will see leis used this way, sometimes; flowers strung by hand are placed reverently on graves or memorial sites as a sign of respect, just as, in other places, a pot of geraniums or, perhaps, a rose, is placed to honor the memory of the dead. The park's eight acres have been tended and planted with 48 distinct and indigenous Hawaiian plants as well as 140 other trees, bushes and flowers that take to the local soil. The park was begun in the 1930s with depression-era Civilian Conservation Corps group labor, and its landscaping was finally completed in the 1950s. Camping is permitted here, and, although there is no water on site, a drive-in restaurant a mile farther down the road has the campers' or cyclists' essentials—soda, juice, food and ice cream.

At Manuka State Park I found a Backroads rider resting. It was Naomi Orsay of St. Louis, Missouri, my favorite cyclist of the group. A nurse with married children, she is a competent rider who feels no great urgency to arrive rapidly at a day's destination. Throughout the trip she would ride for a while and then stop to contemplate the day and, perhaps, read a few chapters of James Michener's *Hawaii* in some shaded spot. Then she would saddle up and ride some more until another spot conducive to relaxation and reflection appeared. Naomi was excited about Hawaii, full of its wonder, and made the trip something of a pilgrimage in which the stops were as important as the motion of travel itself. She was, for example, the last member of the group to arrive at the City of Refuge. Not only had she stopped to read and think but had found a local store along the way which sold traditional Hawaiian musical instruments and toys. Its owners had regaled her with local myths and ways, instructed her in the niceties of a nose flute's use and seen her off, handlebar bag packed with the nose flute and other treasures she eventually demonstrated to the rest of the group.

From Manuka Park, Route 11 runs out and down toward the South Point turnoff, which leads, after 11 miles, to **Ka Lae** ("The Point"), where the first Polynesian settlers are said originally to have landed their canoes. This area is the most southerly settled region of the United States, and, if you accept the Hawaiians' arrival dates as gospel, perhaps the longest under continuous but non-native habitation. In this area there is also a strange green tint to the rock, and a few miles away is **Green Sand Beach**, where the color dominates the sand. It comes from veins of olivine—a green mineral—thrown up at some point from the volcanoes' depths and exposed clearly in this area.

It is a worthwhile detour for those who wish to stop for the day near **Na'alehu,** but cyclists interested in making Volcanoes National Park by nightfall will probably ignore the turnoff and press on. My cyclometer read 44.5 miles from Captain Cook to the rather lovely town of **Waiohinu,** whose stately **Kauahao Church**, on the road's right as you descend into town, is perhaps the most obvious landmark. You can spend the night here at the **Shirakawa Motel,** praised by Riegert in *Hidden Hawaii* and judged by singer James Taylor as "honest digs." Taylor is a leisure cyclist who rode the route from Hilo to Kona several years ago with Ron Reilly and Roberta Baker. They all spent the night at Shirakawa where, Ron told me with a smile, Taylor kicked back and they sang softly together as the sun set.

I'm not sure Ron really knew who James Taylor was or the magnitude of his fame. To him, Taylor was a nice man with a good voice and, as importantly, an amiable touring rider. There is a curious ignorance, amounting sometimes to innocence, on the part of Hawaiian residents when faced with Mainland stars. The television show *Magnum, P.I.*, starring Tom Selleck as a Honolulu-based private investigator, was a network staple in the 1980s and an important part of Oahu's film industry. But when its amiable star came to Island Triathlon and Bike on Oahu one day, the shop's co-owner Frank Smith had no idea who Selleck was. Just another customer, he thought, as Selleck looked at a number of different bicycles. When Selleck asked to take one model out of the shop for a trial ride, Frank said of course—as long as the customer had identification (preferably a motor vehicle license) he could leave as surety against the bike's return.

Other, younger store employees were trying to signal to Frank that the customer was A Name and needed no I.D., but, intent on the sale, Frank was oblivious to their signals. Selleck asked if his studio card would be sufficient and put it on the counter. Frank looked at it and said, politely: "I thought you looked familiar." Selleck test rode and later bought the bicycle but, Ron Reilly says, it remains an open question whether even after that Frank associated his customer with the TV and movie star's roles. One story has it that Frank watched Selleck ride away and suggested that the man's cadence and timing needed work.

Down the road from Shirakawa is the town of **Na'alehu**, where distance riders and those exploring the region will want to stop for refreshments at a wonderful fruit stand on the left just after the local movie theater. A bit more than three miles past Na'alehu is the turnoff for **Whittington Beach County Park**, where camping is permited. Four miles past that is **Punalu'u Beach Park**, a non-camping site, better known as **Black Sand Beach** for its coarse, lava-grained sand. The area is now at least as well known for the upscale Sea Mountain Estates development and the Seamount Ninole Golf Course. Punalu'u is a lovely, black sand beach (strong currents make it dangerous for swimmers) with lovely restaurant facilities. From Shirakawa's, it is a pleasant, relaxing 30-mile round trip for lunch and a bit of sunbathing.

At this point you are riding not south but northeast, up and soon away from the coast toward the entrance to **Volcanoes National Park.** The landscape changes from tropical verdancy in the South Point area, first to arid land and then into tropical desert at the ride's summit, where the road cuts across what my map inelegantly calls the "Great Crack," which separates a volcanic rift zone from an older, more stable island base. The whole is like a piece of jigsaw puzzle in which the last round section just barely fits. On the climb there is another macadamia nut grove to the left, but most riders do not stop to look. Unless you begin early in the morning from Shirakawa Hotel, this climb is done in the early or mid-afternoon when the sun's heat is a physical presence and those whose water bottles were not filled in Punalu'u or before will rue their lack of preparation.

There is little to say about the climb except that the grade is gradual, constant and wearing. Toward the top in the late afternoon it often gets chilly, and it makes sense to carry a windbreaker in your travel bag for this ride. The road's shoulder generally allows riders to concentrate on the climb and not on traffic, although care must be exercised since tourists and huge tour buses regularly race up the mountainside. This is a 4,000-foot altitude climb in thirty miles, which for most folk is sufficiently taxing that few will stop overlong even when the scenery is beautiful. Another problem—and reason for making this climb early in the day—is that on many afternoons the Kilauea region gets hazy when the "vog" (smog from the volcano) settles in.

Finally, on the right, a sign proclaiming Volcanoes National Park appears. Because this is a federal park, there is a nominal admission charge, but after the ride nobody cares because just past this barrier is **Volcano House**, the park's single and justly famous hotel. Campers will be pleased to know there are three different sites in the area where they will be welcomed without reservations by the National Parks Service. One is twenty miles away and 4,000 feet down the coast off Chain of Craters Road, but other, closer campgrounds are available in the park's upper section. For those seeking bed and breakfast accommodations, there are several good establishments two miles farther down the road in the town of Volcano. The addresses of several are included in this chapter's notes. The desk clerk at the Volcano House also has an updated list and will help individuals needing to find lodging in the area.

Ride Seven: Volcanoes National Park

Skill level: Beginner in upper park;
experienced for coastal climb
Connects with Rides One and Six

Volcano House

Kilauea's summit is not a formidable peak but, rather, a plateau surrounding a hugh depression itself bordered by a cliff. The Caldera, which dominate's the region, is two to three miles across and, on its north side, where Volcano House stands, about 400 feet deep. The lodge's dining room overlooks the Caldera, and over an early breakfast I watched the sun rise to suggest, sketch and finally highlight the crater's form. First it is all mist and then, slowly, the totality becomes clear as a plantless, seemingly barren landscape becomes visible in the new day. Wisps of what look like ground mist or fog remain, but they do not burn away. This is steam from the volcano's active, subterrranean layer, and throughout the day and in many parts of the park you will see hot, sometimes sulphurous steam pouring out of vents in the ground. Walking along some trails there is the faint scent of sulphur and, on others, a smell not unlike that of an old-fashioned laundry where the machines that press pants have been at work.

I have never been anywhere where a breakfast is so spectacular or drinks at sunset so rewarding. This vista is Volcano House's greatest attraction and the reason for its being. Adding to the pleasure of the view is the lodge's own beauty. Rooms are furnished exclusively with ohia wood furniture, and the common room is warmed by a huge fireplace, which, *Ripley's Believe It Or Not* noted in the 1930s, had

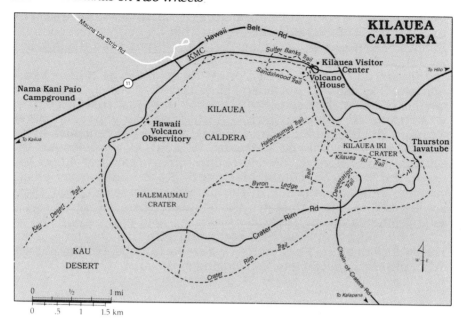

been at the time continuously burning for more than 60 years. The fire is still burning—it consumes, caretakers say, a cord of wood a week—and the well-maintained lodge combines comfort with scenery so unique and spectacular that the usual adjectives employed to praise fine hotels in this case fall short of the mark.

At present Volcano House's only drawback, besides a hefty price for each night's stay, is a total lack of facilities for bicyclists. No, the manager says, bicycles are not allowed in the guest rooms and no, there is no storage place for machines. Lock them up and leave them in front of the Lodge. They admit this policy is a problem and, in late 1989, as the rooms were being upgraded (which will mean higher prices in 1990), its managers told me they will work something out for bicyclists who choose to visit. But it was upsetting to arrive and know the machine that brought me here had to trust itself to a kryptonite lock and the vagaries of the night.

Still, the location is so perfect, the facilities so attractive and the fireplace so warm that I recommend that anyone visiting Volcanoes National Park spend a night at Volcano House and hope that better storage arrangements have been made.

There are campgrounds to stay at and good bed and breakfast facilities in the small town of Volcano a mere two miles away. Those who stay elsewhere may want to cycle in for an early breakfast, a sunset beer or the lavish lunchen buffet the hotel sets out each day. One of the campgrounds, Kamoamoa, is twenty miles away and on the coast, a 4,000-foot descent from the caldera's rim. At present it is a spectacular location from which to study the current coastal flows, which, in 1989, cut Chain of Craters Road a half-mile away. From nearby at sunset I watched Kilauea pour pour molten magma into the sea as part of the continuing activity that began so spectacularly with the 1982 eruptions.

Volcanoes National Park is worth several nights at least. After cycling to the summit, few people want more than a shower and a beer. The next day is usually spent first in an orienting trip to the Visitors Center and then in walking, hiking or cycling the superb system of trails and roads that crisscross the park. The Center has a short movie describing the volcano and its activity and, of course, sells a number of publications on and about the region. The third day (or, for those in a rush and with automobile transportation, the second night) is best spent at road's end on the coast, where the current activity can be seen first hand. Sometimes there is nothing but steam pouring up from underwater vents, but at other times—especially at sunset—the red, molten lava is clearly visible, crawling out of its tube at sea's edge and up into the air as the magma hits the water and begins to cool. It is as if a large, red worm had appeared from the depths of the earth and reared up in anger at the indignity of air before plunging down, darkly, to the cooling ocean. As I write this, yesterday's show was unusually spectacular. A section of the new rock, built up over recent months, collapsed into the sea and a stream of red lava poured like water from a spigot down from remaining rock into the sea. All the TV clips and newspaper pictures and all the words others write cannot compare to the reality of being there and seeing.

Park Trails

There is a 12-mile paved road rimming the Caldera, which tour buses and tourists' automobiles run around in less than an hour. But there is also a series of hiking trails, which I cycled, and the difference is between seeing something on television, and being there in person. It was the difference between reading about romance in a book and being in passionate love. I rode Sulphur Rim trail from the Visitor Center to the Caldera's northeast. The landscape was tall grasses and low ohelo bushes punctuated by open vents that pushed continuous pillars of steam into the air. Riding here in the early morning brought back a hundred childhood memories and dreams of being with The Last of the Mohicans or the Lone Ranger as, at dawn, he moved quietly and undetected through enemy Indian camps on a crucial mission.

In those days I rode a one-speed, red Schwinn, and, cycling near my family's home, I imagined it to be a pony on which I navigated the silent but inhabited native territory. Now, however, I was mounted on a Fuji, and the campfire smoke was the result of the volcano's venting pressure through the tall, harsh grass of the country. Each vent became personified, a cooking fire for unseen inhabitants, and from the grass in which each was located I half expected a member of some elder race to appear and signal me to sit in peace or stand and be at war. The memories were so compelling it was with disbelief and disappointment that I found each vent I explored was inhabited only by my imagination and an extraordinarily complex interplay of plants suited to their specific environment.

In each vent's hole live hardy mosses, which thrive in the heat and live happily with the steam's sulphurous emissions. Around most holes are stands of the high, tough, yellowed grasses and hardy bushes seen so frequently on the Kona Coast. About 50 percent of all the plants closest to a vent are dead—bare branches and emission-coated leaves—but out of the carnage comes even more life. It just will not be deterred, and new bushes and grass grow behind and around that which has been killed as the plants struggle toward the steam's warmth and for a foothold in this region.

The trail carried me past Kilauea Military Camp, a wonderful place to stay, which is closed to the public but open for military personnel (including members of the U.S. military reserves) and their dependents. Then I rode the rim road past the crucial Hawaiian Volcano Observatory (closed to the public) whose seismographs, tilt-meters and other monitors constantly measure the geologic activity of this region. Next to it, in the Jaggar Museum, are working examples of all this equipment, where visitors can see the recorded traces of seismic volcanic events. The plotter's lines waver, jiggle and then firm as paper rolls by, and as that happens the tremors of the subterranean land belch, rumble and then are silent again. Seismic volcanology becomes physically visible—if not necessarily comprehensible—when translated into the records volcanologists use. These records become a chart of the sea changes of the molten core that is the object of scientist's curiosity and the key to the puzzle of Kilauea's future and power.

The landscape of the caldera's west side is bleak and moon-like, littered with huge bare rocks tossed up in the 1950s eruption. Signs date each area of rocks by the year of their eruption, as if the entire area were some petrified vineyard for trolls and the rocks were stands of particularly good, vintage years. As you move to the southeast, the dates become more frequent until you find signs showing where activity occurred in the 1980s. On the south, the Rim road is at crater

level, and here, with others, I walked through a surreal rock landscape scented by sulphur through the great Caldera itself. The crater is like so many images of hell—bare rock, scent of sulphur and the promise of fire as misty steam rises from hidden vents whose power is subterranean—that it seems somehow familiar, a hokey movie mogul's idea of the descent into Dante's *Inferno*. But for me there was a feeling of affirmation growing, of life so raw and new and extreme that I wanted to be active in it.

Walking along I thought again of the most barren sections of the Kona coast and the more fertile uplands whose volcanic ground must have looked, in the not too distant past, something like this rock-hard, almost barren place. Meandering through this landscape, I steadied my bicycle with one hand, my kite bag in the other. In the Caldera I felt a breeze and opened the kite, holding its red sides in hope to the wind, then watched as the red parafoil fluttered weakly in my hand. Briefly it lifted away and carefully I tried to play out string, but the day was calm, and micro-breezes generated by the action of rising steam on a windless day were not enough to hold it stable for long and certainly not sufficient to lift my kite high into the sky. Still, the attempt satisfied me, although the image of a red kite flying high above the somber scene would have been quite wonderful, like an impudent flute rising from and around the depths of a Wagnerian opera or a piccolo chuckling in a somber march.

From there I rode slowly toward the Caldera's eastern side and stopped at Devastation Trail, where the volcano's relation to this island's physical world becomes even more overt. Built on forest almost totally covered in the 1959 flow, Devastation Trail is a research site where scientists are studying how plant life grows and regenerates in new volcanic ash and rock. Parts of the trail are littered with the dead, white branches and trunks of ohia trees burned by the eruption and then tossed aside by the strong winds which accompanied it. But not far away other, newer trees grow, and in those areas where even the tip of an older tree survived the fire, that tip has grown into its own maturity and used its buried sections as primary root and nutrient.

Walking along this trail I remembered the areas of lava rock seen along the northern Kona coast, but now thought of them as more than simply barren and desolate. In retrospect and from the perspective of Kilauea's trails, I instead saw them as a raw beginning which would, in time, take on plants and grass and verdant green. The tufts of grass, bushy growths and stands of trees that made Route 119 so pleasurable a ride were, I now saw, the promise held out to the younger land which dominated the lower, coastal road. This whole island is a treatise on regeneration, I thought. Lush and barren are simply different times on a sliding scale of geologic age, and the volcano's newest moments will become some day like the lushest of older sections. Here is the cycle of it all fed and not hampered, created and not destroyed by a power so elemental and profound that until I first saw it was, simply, inconceivable.

The central fact that volcanoes build and do not simply destroy was hammered home in the **Thurston Lava Tube**, whose entrance is near the end of **Devastation Trail** near Kilauea Iki Crater. The Tube is a tunnel created when a flow of magma cooled and then collapsed, leaving a long, stable, subterranean path in its wake. Entering it, you walk beneath Kilauea Iki Crater's rim along the path the magma took. What is most compelling to me about the walk is not that this was the path hot lava took—wherever you walk above the ground you walk on old lava, after all—but the roots that dangle through the tube's ceiling from the trees which now grow above it. Thurston Tube is surrounded and topped by tropical forest, and here the source of the volcano's attraction becomes clear. Growth and life in almost embarrassing profusion result from apparently destructive volcanic action.

But these are traces, reminders and reconstructions of events which occurred in the past. In 1959, for example, I was ten years old and probably saw but do not now remember pictures published in, say, *Life* of that episode in the saga of Kilauea's eruptive activity. Immediate, actual "real-time" volcanic action occurs now on the Park's coast near where the Chain of Craters Road is buried under lava rock. Here is where I headed next, to a place in which age is measured not in years but in minutes, days and weeks.

For cyclists the trip down is wonderful, a spectacular, twisting, long descent from forest past ever more recent lava fields to the pristine coast and immediacy. There are no shoulders on this route, and the traffic is at times very heavy. But it is glorious not only as a ride (early morning is the best time) but for the views, which constantly unfold as the greater park drops away and behind, as the sea's landscape appears. Parts of the land over which you pedal are flowered and filled with bushes, grass and trees (also two cattle guards you should cross slowly and with care). Other parts of the landscape are lava rock, with a few sprouts of grass or a touch of moss. Throughout the descent and off to the east are what first look like whispers of wind and then become tendrils of fog. Past Kamoamoa Campground they are known for what they are—geysers of steam mixed in the coastal crucible of molten magma poured from undersea vents into the flowing sea.

I spent a sunset here in November of 1989, watching the hordes of tourists who photographed each other capering near the new lava flows and exclaiming to each other that "the ranger said this is only three weeks old, Mom! Wow! Three weeks!" It was as if the newness were the area's sole attraction and that, when the rock ages six months or more, it will become merely boring and barren. Park rangers work to keep people away from the more dangerous and fragile regions, while repeating, again and again, the statistics of the eruption as if they were sports announcers talking about a much beloved football team: number of houses destroyed; area covered by new lava since the eruption began; area covered this year alone; number of active generative vents currently pouring lava into the sea and predictions of future volcanic action. These statistics and other facts are recited 100 times a day to visitors who half listen while photographing each other in seemingly endless rotation where the geysers of steam can be clearly seen as a backdrop.

I sat alone, a half mile away, as the sun set behind wisps of red cloud. The statistics did not matter to me because I had come to believe that this moment, this island, this volcano was my key to understanding all the islands I'd cycled so intently. Hawaii is not different from Molokai, Oahu, Maui or the other islands and atolls which sit to the northwest of Kauai. It is simply a bit younger in geologic time. Oahu once looked like this—bare rock, hardy grass and the indomitable ohia tree. Kauai, whose rounded hills and northern verdancy make it seem so benign, was once the home of similarly angry geysers. It too was molten magma steaming into the sea. I had assumed at the beginning of my trip that this island had its different sides, which were alternately hospitable (the lush windward) and barren (the leeward coast), but Volcanoes National Park reminded me that the two are indivisible and only my arrogance and refusal to see the whole on its own terms and in its own time frame had made the differences seem so vast.

It is all so fragile and yet, strangely, so hardy. Walk off the assigned observation path on Devastation Trail and you trample almost microscopic plant life, slowly breaking down volcanic pebbles, transforming rock into volcanic soil. Lava flows so quickly along the coast—and is cooled so instantly by the sea—that it builds structurally fragile cliffs of rock, which, occasionally, break from their own weight to tumble away. And yet, the whole endures, matures and grows.

Hawaiians personalize the process and make of the volcano Madam Pele, the fire goddess who is said to live still in Hawaii's active volcanic realm. As homes were being burned in a subdivision several years ago, people left offerings to her not in petition and appeasement, not as beggers but as island members who even in extremes wanted to show their respect for her power. I remember a newscast in which a television reporter interviewed a resident whose home was at risk and asked the "victim" if he thought the flows would stop before they engulfed his home. He shrugged, looked up at Kilauea and said, "She stop when She good and ready." "She" was Madam Pele, whose fire formed the islands and whose capricious actions had been a part of the island's mythology and lore for years. Mainlanders laughed at this simple Hawaiian who placed a name and personality on impersonal geologic forces. But it is not that local folk are foolishly ignorant, unaware of seventh grade science and high school geologic lore. They know that the earth has a molten core and most understand that the earth's crust is a series of slowly moving plates whose shifting contributes to earthquakes and volcanic action. And yet, to live so intimately with such cataclysmic power it helps to personify impersonal nature and give it a human face. Madam Pele, whom we know so well from legend and dance, is a personage one can accept when home, crop and life itself may be at stake.

Most visitors see the eruption as destruction, as ruination caused by nature's forces, and are awed, perhaps, by the power. But for those who live here and have given nature and generation a name, the meaning and wonder of Volcanoes National Park is its power of creation. This is genesis, pure and simple, a continuous beginning in the most fundamental sense. Islands are born and plants grow to maturity through the wreckage wrought by lava flows and volcanic dust, just as the world itself has come to being and just as we ourselves, as individuals, have a specific life cycle. That is the meaning of Madam Pele in Hawaiian dance and song and the belief in that message the reason, I think, why so many hold to the myth so strongly with the part of their minds and soul which believe not in pheromones and development but in the power of romantic love and man's hope.

To be in Hawaii at the time of an eruption is to know this in an immediate sense and it is, I think, the source of the reverence local people have for the land not as an abstract, environmental concept but for the reality of its diverse fragility. Hawaii's famous hula master Auntie Edith Kanakaole chanted *Hi'ipoi i ka Aina*—cherish the beloved land—and the phrase has become the battle cry of environmental activists and Hawaiian cultural activists alike. Others have spoken of the land's fragility and power, but nowhere is it more evident than here, as it is created and destroyed simultaneously as new vents open and old ones collapse.

All of this ran through my mind as I watched the flow of subterranean magma and the steam it threw up along Hawaii's coast. Nearby a man was fishing off the shore and farther away a few other people sat, watching the sunset and the day's end, when a large, red head of molten lava reared up from the sea as if angry with the constraint of the lava tube that terminated at the mouth of the undersea vent. A sigh, collective and yet private, issued from all of us who watched from separate solitudes as earth's fire stood out from the sea and pushed away the surrounding steam like a magician who, having disappeared from the stage, reappears in a fury of sound and smoke. Even when it grew dark, the red worm rode high, standing out on the night, and long after I was to see it in my dreams as it weaved and turned like a hula dancer. I knew that my cycling had been not simply an end in itself but a ride to our communal beginning through old islands and over old volcanoes to this simple truth: Genesis is not an ancient myth. Nor is creation a completed fact.

That is Hawaii's lesson and one I would have missed had time not become a physical thing measured in the muscles of my legs and the cramps which sometimes rippled down my back. At the speed of a bicycle, at the scale of travel it had enforced, the various parts of this geologic and social whole had been learned bit by bit until, at the edge of Kilauea's eruption, the relation of the fragments to the whole became clear. Pele lives in the way all our constructs live—through the creation of the land and the quality of our tenure upon it.

Camping Permits

Department of Land and Natural Resources
Division of State Parks
P.O. Box 936
Hilo, HI 96720
961-7200

Department of Parks and Recreation
County of Hawaii
25 Aupuni Street
Hilo, HI 96720
961-8311

For information on Volcanoes National Park, Pu'uhonua o Honau-
nau National Park or Pu'ukohola Heiau National Historic Site:

Superintendent
Hawaii Volcanoes National Park
Hawaii Natonal Park, HI 96713
967-7311

Superintendent
Pu'uhonua o Honauau National Historical Park and
  Historical Site
Honaunau, HI 96726
328-2326

Note: Permits are not required in advance to camp at Volcanoes
National Park.

Hotels

Hilo Hukilau
126 Banyan Way
Hilo, HI 96720
935-0821

Hilo Bay Hotel
87 Banyan Drive
Hilo, HI 96720
935-0861

Naniloa Hotel
93 Banyan Drive
Hilo, HI 96720
969-3333

Hilo Hotel
142 Kinoole Street
Hilo, HI 96720
961-3733

Manago Hotel
P.O. Box 145
Captain Cook
Kona, HI 96704
323-2642

Volcano House
P.O. Box 53
Hawaii Volcanoes Natl.
  Park, HI 96718
967-7321

The (Parker Ranch) Lodge
Route 19
Waimea, HI 96743
885-4100

Kamuela Inn
Route 19
Waimea, HI 96743
885-4100

King Kamehameha
75-5660 Palani Road
Kailua-Kona, HI 96740
329-2911

Kona Seaside
75-5646 Palani Road
Kailua-Kona, HI 96740
329-2455

Kona Bay Hotel
75-5739 Ali'i Drive
Kailua-Kona, HI 96740
329-1393

Kalani Honua Center
P. O. Box 4500
Kalapana, HI 96778
965-7828

Banyan House B&B
Route 130
Keaau, HI 96749
966-8598

Bed and Breakfast, Volcanoes

Kilauea Lodge
P.O. Box 116
Volcano, HI 96785
967-7366

Volcano Cottage
P.O. Box 503
Volcano, HI 96785
967-7683

My Island B&B
P.O. Box 100
Volcano, HI 96785
967-7216

Bicycle Shops on the Big Island

Dave's Bike and Triathlon Shop
Kamehameha Square
75-5626 Kuakini Hwy.
Kailua-Kona, HI 96740
329-4522

C&S Cycle and Surf
Kamuela, HI 96743
885-5005

The Bike Shop
258 Kamehameha Ave.
Hilo, HI 96720
935-7588

Mid-Pacific Wheels
1133C Manono
Hilo, HI 96720
935-6211

Competitive Edge Triathlete Center
75-5744 Ali'i Dr.
Kailua-Kona, HI 96740
329-8141

Hawaiian Pedals Ltd.
Kona Inn Shopping Center
Kailua-Kona, HI 96740
329-2294

Books About Hawaii

Bushnell, *The Return of Lono* (Honolulu: University of Hawaii Press, 1972). Bushnell's retelling of the landing of Captain Cook and the eventual killing of the captain by natives who discovered he was not a god.

Decker, Barbara and Robert, *Road Guide to Hawaii Volcanoes National Park* (Mariposa, Calif.: Double Decker Press, 1986). A good, descriptive guide, including fine maps of trails and paths in the park.

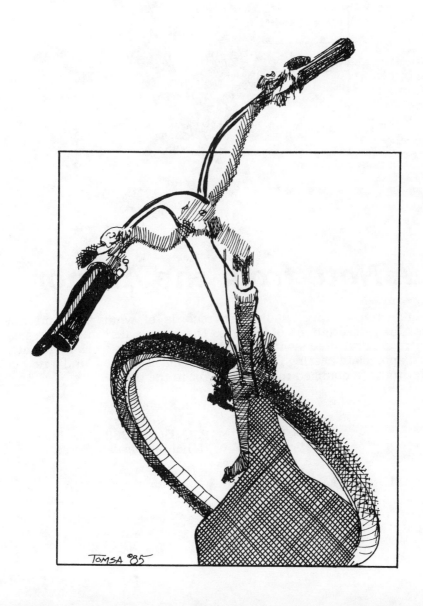

TOMSA °85

A Note from the Author

Like maps, travel books are records of what was and not necessarily descriptions of what is. That's why alert and interested readers are critical to a writer who hopes to keep his work up to date. So I'd appreciate hearing from you, especially if you've found a new or better route, a changed road or an error in the book.

Tom Koch
c/o Bess Press
P. O. Box 22388
Honolulu, Hawaii 96822

NOTES

NOTES

NOTES

NOTES

NOTES

NOTES

NOTES

NOTES